Content Marketing FOR DUMMIES®

by Susan Gunelius

WILEY

Wiley Publishing, Inc.

Content Marketing For Dummies®

Published by
Wiley Publishing, Inc.
111 River Street
Hoboken, NJ 07030-5774

www.wiley.com

Copyright © 2011 by Wiley Publishing, Inc., Indianapolis, Indiana

Published by Wiley Publishing, Inc., Indianapolis, Indiana

Published simultaneously in Canada

For general information on our other products and services, please contact our Customer Care Department within the U.S. at 877-762-2974, outside the U.S. at 317-572-3993, or fax 317-572-4002.

For technical support, please visit www.wiley.com/techsupport.

Wiley also publishes its books in a variety of electronic formats and by print-on-demand. Not all content that is available in standard print versions of this book may appear or be packaged in all book formats. If you have purchased a version of this book that did not include media that is referenced by or accompanies a standard print version, you may request this media by visiting http://booksupport.wiley.com. For more information about Wiley products, visit us at www.wiley.com.

Library of Congress Control Number: 2011928438

ISBN: 978-1-118-00729-7

Manufactured in the United States of America

10 9 8 7 6 5 4 3 2 1

WILEY

About the Author

Susan Gunelius is President & CEO of KeySplash Creative, Inc. (www.keysplashcreative.com), a marketing communications company. Her clients include large and small companies around the world, such as Citibank, Cox Communications, and many more.

She has 20 years of experience working in the marketing field with the first decade of her career spent directing marketing programs for some of the largest companies in the world, including divisions of AT&T and HSBC. Today, Susan often speaks about marketing, branding, copywriting, and social media at events around the world (www.susangunelius.com).

Susan is the author of numerous books about marketing, branding, and social media, including:

- ✔ *Blogging All-in-One For Dummies*
- ✔ *Google Blogger For Dummies*
- ✔ *30-Minute Social Media Marketing*
- ✔ *Kick-ass Copywriting in 10 Easy Steps*
- ✔ *Building Brand Value the Playboy Way*
- ✔ *Harry Potter: The Story of a Global Business Phenomenon*
- ✔ *The Complete Idiot's Guide to WordPress*

She is a featured columnist for Entrepreneur.com and Forbes.com, and her marketing related-articles have appeared on Web sites such as MSNBC.com, FoxBusiness.com, WashingtonPost.com, BusinessWeek.com, and more.

Susan also owns one of the leading blogs for women working in the field of business, Women on Business (www.womenonbusiness.com), which was a finalist in the 2009 and 2010 Stevie Awards for Women in Business in the category of Best Blog, and she is the Blogging Guide at About.com, a New York Times Company (http://weblogs.about.com).

You can connect with Susan on the social Web in the following places:

- ✔ **Twitter:** www.twitter.com/susangunelius and www.twitter.com/womenonbusiness
- ✔ **Facebook profile:** www.facebook.com/susangunelius
- ✔ **Facebook Page:** www.facebook.com/keysplashcreative
- ✔ **LinkedIn:** www.linkedin.com/in/susangunelius

Dedication

To my parents, Bill and Carol Ann Henry, who paid for my marketing education and put me in the position to pursue my career goals.

Author's Acknowledgments

Content Marketing For Dummies is the eighth book I've written, and none of my books would have made it to book stores without the support of my agent, Bob Diforio, who I can't thank enough for his wisdom and guidance.

Of course, this book would not have been written without the unending support of my husband, Scott, who takes charge of the household while I'm holed up writing. Without his encouragement and patience, I wouldn't be able to do the work I do, and for that, I'm forever grateful.

I also need to thank Brynn, Daniel, and Ryan, my children, for making me smile and laugh every day, and my parents, Bill and Carol Henry, for babysitting when I need to write.

Finally, I need to acknowledge the team at Wiley who helped to make this book a reality and get it into your hands. Specifically, thank you to Amy Fandrei who brought this project to my attention and Jean Nelson for smoothly managing the editing process.

Publisher's Acknowledgments

We're proud of this book; please send us your comments at http://dummies.custhelp.com. For other comments, please contact our Customer Care Department within the U.S. at 877-762-2974, outside the U.S. at 317-572-3993, or fax 317-572-4002.

Some of the people who helped bring this book to market include the following:

Acquisitions, Editorial, and Media Development

Project Editor: Jean Nelson

Acquisitions Editor: Amy Fandrei

Copy Editors: Brian Walls, Melba Hopper

Technical Editor: Michelle Oxman

Editorial Manager: Kevin Kirschner

Media Development Project Manager: Laura Moss-Hollister

Media Development Assistant Project Manager: Jenny Swisher

Media Development Associate Producers: Josh Frank, Marilyn Hummel, Douglas Kuhn, Shawn Patrick

Editorial Assistant: Amanda Graham

Sr. Editorial Assistant: Cherie Case

Cartoons: Rich Tennant (www.the5thwave.com)

Composition Services

Project Coordinator: Katherine Crocker

Layout and Graphics: Corrie Socolovitch, Kim Tabor

Proofreaders: Lindsay Amones, BIM Indexing and Proofreading Services

Indexer: WordCo Indexing Services

Publishing and Editorial for Technology Dummies

> **Richard Swadley,** Vice President and Executive Group Publisher

> **Andy Cummings,** Vice President and Publisher

> **Mary Bednarek,** Executive Acquisitions Director

> **Mary C. Corder,** Editorial Director

Publishing for Consumer Dummies

> **Diane Graves Steele,** Vice President and Publisher

Composition Services

> **Debbie Stailey,** Director of Composition Services

Contents at a Glance

Table of Contents

Introduction

. . . .

Content marketing is more than just a trendy buzz phrase. It's an effective way to build your brand and business. By reading this book, you're taking the first important step to seizing an opportunity that is wide open to you.

The challenge with content marketing is two-fold:

- ✔ It's still a very new form of marketing, and therefore, no one knows the recipe for success yet.
- ✔ It's a continually evolving form of marketing, so the tactics you use today might not be the right ones to use tomorrow.

The trick to achieving content marketing success isn't just understanding the tools available to you to publish content online and offline. You also need to think strategically to leverage content and conversations to boost your brand, your business, and your bottom line.

Content Marketing For Dummies introduces you to the world of content marketing so you can develop your own strategies and implement those strategies in ways that set you up for the long-term success you and your business need. By reading this book, you gain the knowledge you need and the ability to find the tools that you need to implement your own content marketing plan.

About This Book

Content Marketing For Dummies provides a huge amount of information, including fundamental marketing theory and step-by-step instructions to implement specific tactics immediately. Some of the information you can glean from this book includes:

- ✔ Understanding the basics of the content marketing opportunity
- ✔ Creating a content marketing strategy
- ✔ Executing a content marketing plan
- ✔ Discovering the tools of long-form content marketing
- ✔ Marketing with short-form content
- ✔ Using conversations to promote a brand and business
- ✔ Using search engine optimization tricks to boost your content marketing success

- ✔ Following the rules of content marketing
- ✔ Integrating your content marketing efforts
- ✔ Analyzing the results of your content marketing efforts
- ✔ Building a content marketing team to help you

Content marketing is a unique form of marketing that any brand or business can use to connect with a wider audience and drive business. Don't be overwhelmed by the content marketing opportunity. Instead, be inspired by it and dive in!

Foolish Assumptions

Content Marketing For Dummies is written for those just beginning a foray into content marketing, but it also includes a great deal of information that benefits more advanced content marketers. However, even though this book is written as a beginner's guide, I have to assume you know a few things:

- ✔ You have a computer and have basic computing skills, such as how to access and browse the Internet.
- ✔ You have a brand or business that you want to build (your brand might be yourself).
- ✔ You understand what marketing is at the most basic level.
- ✔ You're familiar with blogs, Facebook, and other social Web tools, even if you haven't used them before.

If you're not familiar with marketing and the tools of the social Web, you can still read and benefit from this book, but you might want to check out *Marketing For Dummies,* 3rd Edition, by Alexander Hiam and *Social Media Marketing All-in-One For Dummies* by Jan Zimmerman and Doug Sahlin.

Conventions Used in This Book

This book includes a couple of conventions, which are used to present information consistently. For example, an *italicized* word or term notifies you that its definition is nearby. Text in **bold** indicates text you should type on your computer to complete the instructional step. Finally, Web site addresses and e-mail addresses are displayed in monofont, so you can't miss them.

What You Don't Have to Read

Content Marketing For Dummies is divided into seven parts. Each chapter is written modularly, meaning each chapter stands on its own. In other words, you don't have to read the chapters in order. In fact, you don't even have to read all of the chapters. Instead, you can select the parts or chapters that apply to you.

Although you'll get the most out of this book by reading it in its entirety, that isn't a requirement. How you choose to read and use this book is up to you, and you'll benefit from reading any part of it regardless of the parts you choose.

How This Book Is Organized

Content Marketing For Dummies includes seven distinct parts. Here is what you can find in each part.

Part I: Getting Started with a Content Marketing Plan

Part I introduces content marketing. You find out what content marketing is, how content marketing can benefit you, and how to create a content marketing strategy for your brand and business. You also discover how to take the first steps to implement that content marketing strategy.

Part II: Marketing with Long-Form Content

In Part II, you find out about the long-form content marketing opportunity that focuses on creating in-depth content that takes more than a few minutes to create and consume. You read about specific types of long-form content marketing, as well as how to write long-form content for the Web and optimizing that content to improve performance and results.

Part III: Marketing with Short-Form Content

Part III introduces you to the tools of short-form content marketing and shows you how to create short-form content that effectively promotes your business (both directly and indirectly) within seconds. You also get tips that help you improve your short-form content so you follow rules of etiquette while boosting your brand and business at the same time.

Part IV: Engaging in Online Conversations to Share Content

Part IV shows you that talking about content and sharing content is a form of content marketing. In this part, you find out where you can participate in conversational content marketing as well as how to improve your conversations to increase results and ensure you're a welcome participant in the online conversation.

Part V: Achieving Long-Term Success

Creating content and using the tools of content marketing aren't the only parts of content marketing that you need to consider in order to achieve long-term success. Part V shows you how to integrate your online and offline content marketing efforts with each other as well as with your other marketing initiatives to get the biggest bang for the buck. You also read how to analyze your content marketing performance so you can fine-tune and improve your efforts over time. Finally, you discover how to build a content marketing team to help you reach your goals.

Part VI: The Part of Tens

The Part of Tens is a handy feature included in all *For Dummies* books. In *Content Marketing For Dummies*, the Part of Tens offers quick lists with useful information, such as free tools to get started with content marketing and tools to publish your content, as well as resources to get additional help if you need it.

Part VII: Appendixes

Content marketing can be intimidating and overwhelming. Sometimes it's hard to know where to start. Appendix A includes three sample content marketing quick start plans to help you get started with content marketing quickly.

The world of content marketing includes a wide variety of words and terms that you need to understand. Use the glossary in Appendix B to make sense of terms you haven't heard before while you read this book.

Icons Used in This Book

An excellent feature of all *For Dummies* books is the use of helpful icons that offer quick tips, tricks, and warnings. The icons used in this book are

The Tip icon points out helpful information that will make a content marketing task or job easier.

The Remember icon indicates an interesting or useful fact that you might want to use later.

When you see the Warning icon, stop and read the information provided. This icon signals lurking danger that you need to recognize and consider before proceeding.

The Technical Stuff icon highlights information that the tech-savvy reader might want to make note of.

Where to Go from Here

This book is written for those new to content marketing; it makes this overwhelming and complicated topic easy to understand so you won't be intimidated. If you're just getting started, turn to Part I. If you have a question or are curious about a topic, turn to the index or table of contents and head right to the chapter or section that covers that topic. When you finish reading this book, you're likely to wonder why you waited so long to add content marketing initiatives to your marketing plan.

Part I

Getting Started with a Content Marketing Plan

The 5th Wave   By Rich Tennant

In this part . . .

Congratulations! You've taken the first step to growing your brand or business with content by reading this book, and you're about to embark on an adventure that can deliver real results. But don't be tempted to start churning out content until you take some time to discover what content marketing is and how it can help you.

Part I covers all the content marketing basics, so you can effectively develop your own content marketing strategy and then appropriately execute a marketing plan based on that strategy. You find out about content etiquette, laws that affect content marketers, and how to forget how to think like a marketer and instead, think like a publisher.

Chapter 1

Defining the Content Marketing Opportunity

Congratulations! You've made the decision to use content to promote your business, and you're ready to get started. This book introduces you to the content marketing opportunity. Thanks to the free and open nature of the social Web, businesses can build brand awareness, develop relationships, and boost their profits in amazing ways. The trick is understanding the why's and how's of content marketing so you can produce and publish content that actually helps you reach your goals rather than creating the opposite effect — or no effect at all!

Before you dive into the world of content marketing, you need to prepare yourself by taking the time to find out how content marketing evolved and what you need to do to create content that drives traffic, conversation, sharing, and ultimately, purchases. In other words, there is more to content marketing than simply publishing words. Set yourself up for success from the start by mastering the fundamentals.

Understanding What Content Marketing Is

Content marketing encompasses all forms of content that add value to consumers, thereby directly or indirectly promoting a business, brand, products, or services. Content marketing occurs both online and offline, but the free and simple tools of the social Web have opened up the ability for companies of all sizes to compete alongside one another, not for market share but for voice and influence.

Marketing a business using content isn't a new concept; however, it has evolved in recent years to mean far more than creating a company brochure filled with overtly promotional messages and images. Today, content marketing focuses on creating content that is meaningful and useful to consumers with promotion taking a backseat to adding value, particularly adding value to the online conversation happening across the social Web.

Evolving from interruption marketing to engagement marketing

In the 21st century, consumers actively try to avoid being interrupted by ads and marketing messages. While companies used to have to rely on catching the attention of consumers using tactics such as shock advertising and sexual innuendos, the same tactics aren't as effective today when consumers can simply click away from an online ad or skip commercials on their DVRs. Even the most attention-getting ads go unnoticed by consumers who fast-forward over them.

At the same time, consumers are now hyper-connected. They have access to enormous amounts of information, such as instantaneous access to real-time news, from their homes, offices, and mobile devices. In other words, simply interrupting consumers and delivering marketing messages won't get the job done anymore. Instead, companies have to quickly demonstrate the added value they can deliver, particularly if they're interrupting consumers in order to deliver that value.

To achieve success, companies need to engage consumers rather than interrupt them. Consider a pop-up ad appearing on a Web site today. It wasn't so long ago that pop-up ads were all the rage among marketers. Today, they're a sure-fire way to annoy customers and cause them to turn away from your brand. Rather than taking control of consumers' online experiences, businesses need to enhance those experiences, and they can do it with content that adds value and engages consumers.

Breaking through the online clutter

Given how cluttered the Web is with content, messages, spam, and so on, you're undoubtedly wondering how you can get consumers to notice you without doing something drastic to catch their attention. That's where you can apply the steps of brand-building to your content marketing strategy.

Just as a brand isn't built overnight, neither is an effective and influential content marketing plan quickly built. Start thinking of content marketing as an essential part of building your brand and online reputation. A powerful brand can lead a business to fantastic places. For example, the Disney brand adds immense value to the Walt Disney Company. You can build your own brand through content marketing and position yourself for success through long-term, sustainable growth.

You can apply the following three fundamental steps of brand building to your content marketing initiatives:

- ✔ **Consistency:** All of your messages and activities must consistently communicate your brand image and promise, or consumers will become confused. They'll turn away from your brand and look for one that does consistently meet their expectations in every interaction.

- ✔ **Persistence:** Brands are built over time and through continual efforts in spreading messages and meeting customer expectations.

- ✔ **Restraint:** Brands must stay focused and resist extending into areas of business or activities that run counter to the brand promise.

Just as a brand represents a promise that consumers can rely on to meet their expectations again and again, so should your content marketing. By publishing valuable content that consistently communicates your brand promise, consumers will develop expectations for your brand and become loyal to it. Loyal consumers talk about the brands they love. This is a marketer's dream come true. In other words, you can build your brand and your business through content with little or no monetary investment. Instead, you simply need to commit your time and effort. It's an opportunity that businesses would be crazy to pass up!

Understanding 21st century buying behaviors and purchase processes

Changes in the ways consumers make purchasing decisions is another reason content marketing has become a critical element of a business's marketing plan. No longer do consumers rely on television or print ads to get information about products and services; with the growth of the social Web, the pool of people and resources consumers can go to and get reviews and referrals has grown exponentially.

Research shows that prior to making a purchase, consumers conduct the majority of their research online. They read reviews from experts and everyday consumers. They search for comparison-shopping sites, and they publish questions on forums, blogs, social networking profiles, Twitter, and more. Consumers can learn about products and services and decide on which purchase is best for them in the privacy of their homes, either anonymously or otherwise. It's entirely up to each individual.

Within seconds, consumers can find honest opinions online through simple searches and by participating in conversations. Of course, not all reviews are created equal, but the fact is that this is where consumers do their research, and this is the stage on which they make the majority of their purchasing decisions, including where and what to buy. So, you not only need to represent your business in the online space, but also you need to monitor your business and industry across the Web conversations to ensure that they accurately reflect your brand, products, and services.

Again, you can achieve that goal with great content! However, as discussed earlier in this chapter, that content can't consist entirely of promotional messages. The content must be interesting and engaging, or it will be ignored, simply because that's the type of interruptive content that consumers are *not* looking for online.

Being customer-centric

When companies first started creating Web sites, the sites were highly navigational, meaning they offered static information through one-way information delivery. As the Internet evolved, business Web sites became transactional, and consumers could actually make purchases online. Nevertheless, online communication remained primarily one-way until the evolution of the social Web, which changed the world of communication and business. Suddenly, businesses could participate in public two-way conversations. However, many businesses still haven't modified their Web sites and online destinations to focus more on consumers' needs than on the company's goals. In other words, business sites are still talking *at* people about topics that matter to the business and in a transactional manner rather than talking *with* people about topics that matter to those people and in a social manner.

Today, online communication trumps many traditional forms of communication, particularly as smartphones enable people to easily communicate via the tools of the social Web faster than they can via e-mail, telephone, or in person. This fact doesn't mean a company should move all of its communications to the online space, but it does mean that the online space needs to be a priority in every company's marketing communications plan. The most successful business Web sites in the 21st century have evolved, too. Those sites are now customer-centric (or audience-centric), and the content published is created with consumers' wants, needs, and expectations as the top priorities.

Consumers are fickle and impatient. You need to give them information that makes them smarter consumers and that helps them in multiple aspects of their lives. Create a Web site and other branded online destinations (see Chapter 2 for more on this topic) that are customer-centric. In every branded interaction, give customers a reason to want to visit your Web site and engage with you and your content by adding value to the online conversation. A destination-centric content strategy that focuses more on your business than on your target audience won't get the job done anymore.

Comparing traditional online marketing, social media marketing, and content marketing

Most people, including many marketers, are confused about the differences among traditional online marketing, social media marketing, and content marketing. These three forms of digital marketing overlap frequently, so making a distinction among them is challenging. However, you need to understand the underlying differences if you want to be successful in marketing your business with content.

The three primary forms of digital marketing are as follows:

- **Traditional online marketing:** All forms of marketing related to the Internet are considered to be online marketing. Traditional forms predate the social Web and include all forms of online ads (such as banner, pop-up, flash, interstitial, video, and so on). Traditional forms of online marketing rely on "push" marketing strategies and are typically direct marketing efforts, meaning companies push messages at consumers with a specific action or response in mind from consumers.

- **Social media marketing:** Social media marketing can include direct and indirect marketing efforts and includes all forms of marketing executed using the tools of the social Web. For example, writing a business blog providing tips or participating in a Facebook conversation related to your industry are both forms of indirect marketing through social media. Alternatively, publishing a discount code in your Twitter feed is a direct marketing tactic through social media. The tools of the social Web include all online publishing tools that enable people to publish any form of user-generated content such as articles, comments, videos, images, audio, and so on.

✔ **Content marketing:** Content marketing is less social and more informational in nature than social media marketing (although great content can and should lead to conversations and sharing). All content that adds value and could market a business (directly or indirectly) is considered a form of content marketing. Content marketing can come in long-form (such as blogs, articles, ebooks, and so on), short form (such as Twitter updates, Facebook updates, images, and so on), or conversation and sharing (for example, sharing great content via Twitter or offering helpful information in an online forum).

As you might expect, an online article is a perfect example of content marketing. However, as consumers and audience members share and discuss the content, it becomes a social media marketing opportunity. In other words, content marketing involves understanding what consumers want and need, and then creating and publishing content that is relevant and useful. By publishing content that helps consumers, your brand and business become a part of their lives that they come to rely on and trust over time. As that content is discussed and shared across the social Web, what started as an indirect content marketing effort can become a powerful form of social media marketing. The opportunities are practically limitless!

Understanding how different departments in an organization can use content marketing

Despite its name, employees from varied departments within an organization can participate in content marketing initiatives. Remember, content marketing doesn't have to include direct marketing messages at all, and that's where members of your organization outside the marketing department can get involved. Chapter 17 has more about building a content marketing team, but right now, the focus is on how content marketing can spread across an organization and become an organic part of employees' everyday responsibilities.

Content marketing is all about publishing useful information that helps your target audience, which means your executives can write blog posts, ebooks, or presentations that offer their thoughtful leadership. Customer service team members can create answers to frequently asked questions or solutions to common problems, and the marketing team can create videos, conduct interviews, and publish tutorials. Figure 1-1 shows a breakdown of activities that different departments within a company can pursue via content marketing, as well as the social media marketing opportunities that evolve from great content.

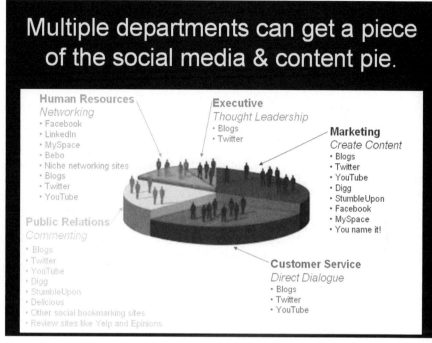

Multiple departments can get a piece of the social media & content pie.

Human Resources
Networking
• Facebook
• LinkedIn
• MySpace
• Bebo
• Niche networking sites
• Blogs
• Twitter
• YouTube

Executive
Thought Leadership
• Blogs
• Twitter

Marketing
Create Content
• Blogs
• Twitter
• YouTube
• Digg
• StumbleUpon
• Facebook
• MySpace
• You name it!

Public Relations
Commenting
• Blogs
• Twitter
• YouTube
• Digg
• StumbleUpon
• Delicious
• Other social bookmarking sites
• Review sites like Yelp and Epinions

Customer Service
Direct Dialogue
• Blogs
• Twitter
• YouTube

Figure 1-1:
Multiple departments can get a piece of the content marketing pie.

Of course, if you're a solo entrepreneur or have very few employees, you'll wear multiple hats and create varied content to leverage the multiple opportunities to connect with consumers. The trick is to publish varied content so your audience is continually engaged and its expectations are met again and again.

Discovering how you can benefit from content marketing

The primary benefits of content marketing are building brand awareness and developing relationships with your target consumer audience *and* online influencers. (See Chapter 2 for more about finding and connecting with your target audience and online influencers.) The idea, at this point, is to understand how content marketing can enable you to build your brand and business by putting you in front of audiences that matter.

By publishing content, you can put yourself on the map. As you build your business's online presence through consistent and persistent publishing of interesting and useful content, more and more people will find you or hear about you. If your content is relevant and interesting, they'll want more of it. They'll remember who you are, and they'll share your content with others. They'll want to talk about your content with you and with their own online (and offline) connections. In other words, your content opens the virtual door between your business and a global audience.

Your content helps people understand your brand message and promise, and it allows people to develop their own perceptions for your brand and business. They develop expectations for your brand based on the information you consistently share. They reach out and communicate with you via social Web conversations, and in time, they become loyal brand advocates who talk about your brand, creating a form of word-of-mouth marketing that business owners could only dream about years ago.

Think of it this way — two decades ago, business owners like you would have done anything (well, maybe not *anything*) to get together with an audience of engaged consumers to talk about products and services. Today, a larger engaged audience than you can imagine is available to you, thanks to the power and reach of the social Web. You just have to discover what they want to hear from you, and then deliver it again and again.

Defining the three forms of content marketing

Content marketing comes in three basic forms — long-form, short-form, and conversations. It's important to understand that content marketing is still a new form of marketing, and no one knows the recipe for success. Only a few rules and some loose guidelines are available for businesses and marketers to follow. In fact, you're really limited only by your creativity and dedication. Truth be told, any content that you make publicly available online and offline could be considered a type of content marketing, because all content is a reflection of your brand and business. Furthermore, all content opens up a potential talking point for consumers to consider, dissect, analyze, and debate. The social Web offers a perfect (and very public) place for them to do so.

Also, the forms of content marketing are constantly changing as new tools to create, publish and share that content are launched and others are shut down. Enhancements and new functionality are added to content publishing tools every day, which means the tools you're using to create, publish, and share content today might not be the tools you're using tomorrow.

The three forms of content marketing that you can create, publish, and share as part of your content marketing plan follow:

- ✔ **Long-form content marketing:** Includes all published content that's longer than a few sentences and that offers deep value, such as blog posts, articles, ebooks, press releases, white papers, presentations, videos, podcasts, webinars, and so on.

- ✔ **Short-form content marketing:** Includes all published content with no more than a few sentences and that communicates useful information, such as Twitter updates, Facebook updates, LinkedIn updates, images, and so on.

- ✔ **Conversations and sharing content marketing:** Can happen through conversations about published content and through the sharing of published content, such as blog comments, forum comments, Twitter updates, link sharing via social bookmarking, comments on videos and images, and so on.

Each of the preceding forms of content marketing is described in detail later in this book. The important thing to remember is that you're likely to see overlap between the three forms as well as overlap with social media and traditional online marketing efforts. That's a good thing!

The best marketing plan is a fully integrated strategy where one piece connects to the next. For example, the phrase, "If you build it, they will come," doesn't apply to content marketing. Simply publishing content isn't enough. You also need to promote that content. You can do so through conversations and sharing as well as through social media and digital marketing efforts. In fact, you can even integrate your offline marketing efforts with your online content marketing efforts (see Chapter 15 for more on this topic).

Understanding the Google Effect: How to Leverage the Power of Search

There has never been a better time in history for a small business to compete on a level playing field regardless of its budget. If you can spare even just an hour a day on content marketing-related activities, you'll see results in terms of increased word-of-mouth marketing, repeat business, and new business. But many people don't understand how to connect content marketing efforts with bottom-line business growth. If you're wondering how content marketing can help you build your business, you simply need to think of a single word — Google.

Ask yourself the following question — how do you find information about a type of product, service, or business? Do you pick up the local Yellow Pages or newspaper in search of an ad? Probably not, and it's fairly safe to assume that most people are just like you. When they need information about a product, service, or business, they turn on their computers or smartphones, open up their Web browser, and visit their preferred search engine. For the vast majority of Internet users, that preferred search engine is Google. Next, they type keywords related to the product, service, or business they need to find, and click the various links provided in the search results. In simplest terms, your business needs to be represented in keyword searches related to your products and services, and it's easier than ever to get there through content marketing.

Creating entry points

Consider the following scenario, which demonstrates how content marketing can help you ensure that you're represented on search engines and across the social Web. First, imagine that your business has a Web site. You invest in great design and copywriting and launch a 10-page Web site that looks fantastic and tells the complete story of your business and products. That site creates ten entry points on which Google or other search engines can find you.

Next, imagine that you connect a blog to your Web site and publish a new blog post every day for a year. Now, you have 365 *more* entry points to your Web site. Google and other search engines can find all these entry points and then deliver those pages to people searching for your type of business and products.

Now, imagine that the content you publish throughout the year on your business blog is interesting, useful, and meaningful content that meets your target audience's needs. Your audience will undoubtedly want to share that content with their own online connections. They'll tweet about it, post it on Facebook, blog about it, and more. When you write amazing content that people want to share, which I call *shareworthy content*, you're opening up the floodgates for even more entry points to your business blog and Web site. Suddenly your 375 entry points turn into hundreds or thousands more, all from the conversations and sharing of your shareworthy content.

I call this the *compounding effect of blogging*, and it's a powerful thing. You simply can't buy that kind of access to consumers! By publishing amazing content that is relevant and useful to your target audience, your entry points will grow over time. Every day you wait is a missed opportunity to create those valuable entry points that every business needs in order to reach full potential.

Researching keywords

Before you begin creating a lot of content and publishing it online, take some time to discover what keywords and keyword phrases you need to focus on. Drill down and find the specific keyword phrases that will drive your targeted traffic to your content — and that will help you avoid competing with larger competitors with bigger budgets to spend on search engine optimization.

Throughout this book, you can find specific search engine optimization techniques as part of the tips provided for implementing the three forms of content marketing, but you can't use search engine optimization techniques unless you do your research upfront (specifically, keyword analysis).

Following are several free and paid tools that can help you determine which keyword phrases to target in your content:

✔ **Google AdWords Keyword Tool** (`https://adwords.google.com/o/ Targeting/Explorer?__u=1000000000&__c=1000000000&ideaRe questType=KEYWORD_IDEAS#search.none`): The free Google AdWords Keyword Tool enables you to find out the popularity of keywords in terms of traffic and the cost-per-click that advertisers are paying for those keywords. Additionally, when you enter a keyword into the search tool, a list of related keywords is returned to you as well, making it easy to broaden your research and find the best keywords for your content. See Figure 1-2, which shows the results for the keyword *sports*.

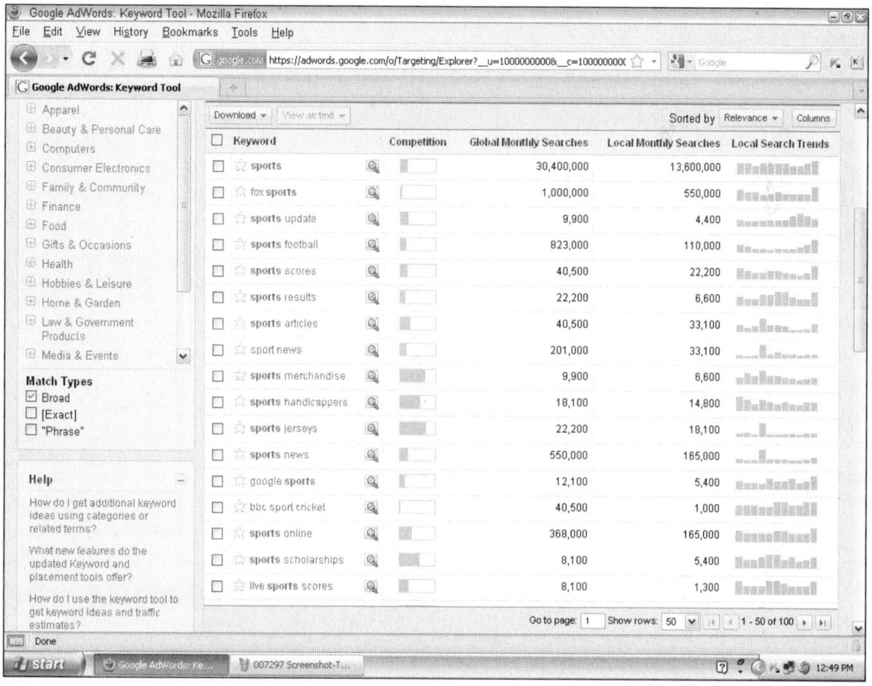

Figure 1-2:
The Google AdWords Keyword Tool provides search popularity data and related keyword suggestions.

- **Google AdWords Traffic Estimator** (`https://adwords.google.com/o/Targeting/Explorer?__u=1000000000&__c=1000000000&ideaRequestType=KEYWORD_STATS#search.none`): The free Google AdWords Traffic Estimator tool helps you discover how much advertisers are paying for certain keywords. Advertisers bid on keywords and serve ads on Web pages with relevant content. Popular keywords typically have higher price tags and higher traffic estimates. The key to using Google AdWords Traffic Estimator for keyword research is to find the middle ground. Look for keywords related to your blog's content that are neither the most trafficked and highest priced nor the least trafficked and lowest priced. This way, you'll strike a balance between too much competition (meaning many other sites are already creating content related to those keywords) and too little traffic (meaning no one is searching for those keywords).

- **Wordtracker** (`www.wordtracker.com`): To use Wordtracker, you have to pay a fee, but a free trial is available. If you're serious about keyword research, then Wordtracker is probably the best tool currently available with a fairly reasonable price tag.

- **Keyword Discovery** (`www.keyworddiscovery.com`): Keyword Discovery is another excellent tool for keyword research, but it also has a fee associated with it. A free trial is available, so you can give it a test drive before you pay anything. The results you'll get from Keyword Discovery are extensive and best for someone who really wants to drill down deep into keyword research.

Don't let search engine optimization take center stage. Your content is always the top priority. Make sure what you say is the cornerstone of your content marketing efforts. Everything else should be secondary and used to complement what you say. If you have any chance of getting people to talk about you and share your content in the long-term, which helps you build your brand and business, you need to make sure your content is always meaningful, relevant, and useful.

Keyword research is constantly evolving, and it's a very detailed topic. You can read much more about search engine optimization in *Search Engine Optimization For Dummies* by Peter Kent (Wiley). And don't forget to check out the additional search engine optimization tips included in Chapters 7, 10, and 14 of this book.

Search engine reputation management

There is more to search engines than keyword results. You can also use search engines to stay abreast of content and conversations related to your brand and business reputation. In this way, you can take the necessary steps to ensure those results are the ones you want people to see. In other words, when consumers type keywords related to your business into their preferred search engines, you need to know that the results they'll get not only point them in the direction of your business, but also point them to places that paint your business in a positive light.

You can use several tools to monitor your search engine reputation. Following are some easy tools that you can use free:

- ✔ **Google Alerts:** You can set up Google Alerts (www.google.com/alerts) to send you e-mail messages when content that uses your chosen keywords (for example, your business name) is published online.

- ✔ **Google Advanced Search:** You can conduct daily or weekly Google Advanced Searches (www.google.com/advanced_search) using your chosen keywords (such as your business name) to find content that Google Alerts may have missed.

- ✔ **Twitter alerts:** Twitter alerts work similarly to Google Alerts. You receive e-mail messages telling you about Twitter posts that include your chosen keywords. TweetBeep (www.tweetbeep.com) is a good choice for automating Twitter alerts.

- ✔ **Twitter Advanced Search:** You can conduct Twitter searches using very specific criteria to find tweets related to your chosen keywords using the Advanced Twitter Search form (http://search.twitter.com/advanced).

- ✔ **Twitter apps:** A number of Twitter applications can help you monitor tweets and conversations on Twitter that are related to your business. Monitter (www.monitter.com) is a great Twitter app for keeping tabs on conversations using your chosen keywords.

Again, content marketing can't occur in a silo. You need to be aware of what's being said about your business, brand, products, competitors, and so on. In this way, you will be able to respond and create content that's even more relevant to your targeted audience's wants and needs. Be sure to check out Chapter 16 to read about how to best respond to negative conversations and content about your business that you find online.

Revealing the Broad Reach of Online Content

Your business operates in a truly global environment, and content marketing via the Internet has the ability to put your business in front of more people than ever. In 2009, comScore reported that the number of Internet users around the world had surpassed one billion, and that number didn't even include people who accessed the Internet via smartphones or public computers such as Internet cafés and libraries. Furthermore, the majority of those users were in the Asia Pacific region, followed by users in Europe, North America, the Middle East and Africa, and Latin America (www.comscore.com/Press_Events/Press_Releases/2009/1/Global_Internet_Audience_1_Billion). And the growth in Internet use shows no signs of slowing down. According to predictions by Forrester research, the number of Internet users across the globe will more than double to 2.4 billion by 2014.

In fact, many small businesses have grown into global companies with millions of dollars in annual revenue simply through minimal efforts to build an online presence and by publishing valuable content. The sidebar, "The success of Gary Vaynerchuk and Wine Library," describes one of the most popular examples of a small business expanding beyond anyone's wildest dreams, thanks to a blog and online video content.

It's amazing to think that people around the world can see the words you publish online instantaneously. Therefore, the question for businesses isn't "Why should you use content marketing?" but rather "Why *aren't* you *already* using content marketing?"

It comes down to earning a share of the online voice as mentioned earlier in this chapter. If you're actively participating in the online conversation (or at least being mentioned in that conversation), then you're earning valuable publicity without spending any money. The value of this *earned media* is incalculable. The sidebar, "The success of Gary Vaynerchuk and Wine Library," is the perfect example of how earned media born of amazing content can catapult a business to new heights of success. But you can't get there unless you're consistently and persistently publishing your own shareworthy, amazing content that your audience finds useful.

The success of Gary Vaynerchuk and Wine Library

Gary Vaynerchuk's father owned a small wine store in Springfield, New Jersey. As Gary grew up, he spent a lot of time at his father's store and developed a love of wines. One day, he asked his father if he could start a blog for the store. His father acquiesced, and Gary began publishing content about his love of wine, his unique ways of tasting wines and comparing the flavors of those wines to unusual objects like rocks. Soon, he added an online video element where he used his own video camera to record himself talking about wine to the Wine Library blog, and Wine Library TV (http://tv.winelibrary.com) was born.

Gary's passion for his subject matter and his enigmatic personality were contagious, and his audience grew and grew. Today, Wine Library is a $60 million-per year business with over half of those sales coming from the Internet. Gary is a sought after social media speaker, and he signed a multi-million dollar contract to author a series of books about social media marketing. And it all started from a blog.

Shifting from a Marketer to a Publisher Mindset

One of the first things you must do in order to be successful with content marketing is to forget everything you know about marketing. That's a scary concept for many people. For years, businesses have been following marketing strategies based on interrupting consumers. For your content marketing efforts to work, you need to put the aggressive marketing mindset on the backburner and focus on writing and publishing shareworthy content, as mentioned earlier in this chapter.

Therefore, as you're creating content, do so with your audience in mind, not your business goals. Deliver the content your audience wants and needs and then promote that content separately through your social media interactions. Inevitably, as I mentioned earlier, your content and social media marketing activities will overlap, but your content should be able to stand on its own, separate from your social media marketing tactics. This section offers some helpful suggestions to better enable you to separate your content marketing and content publishing thoughts.

Applying the 80-20 rule

In marketing theory, the 80-20 rule states that 80 percent of business comes from 20 percent of the customers. I like to use a similar concept when it comes to content marketing and social media marketing. Remember, you have to think like a publisher to be successful with content marketing. If you apply the 80-20 rule to your content marketing efforts, 80 percent or more of the content you develop should *not* be self-promotional and 20 percent or less should be self-promotional. That means the vast majority of the time you spend on content marketing activities won't be directly related to marketing at all.

But hold on! Just because 80 percent of your efforts aren't directly self-promotional doesn't mean they're not indirectly marketing your business. In fact, it's indirect marketing that makes content marketing so powerful. Every piece of content you publish or share can add value to the online experience and further strengthen your relationship with your online audience of brand advocates who will talk about your content and share it with their own audiences. Don't think content that doesn't directly promote your business isn't helping drive revenues. It's just happening indirectly and might not be apparent immediately.

Adding value, staying relevant, and being shareworthy

If you're following the 80-20 rule, you know that 80 percent of your content should add value to the online experience, particularly for your target audience. This is how you build relationships and set expectations for your target audience and among online influencers who can help to spread your messages even farther across the global Web community. You need to take the time to research what type of information, messages, and content your target audience wants from a business like yours, and then deliver that content in a professional manner. Read Chapter 2 for more on researching your audience and online influencers.

In addition, you need to offer content that your audience will share with others. Traditional publishers use this strategy to create content that not only sells newspapers or magazines but also offers a pass-along value that may convert secondary readers into subscribers. The same concept holds true for content marketing today. The difference is that today anyone, including you, can be a content publisher and use that content to lead to bigger and better things, such as brand awareness, business growth, and sales.

Never has there been such an exciting opportunity for small and mid-size businesses to stake their claims and position themselves for success — because now it's not necessarily the depth of your wallet that leads to success through content marketing but rather the depth of your words. Content marketing enables businesses to continually meet customer expectations and to add something extra to the consumer experience that helps develop trust, security, and loyalty.

Content marketing offers the perfect way for businesses to leverage the three S's of Customer Loyalty:

- ✔ **Stability:** Customers become loyal to a product, brand, or business when it sends a consistent message they can trust and rely on.
- ✔ **Sustainability:** Customers become loyal to a product, brand, or business when they believe it will be with them for a long time or at least for a specific amount of time with a predetermined end.
- ✔ **Security:** Customers become loyal to a product, brand, or business when it gives them a feeling of comfort or peace of mind.

As you can see, consumers actively look for products, brands, and businesses that they feel they can trust and that won't abandon them. They become emotionally involved in the products, brands, and businesses that help them feel a sense of comfort. A well-executed content marketing strategy can offer the stability, sustainability, and security that consumers seek, and it can help them develop an emotional connection and relationship with a product, brand, or business.

Developing Content to Build Your Brand and Form Relationships

Content marketing, paired with social media marketing, is the single largest opportunity for individuals, organizations, and companies of any size to build their brands and build their businesses.

Content marketing offers a unique opportunity for you to engage with current and potential employees, position your brand as a brand of choice, develop an ongoing dialogue with consumers and influencers that ultimately creates brand advocates and brand guardians, and to learn an incredible amount about your target audience and competitors. What's not to love?

Understanding what a brand is

Branding is a difficult concept for many people to understand. That's because a brand isn't truly a tangible or quantifiable thing. Although a brand can be represented by tangible elements, such as a logo, color palette, and so on, intangible elements work with the tangible elements to create consumer perceptions, as illustrated in Figure 1-3. In other words, brands are built by consumers, not companies. Companies might nudge consumers in a desired direction, but consumers create brands through experiences and emotions.

The easiest way to think of a brand is as a promise to consumers. A brand sets expectations for consumers through that promise and meets those expectations in every interaction. Brands that don't meet those expectations fail.

As consumers experience brands and make them their own, the brands grow. The most powerful brands are relationship brands. These brands are typically shared by groups of people and provide opportunities for consumers to select how they want to interact with the brand they love through a wide variety of experiences. You can set the wheels in motion to turn your brand into a relationship brand by consistently and persistently publishing interesting, shareworthy content relevant to consumers' wants and needs, thereby adding value to their lives.

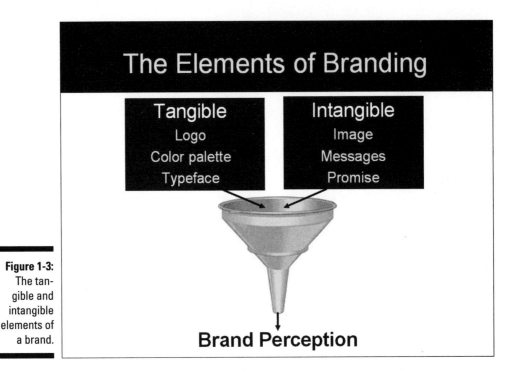

The Elements of Branding

Tangible
Logo
Color palette
Typeface

Intangible
Image
Messages
Promise

Brand Perception

Figure 1-3:
The tangible and intangible elements of a brand.

Positioning your brand

Before you can create content that sets brand expectations in consumers' minds, you need to determine where your brand is positioned in the marketplace relative to your competitors. The most powerful brands own a word in consumers' minds. For example, in the auto industry, Toyota owns reliable in the minds of U.S. consumers, Hyundai owns affordable, and Cadillac owns luxury. Take some time to determine where your business should be positioned relative to your competitors, and work on creating content that accurately reflects that position.

If you own a gourmet food store, for example, publishing content that shows consumers how to make meals for under $10 doesn't match your brand's position. Doing so will confuse consumers and could cause them to turn away from your brand in search of one that does meet their expectations based on the brand's promise. In other words, don't promise high-end, gourmet products and shopping experiences and then deliver low-end, cheap information and content experiences. That content doesn't add value to your target audience's lives, so they won't talk about it or share it with other people who might help your business grow.

You can determine your brand's position by taking the Brand Perception Snap Shot, which requires you to answer the following three questions:

1. What five words would you use to describe your brand today?

2. What five words would your customers use to describe your brand today?

3. What five words do you want customers to use to describe your brand in the future? What is your ultimate goal?

Be honest in answering these questions and then take some time to review your results. Find the gaps and opportunities and fill them. You can do this through your content marketing efforts and easily position your brand in consumers' minds. Your consistency and persistence will pay off over time as you continually develop audience expectations and perceptions of your brand.

Establishing credibility and becoming the go-t0 person for a topic

Your business is nothing if it's not credible. Your amazing content can help you develop an online reputation that is built on authority and that clearly demonstrates your knowledge and expertise in your area of business or topic. When you publish content, do so with the goal of always making sure the content helps to establish you as the go-to person for information related to your business.

The more you publish valuable content and the more people talk about that content, the more your reputation will grow and spread across the online community. One day you'll start getting e-mails or phone calls from people who want to use you as an expert for an article or interview. That's a sign your efforts are starting to pay off! Pat yourself on the back and keep publishing shareworthy content that helps to position your brand and yourself in the eyes of consumers and online influencers.

Just as Gary Vaynerchuk (see the sidebar earlier in this chapter) wasn't always the go-to person for social media marketing, you'll need time to establish your reputation and become a popular source for topics related to your own line of business. Don't give up too soon!

It's also important to determine the style and voice you want to use in your content marketing efforts. That style and voice needs to be appropriate for your brand image and should match consumer expectations for your brand, but it also must be real and honest. If your personality and your passion for your business don't shine through, you're unlikely to retain an audience and build relationships based on that content.

Similarly, you need to be accessible to your audience. Communicate with them and respond to their questions, e-mails, comments on your blog, tweets, and so on. Content marketing and social media marketing go hand-in-hand. You can't publish content and then disappear. Instead, actively engage with your audience to deepen your relationships with them as well as their relationships with your brand.

Understanding the ARMS Theory of Brand Building

Four primary steps to brand building strategy can help you understand where you are on the path to building a successful brand and where you still have to go to reach the level of success you want and need. I call this the ARMS Theory of Brand Building, broken down as follows:

- ✔ **Awareness:** Consumers move from an unaware state to an aware state. They have heard of a brand but don't remember it without a prompt and can't remember any details about it.

- ✔ **Recognition:** Consumers move from an aware state to a state of recognition where they remember a brand when they are prompted and know what it is and what it's for.

- ✔ **Memory:** Consumers move from a state of recognition to a state of memory when they can recall a brand and what it's for without being prompted in any way.

- ✔ **Spreading the word:** Consumers move from a state of memory to spreading the word when they have tried a brand, believe the brand promise, and want to share their knowledge and experiences with other people.

The ultimate goal of brand building is reaching the "spreading the word" stage where consumers aren't only loyal to your brand but also advocate it and defend it against naysayers. Therefore, it's essential that on the social Web you focus your efforts on building a band of brand advocates who will share your content, promote your content and your brand, and stick up for your content and your brand when it is questioned. You need to cultivate relationships with your brand advocates just as they cultivate relationships with your brand. Again, there's more to content marketing than simply publishing content. If you don't pursue the activities that can help the content thrive and work as indirect marketing tools, you won't get the results you want and need.

Committing to a Long-Term Strategy

As discussed earlier in this chapter, brands aren't built overnight and content marketing is a long-term strategy to build brands and businesses. You need to commit to pursuing content marketing initiatives for years to come in order to be successful. Remember the compounding effect of the blogging concept described earlier in this chapter (in the section, "Creating entry points"). That kind of domino effect can't occur without a lot of dominos already in position (that would be your varied pieces of content). Each new piece of shareworthy content that you publish plays an important part in expanding the domino effect. Keep adding dominos!

It's also important to set reasonable expectations for your content marketing success. That's because your success is directly dependent on the amount of time you commit to content marketing. The more time you put into publishing great content and engaging with your audience online and offline, the better your chances are of seeing real results sooner rather than later. However, much of your content marketing efforts will rely on your willingness to experiment and tweak your efforts. That's because content marketing is still too new to have a defined roadmap to success. Instead, carve out your own roadmap. Just don't expect to become an Internet sensation overnight!

Perhaps one of the most important things to keep in mind as you're pursuing your own content marketing plan is . . . don't get too caught up in the numbers. When it comes to content marketing, quality trumps quantity.

If you must measure your results, focus on hard and soft metrics, as described in Chapter 16.

Think of it this way. If you publish 1,000 pieces of poorly written content, they won't help you much. In fact, they could do more harm than good if they don't live up to consumers' expectations for your brand. However, if you publish 100 pieces of interesting, shareworthy content, the chances of that content spreading to your target audience and driving those people to visit your Web site, blog, or other branded online destination for more information are much greater.

Similarly, having 10,000 blog subscribers who don't share your posts or publish comments is far less helpful than having 1,000 blog subscribers who link to your posts, share them on Twitter and other social sites, join the conversation through comments, and so on. Quality relationships with your target audience can help you build your business far more effectively than can big numbers that are meaningless in terms of converting sales. It might be tempting to focus on numbers, but try to refrain!

Benchmarking Other Businesses That Are Doing It Right

Before you begin your own content marketing plan, it's helpful to look at other businesses that are doing great things in the online space. Of course, you don't have to do the same things that the businesses mentioned in this section are doing with content marketing, but you can get some ideas and implement some similar tactics if they're right for your business, brand, and audience. The key is to avoid reinventing the wheel. Take some time to research what other companies are doing well or mistakes they've made, and learn from those companies. If similar tactics might work for you, try them. Also, make sure you know what your competitors are doing so you can act appropriately to retain your brand's position in consumers' minds.

Following are several businesses that are doing great things with content marketing:

- **Gary Vaynerchuk:** As mentioned earlier in this chapter, Gary Vaynerchuk of Wine Library is a great person to follow to see how video content can help a business grow. http://tv.winelibrary.com

- **Naked Pizza:** Naked Pizza uses Twitter for both social media marketing and content marketing. The New Orleans-based pizza retailer publishes direct marketing messages such as discount offerings as well as newsletter content, all in 140-characters or less. http://twitter.com/nakedpizza

- **Dell:** A large company that has evolved into a content marketer to benchmark is Dell. The company effectively surrounds consumers with branded content through varied Twitter profiles, blogs, forums, social networks, and more, many of which can be found by visiting the online Dell Community site as shown in Figure 1-4. http://en.community.dell.com

- **Whole Foods Market:** Whole Foods Market publishes content that adds value to users' lives through a large number of national and local Twitter profiles, blogs, Facebook, Flickr, and more, all of which give Whole Foods a personality that matches the brand and a way of engaging with consumers. Many of these branded destinations can be found from the Whole Foods Market Web site map at www.wholefoodsmarket.com/sitemap.php.

As you spend time online, always be on the lookout for great content marketing examples and companies doing amazing things through content marketing. There is always something new to discover, and you never know when you might stumble upon an idea that will work perfectly for your own business!

Figure 1-4:
The Dell
Community
provides
access to
a variety
of content
through
blogs,
forums, and
more.

Chapter 2

Creating a Content Marketing Strategy

*W*hen you fully understand how content marketing can help you build your brand and business, as discussed in Chapter 1, it's time to put together your own content marketing strategy. As with all marketing strategies, you need to analyze the market, competitors, and customers in order to find opportunities to effectively position and promote your company through content.

Your overall business marketing strategy should provide a clear direction for your business with content marketing efforts playing an important role in that strategy. When your strategy is defined, you can execute a marketing plan, as discussed in Chapter 3, and pursue the various tactics you expect to use in order to achieve the goals defined in your marketing strategy. This chapter explains how to create the content marketing strategy within your overall business marketing strategy. To that end, both a Content Marketing Strategy Worksheet and a Content Marketing Strategy Template are included in the online Cheat Sheet at www.dummies.com/cheatsheet/contentmarketing to help you get started.

Researching Your Competition

You'll find it very difficult to achieve higher levels of business success if you don't know what your competitors are doing. In order to develop your content marketing strategy, you need to know your competition as well as you know yourself. Researching your competition allows you to react appropriately to their content marketing tactics and even to anticipate some of those potential tactics. In other words, by knowing your competition, you can more effectively position your business in the minds of consumers and meet their needs and expectations. More specifically, competitive research enables you to find and exploit your competitors' weaknesses, position your brand as a brand of choice, establish your unique niche, and differentiate your business from other businesses.

Don't be tempted to assume that you already know everything about your competitors from years of experience. The social Web is a completely different space, and what worked offline through traditional marketing strategies and tactics is unlikely to work as effectively online. Consumers are actively looking for information. Give it to them, and know what your competition is doing so you can give consumers the information they're actively seeking better than your competition does.

Finding your competition online and monitoring their activities

The first step to researching your competitors is finding them across the social Web. However, you need to analyze more than your competitors' Web sites. Fortunately, a variety of tools are available to help you find your competition online, just as they help you monitor your own online reputation, as discussed in Chapter 1. When you find your competitors, you need to analyze what they're doing on their branded online destinations as well as on sites they don't own but simply maintain a presence.

Following are a number of methods and tools you can use to conduct your competitive online research:

- ✔ **Google Advanced Search:** Conduct a daily or weekly search on your competitors' names using the Google Advanced Search tool (www.google.com/advanced_search) to find content or conversations recently published about them.

- ✔ **Google Alerts:** Set up Google Alerts (www.google.com/alerts) to send you alerts for your competitors' names.

- ✔ **Monitter:** Use monitter (www.monitter.com) to conduct real-time Twitter searches with competitors' names as the keywords.

- ✔ **Twitter:** Follow your competitors on Twitter (`www.twitter.com`) and read their tweets. Use the Twitter profile search tool to find accounts (`https://twitter.com/invitations/find_on_twitter`). Note that you have to be logged into your Twitter account to use the Twitter profile search tool.

- ✔ **Facebook:** Follow your competitors' profiles and business Pages on Facebook and read their updates. You can use the Facebook People Search tool (`www.facebook.com/search.php?type=users`) to find profiles on Facebook, but if a profile is set to private, you can't view it unless you're "friends" with that profile owner. You can search for Pages from the Facebook Page Directory search (`www.facebook.com/directory/pages`).

- ✔ **LinkedIn:** Follow your competitors' profiles on LinkedIn and read their updates. If you know the names of your competitors' executives or employees, you can search for them on LinkedIn using the search tool found at the bottom of the LinkedIn home page or at the top of any page in your LinkedIn account. Note that you can't view a private profile unless you're connected with that person.

- ✔ **On-site searches:** Visit your competitors' Web sites and blogs and look for links to other online profiles or branded destinations such as YouTube channels, Flickr profiles, and so on. Companies that are implementing a social media marketing or content marketing plan should have links to their various branded online destinations prominently displayed on their Web sites and blogs. A good example is shown in Figure 2-1.

 As you find your competitors' online destinations and conversations, analyze them to discover what kind of content your competitors are publishing. Can you find any gaps or any opportunities to "borrow" a share of voice or to offer content that your target audience isn't already getting from your competitors? Is there a way to repackage the type of information they're publishing to make it more useful and interesting to consumers? What content are your competitors publishing that sparks conversations or sharing? Your findings can help you determine what kind of content to create and where to publish it.

Eavesdropping on your competitors' online conversations

Thanks to the social Web, you can listen in on the conversations your competitors have with their customers and the online audience at large. This is an opportunity you can't pass up! Ten or twenty years ago, business owners would have done anything to be a fly on the wall and listen to their competitors' conversations, but there was really no way to do it legally. The public nature of the social Web places many of those conversations right at your fingertips. Look for them, listen to them, and learn from them! They can have a significant impact on your marketing strategy.

Links to branded online destinations

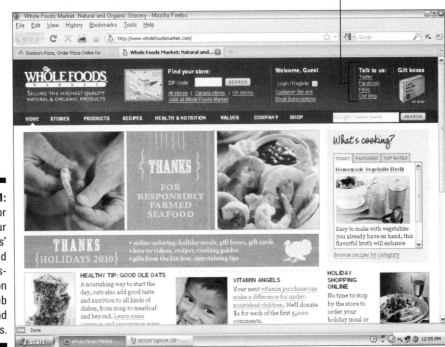

Figure 2-1:
Look for links to your competitors' branded online destinations on their Web sites and blogs.

You can start listening to your competitors' online conversations by analyzing their various online profiles and branded destinations as described in the previous section. However, other ways of listening in on your competitors' conversations can give you even more insight. Following are several tricks you can try to get the inside scoop on your competitors' messages and relationships with consumers:

- **Friends and connections:** Review your competitors' profiles on Facebook, LinkedIn, and other social networking sites and find out who is connected to them as well as whom they're following. Follow those people, too, and keep track of the related conversations and sharing.

- **Groups:** Review your competitors' profiles on Facebook, LinkedIn, Google Groups, and other social sites and find the groups they belong to and participate in. Join those groups and monitor your competitors' conversations within those groups.

- **Followers:** Review your competitors' profiles on Twitter and see both whom they're following and who is following them. Follow those people, too, and find out what content is being discussed and shared.

✔ **Blog comments:** Read your competitors' blogs and pay close attention to the comments section on each blog post. Follow links within profiles, particularly the links that lead you to the site of the person who published a comment. Learn more about the people participating in these conversations and reach out to them. If your competitors' accept and publish *trackback links* on their blog posts, follow those links to discover who else is writing about the content published on your competitors' blogs. If they're linking to your competitors' content, you need to connect with them so they'll link to your amazing content in the future. You can see an example of a trackback link published on a blog post in Figure 2-2.

TECHNICAL STUFF

Trackback links are published within the comments section on some blogs providing an easy way for bloggers to see what other sites and blogs are linking to their content and potentially driving additional traffic to those sites and blogs from interested readers.

✔ **Incoming links:** Use a link checker tool like Google's to find out what sites and pages are linking to your competitors' Web sites and blogs. The owners of those sites and pages are actively discussing your competitors and sharing their content. You need to get a piece of that action, too, so reach out to those site owners and start building a relationship with them. To find incoming links to your Web site or blog, you can conduct a link search through Google by typing **link:***yourURL* into the search box at `www.google.com` (where *yourURL* is the URL for your site, such as **link:www.keysplashcreative.com**). Google Webmaster Tools also offers more comprehensive link research results (`www.google.com/webmasters/tools`).

✔ **LinkedIn Answers:** If your competitors answer questions on LinkedIn (`http://learn.linkedin.com/answers`), then you can find people looking for information related to your business and provide your own answers, too.

Finding gaps and opportunities

As you monitor ongoing conversations and your competitors' involvement in those conversations and related content, look for opportunities to fill gaps and offer something different or offer similar information in a better way. In other words, don't market scared. Just because your competitors are publishing a specific type of content in a specific way doesn't mean those strategies or tactics are right for you and your audience. However, knowing what those strategies and tactics are can help you differentiate your business or better position your brand as the brand of choice.

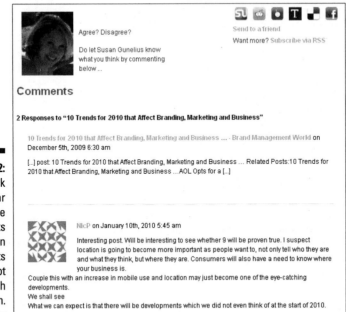

Figure 2-2:
Trackback links appear in the comments section in blog posts that accept and publish them.

Just as each piece of content that you publish becomes part of the larger compounding effect that can deliver long-term sustainable growth to your business, so do your research and analysis efforts. All together, your activities will enable you to drive organic buzz about your business that can be far more powerful than a simple banner ad.

Try to think out-of-the-box and come up with new ways to offer content that your audience wants and needs. For example, if you sell customized gift baskets online, allow consumers to view those baskets through online video so that they can see exactly what their money will buy and make changes on demand. This visual approach provides a creative way to add a tangible element to an online buying process. A business that once could thrive only offline can now thrive online, thanks to creative content marketing and communications via the user-generated content of the social Web.

If you own a business that can help customers by offering step-by-step tutorials, don't just provide in-person training classes or instruction manuals. Instead, add a content marketing aspect by offering webinars or screencast tutorials. You can even turn tutorials into videos that can be shared across the social Web to broaden the reach of your content and indirectly market your business. By offering useful information to consumers, you build a relationship with them based on appreciation and trust. In this way, you can deliver positive word-of-mouth marketing as well as tangible results to your business for years to come.

Identifying Your Audience

As you research your competitors, you also need to research your customers. The social Web is an amazing market research tool that can give you an incredible amount of information about your existing customers, prospective customers, target audience, and audience segments. All you have to do is find your audience, pay attention to what they're doing online, read their content, and listen to their conversations. Sometimes you can even ask them questions.

Many of the tools and techniques that you use to find and research your competitors are the same ones you can use to find your audience. That's because competitors who are effectively using content marketing to build their businesses should already be present in the online destinations where your target audience spends time. However, simply finding your competitors and target audience isn't enough. You also need to evaluate what's happening on those destinations to determine which activities are truly right for you to invest your time and effort.

As you discovered earlier, don't fall into the trap of marketing scared. Instead, create your own roadmap based on your own research and analysis of your market, competitors, and audience.

Determining your target audience and segments

Part of leveraging the social Web to market a brand or product involves changing your marketing strategy in terms of segmenting your customer base. Finding your best customers is a fundamental step in building a business. When you determine the customers you want to target, you need to define ways to find more people like your best customers in order to target that market with meaningful advertising, promotions, and so on — or in the case of content marketing, more useful and shareworthy content. The traditional way of taking this step is to segment your customers by focusing on similar demographic characteristics, such as age, income level, gender, and so on, and then to find similar people based on those demographics.

However, this approach is not necessarily the most effective way to segment and target customers in the world of the social Web. It's true that you need to know the primary demographic profiles of your best customer audiences and whether those profiles match sites where your audience might spend time; however, those factors aren't the only ones that matter — because the social Web can be analyzed using behaviors in addition to demographics. In fact, behavioral targeting is often more powerful than demographic targeting because, while using the Internet for researching, communicating, shopping, building relationships, and more, people don't necessarily reveal personal demographic information. Furthermore, the social Web is filled with people who participate in conversations and publish content anonymously or by using pseudonyms, so it can be very difficult to actually compile demographic information about these people.

Clearly, relying on demographic segmentation when building a content marketing strategy may lead your business down a path to failure. Instead, Internet users need to be segmented and targeted based on their online behaviors. What sites do they visit? What conversations do they join, and what do they say in those conversations? What content do they share with their own audiences? Those are just a few of the relevant questions marketers need to ask to understand their current and potential online audiences.

By continually evaluating online customer behaviors and adjusting the marketing strategy to address those behaviors, marketers can find similar people and introduce the best content, in the best places, and at the best time.

The best content marketing strategy is to find your audience and publish the right kind of content to interest these people and add value to their lives. A combination of demographic and behavioral targeting is essential to creating a solid content marketing strategy.

Finding your audience's hangouts

One of the most important steps you need to take before you launch your content marketing plan is to find where your target audience already spends time interacting and sharing online. You can use some of the tricks suggested earlier in this chapter to eavesdrop on your competitors' conversations by researching your competitors' followers and connections across the social Web. Chances are many of those people will be part of your target audience, too.

However, the first step is to refer to your keyword research, discussed in Chapter 1, and use those keywords to conduct Google searches (since that's the tool most people use to search for information online). In other words, pretend you're a potential customer looking for the type of business, products, or services you offer. Follow the links delivered in the search results just as a consumer would. As you follow the paths provided, you'll be following your target audience. Inevitably, you'll find blogs, Web sites, forums, groups, and so on that your target audience is reading, participating in, and sharing with their own audiences. You need to get involved on those sites, too.

Begin by joining the conversations happening on those sites and offering useful information that adds value to the existing dialogue. Do not self-promote yet. It's critical that you begin developing relationships with your target audience on the destinations where they already spend time, and you can't do that if you're trying to sell. If you want to be a welcomed member to the party, you have to bring something to the table that is meaningful, or no one will want to hang out with you.

When you become a recognized part of the community on a specific destination where your target audience spends time, you can begin bringing those people back to your own branded online destinations, as discussed later in this chapter, where you can offer even more information through your amazing, shareworthy content and deepen your relationships with them. That's how you build lasting relationships that lead to brand loyalty, brand advocacy, and long-term sustainable growth.

Discovering what your audience wants and needs

If you're not delivering the type of content your target audience wants and needs, they won't read or view your content nor will they share it. In fact, they might ignore you or publish negative responses to your content. You don't want that to happen.

Just as you need to determine what your audience wants and needs from your products and services to develop effective advertising, you need to determine what your audience wants and needs from content. It can be intimidating to try to think of new, amazing content to publish consistently and persistently. Don't worry. Every piece of content you publish doesn't have to be amazing. However, you don't want to dilute your value by publishing too much content that isn't discussion-worthy or shareworthy. The majority of your content should be meaningful, but everyone has days when they're simply not up to their full potential. It's acceptable to have off days when it comes to content marketing, and particularly if you don't have a large staff to cover for you. Just don't let it become a habit, or all of your hard work will have been for naught.

To find out what your audience wants and needs from your content, you can start by listening. In fact, listening is one of the most important parts of any successful content marketing strategy. You need to constantly be listening to the online conversation so that you can modify your content marketing strategy as necessary. Consumers move quickly and change their minds even more quickly. If they find your content to be stale or outdated, they'll move on in search of another business or destination that offers the type of value-added information they want and need.

Use the tools suggested earlier in this chapter to find your audience and listen to their conversations, just as you did to find and listen to your competitors. Furthermore, ask your customers both in person and online what kind of information they want and need. Publish a poll on your blog using a tool like Polldaddy (www.polldaddy.com) or SurveyMonkey (www.surveymonkey.com), or pose the question on a forum or group you belong to where your target audience spends time. Additionally, pay attention to your own Web site and blog analytics to see what content is driving a lot of traffic, comments, and incoming links. You can find out more about evaluating Web analytics and content performance in Chapter 16.

Your focus should be on long-term growth and trends. There will always be a few audience members who are louder than others, and certain pieces of content might attract a lot of attention. It's up to you to pick out fluctuations that spell opportunities and anomalies that won't drive business in the long run. Pursue the opportunities aggressively, and put the anomalous traffic spikes on the backburner.

Finding and connecting with influencers

While you're researching your competitors and finding your target audience, you should also be looking for the online influencers who can help you drive more traffic and conversations around your content. For example, if you own a dating service company, you need to search for the top dating and relationship experts on Twitter and Facebook or the top dating bloggers. These people already have audiences that will be good matches for a dating service business, and if they're very popular, they probably have relationships with many of those audience members and have influence over them.

A number of search tools can help you find influencers across the social Web. Several options to get you started are listed here:

- ✔ **Twitter apps:** Use Twitter apps such as WeFollow (`www.wefollow.com`) or Twellow (`www.twellow.com`) to find people by keyword or interest on Twitter. For example, as shown in Figure 2-3, a search using the tag *organicfood* on WeFollow delivered 88 results that a business selling organic foods would be wise to research. Look for people with a lot of followers and a lot of retweets and @replies to show they're truly engaged with their audiences.

- ✔ **Blog searches:** Conduct a search for blogs by keyword using Google Blog Search (`http://blogsearch.google.com`), Technorati (`www.technorati.com`), or IceRocket (`www.icerocket.com`). Look for blogs that are updated frequently with quality content and have high subscriber numbers (if they're published on the site), Alexa rankings (`www.alexa.com`), and Compete rankings (`www.compete.com`). While these ranking tools aren't 100 percent accurate, they can give you an idea of a blog's reach and influence.

- ✔ **Video searches:** Many online influencers publish video content. You can conduct video searches on a number of Web sites, including the largest online video site, YouTube (`www.youtube.com`), or Google (`http://video.google.com`). Look for video publishers whose videos get a lot of views and comments and whose profiles link to their blogs and other branded online destinations so that you can get a better idea of their positions and influence in the online space.

✔ **Groups:** You can search for groups on Facebook, LinkedIn, or Google (http://groups.google.com/). Not only will your target audience participate in relevant groups, but group leaders could be highly influential voices online. Look for groups with a lot of active members in order to find the best groups to target.

When you find online influencers who seem to have an engaged audience of people who match your target audience profile, work to get on those influencers' radar screens. Follow them on Twitter and retweet their content or send them @replies. Friend them on Facebook, like their Facebook Page if they have one, and converse with them. Read their blogs and publish comments. However, don't self-promote immediately. Instead, work to demonstrate your knowledge and ability to add value to the online influencers' conversations through social media marketing efforts before you share your own content with them.

An aggressive approach of self-promotion is unlikely to keep you in the good graces of online influencers. Instead, build a relationship first, and then when the time comes when you'd like to ask an online influencer to help you spread the word about your content or business through a tweet, guest blog post, or other tactic, that online influencer is more likely to be willing to help you.

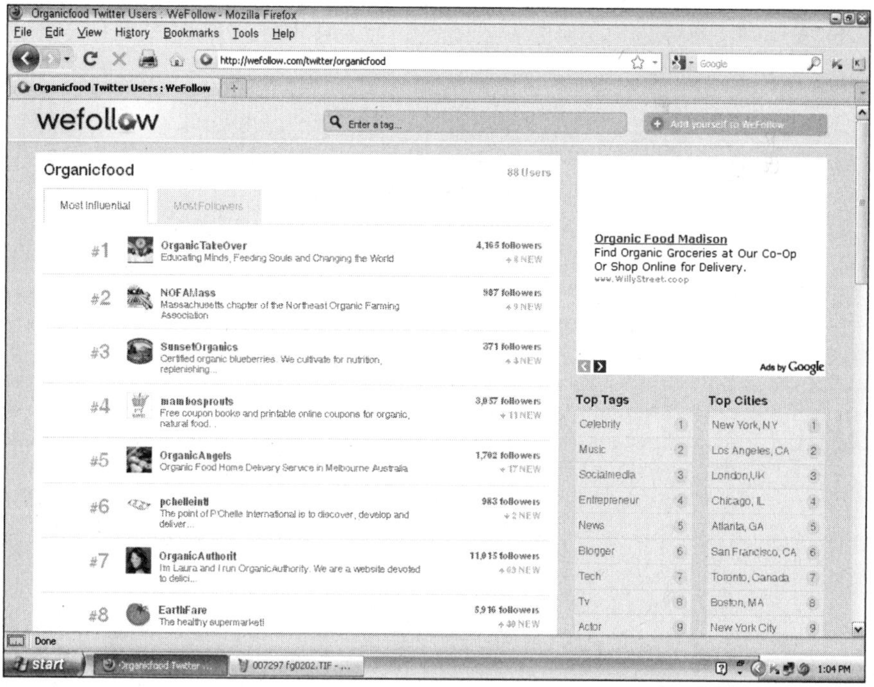

Figure 2-3:
Search for influencers on Twitter using an app such as WeFollow.

Establishing Goals and Choosing the Best Forms of Content Marketing

As you develop your content marketing strategy, you need to do so with goals in mind. Because content marketing is very much a long-term marketing strategy, you must define where you want your business to be in the future. This strategy includes determining how much time you can devote to content marketing, the resources available to help you with your content marketing efforts, and the results you want to attain from those efforts.

This book has more information about the various forms of content marketing that can help you choose the best forms to pursue as part of your content marketing plan. However, you do need to approach content marketing realistically, or you won't be satisfied with your results. Remember, content marketing success comes in the form of long-term sustainable growth through brand building and relationship development, which lead to loyalty and word-of-mouth marketing. You can supplement your long-term strategy with short-term tactics such as discount promotions, contests, and so on, but the power of content marketing comes from the organic growth it creates.

With that in mind, you need to move forward with a highly focused content marketing plan. You can't be all things to all people. In fact, trying to spread yourself too thin will reduce your own content quality and confuse consumers. If you can't meet their expectations through your content, they'll leave you behind and find someone who can. The most powerful brands are highly focused brands, so it makes sense that with all the clutter and competition for a share of voice online, niche-focused content can help you stake your claim in the online space. You can read earlier in this chapter about establishing credibility and being the go-to-person for information related to your business. Your brand, online reputation, and business will benefit immensely if you take the time to choose a specific area of focus and related keywords to *own*.

Your content marketing goals need to be realistic. For example, you might create a goal to develop three viable branded online destinations within the next three months, or you might create a goal to attract 1,000 quality Twitter followers over the next six months. Make sure your content marketing goals are always based on quality, not quantity, because if you publish quality content and focus on developing quality audiences, quantity will come organically in time. In other words, your content marketing strategy is successful when the compounding effect begins to truly work for you and you see your numbers growing simply because your content and conversations are meeting customer expectations.

Quality content and relationships help you increase your sphere of influence in the online space, which is a valuable intangible business asset.

Before you define your goals, you also need to think about the types of content marketing you can realistically pursue given the amount of time and technical savvy they require. The best part about content marketing is that the tools of the social Web that enable you to publish content are fairly easy to use. If you can use word-processing software and an Internet browser, then you can use social Web tools.

Take some time to create accounts on the most popular sites that enable you to publish content such as WordPress.org for a blog, Facebook.com for social networking, and Twitter.com for microblogging. Before you announce that you're joining the social Web or start reaching out to other people online, play around with the features and start publishing content to build up an archive of amazing content. Get an idea of which tools you enjoy or think you can stick with for the long-term, and begin to define your marketing strategies using those tools as your top branded online destinations.

Creating a Core Branded Online Destination

When you pursue a content marketing strategy, you need to have some place to publish content online. In other words, you need to have a core branded online destination that serves as the centerpiece of your content marketing activities. Remember, not all of your content marketing efforts will happen on your own sites, particularly as your social media marketing activities overlap with your content marketing efforts. Your online conversations that happen across the social Web both on and off your own sites should all lead back to your core branded online destination.

Where: Location! Location! Location!

You can use many tools to establish your core branded online destination. A blog is the best choice, because it gives you the most flexibility in terms of the type of content you can publish in one place. Blogs are also very search-engine friendly and are very powerful in terms of the compounding effect of blogging and building your online presence.

But what if blogging isn't right for you? What if the idea of writing even a single paragraph blog post sounds like a monumental effort to you? That's okay. Choose another tool that you do enjoy and make that your core branded online destination. Some of the most popular core branded destinations other than blogs are Facebook Pages, LinkedIn profiles, YouTube channels, or Twitter profiles. You can make any social site your core branded destination, because the value comes from the content you publish there, not the name of the tool.

I describe the story of Naked Pizza told in Chapter 1. It's the perfect example of a brick-and-mortar retailer that successfully uses Twitter as its core branded online destination. The most important thing that you need to do is to ensure that your core branded destination offers the most information to enable you to connect with and build relationships with your target audience. If Naked Pizza can achieve that in 140-character or fewer tweets, so can you.

Designing your central hub

If your core branded destination is the central hub for all your content marketing efforts to which all roads lead, then you need to make sure that central hub accurately reflects your brand image and promise. It needs to meet consumers' expectations for your brand both in content and visual appeal.

For example, a technical company positioning itself as expert in Web development should have a core branded destination that looks great, loads quickly, and is designed with intuitive navigation with all the bells and whistles people expect from a top Web development provider. If that company's core branded destination looks like an out-of-the-box, standard site that anyone could create with little technical knowledge, consumers will be confused and search for another site and company that meets their expectations.

Therefore, take time to make sure your core branded destination looks great, works well, and accurately reflects your brand. If you invest money in your content marketing strategy, then the design of your core branded destination should be at the top of your priority list when it comes to setting your budget.

Fortunately, you can find designers who can help you create branded blogs, Twitter backgrounds, Facebook Pages, and more. Following are several sources to help you find affordable design help:

- ✔ **Twitter backgrounds:** You can get custom Twitter background design help from many freelance designers as well as from sites like Social Identities (www.custombackgroundsfortwitter.com), which provides custom Twitter and Facebook design services.

> ✔ **Freelance blog designers:** You can search for freelance blog design-
> ers on Google or check the footer in blogs you like to see if a link to the
> designer is provided. Alternatively, you can publish a design request
> opportunity on Craigslist (www.craigslist.org) or a freelancer Web
> site such as Freelancer.com (www.freelancer.com), Elance (www.
> elance.com), or iFreelance.com (www.ifreelance.com). Some of
> these sites require that you pay a fee to publish a listing, so be sure to
> read all of the site requirements.

Blog design doesn't have to cost thousands of dollars. Thanks to the many
premium themes available for the most popular business blogging application,
WordPress, you can purchase a premium theme and hire a designer to help
you tweak it to match your brand and needs for anywhere from a few hundred
dollars and up, depending on the extent of your customization requests and
the designer you choose. To find out more about blog design and themes,
check out *Blogging All-in-One For Dummies* by Susan Gunelius (Wiley).

Adding value and making it easy to buy

Of course, your core branded destination should offer a wealth of content
that adds value to your target audience's everyday lives so that they talk
about it, share it, and come back for more. But there is more to creating your
core branded online destination than publishing amazing content on a site
that's well designed. You also need to make sure it's extremely easy for your
audience to buy from you or perform the action you want them to do when
they visit your site, such as submit an inquiry form.

No matter how important it is to publish amazing content and indirectly
market your business through your content, you're still running a business,
and you need to make money. While you don't want to be overly aggressive
through your content in promoting your business (review the 80-20 rule
described in Chapter 1), you do want to make sure that visitors can easily
make a purchase or perform your desired action when they come to your
core branded destination. You don't want to make them feel like they're
being pushed to buy something, but you do want to make sure the option
is always available and easy to do.

Therefore, make sure links to your online catalog or inquiry form (or other
page or action you want visitors to follow) are prominently displayed on
every page of your core branded destination. Don't interrupt the audience's
experience as they read your content and engage with you. For example, a
pop-up window that appears when visitors navigate around your site is a
sure-fire way to annoy them. Instead, provide links for convenience in your
blog's sidebar or core branded destination profile, so they're easily accessible but not overbearing and interruptive.

Surrounding Consumers with Branded Content

When your core branded destination is set up and you're building an archive of amazing content on that central hub, it's time to begin spreading your tentacles across the social Web. Ultimately, you want to surround consumers with your branded content by creating branded online destinations that allow consumers to choose how they want to experience and interact with your brand.

Not everyone likes the same type of content or experiences, which is why companies like Disney offer varied ways for consumers to experience their brand. For example, a consumer can watch the Disney Channel, visit Walt Disney World, or shop at the Disney Store. Each experience is very different and is likely to appeal to different audiences and consumers. In the online space, Disney offers varied branded experiences as well, including blogs, online games, a Facebook Page, online shopping, forums, and more. Consumers can select how they want to experience the Disney brand online, too.

The more time you spend publishing content and engaging with your audience, the more you're likely to enjoy content marketing. In time, setting up multiple branded online destinations won't seem like an overwhelming task. If necessary, you can recruit employees or hire freelancers to help you maintain your varied online branded destinations without breaking the bank. Chapter 17 provides more information about building a content marketing team when the time comes.

As you build your branded online destinations, you must make sure that all of those destinations accurately reflect your brand, add value, and lead back to your core branded online destination. Never forget that all roads lead back to that central hub, and that's where you want to try to lead as many people as you can so you can share even more information and deepen your relationships with them.

Figure 2-4 shows a representation of a business using a blog as its core branded online destination with varied branded online destinations leading back to that central hub.

Don't feel like you need to create numerous branded online destinations right away. Quality trumps quantity, so only pursue extending your brand to new online destinations if you're certain you can commit to them for the long-term with quality content and interactions. You don't want to focus on varied branded online destinations at the expense of your core branded online destination.

Figure 2-4:
All roads
lead back
to your core
branded
online
destination.

Comparing Free versus Premium Content Strategies

As you move forward with your content marketing strategy, you're likely to find some businesses that offer only free content and some that offer both free content and premium content that is available with a price tag. For example, premium content could come in the form of an ebook available for purchase, a newsletter available for a monthly subscription, a membership fee to a site that gives people access to more content, and so on. Businesses can get very creative in how they package content in order to make money.

Before you can determine if putting a price tag on your content is right for your business, you need to review your content marketing goals. Ask yourself the following questions:

✔ Why am I offering content online?

✔ What do I want to get from my content?

✔ What do I want people to do with my content?

✔ Who do I want to read or view my content?

Answer the preceding questions and compare them to the benefits that putting a price tag on your content could give you in terms of revenue. Would the money you could potentially make from your content mean more to you than the word-of-mouth marketing, brand loyalty, brand advocacy, and search engine optimization that free content gives your business?

Bottom line, a true content marketing strategy offers all content for free in an attempt to drive an online buzz, create entry points to your branded online destinations, surround consumers with branded experiences, engage consumers, encourage sharing, and indirectly market your business for long-term, sustainable, and organic growth. A content marketing strategy that includes a premium component adds a direct sales and revenue-generating element to the strategy that may run counter to the true purpose of content marketing. Again, only you can decide if the potential revenue outweighs the indirect marketing benefits of a true and free content marketing strategy.

Chapter 3

Taking the First Steps to Executing Your Content Marketing Plan

In This Chapter

▶ Interlinking and cross-promoting

▶ Understanding link building strategies

▶ Delving into the do's and don'ts of content marketing

▶ Letting your content spread

▶ Enhancing content with images and sound

*W*hen you've defined your goals and created your content marketing strategy, you're ready to put together an actionable content marketing plan filled with specific tactics that you commit to pursue over the course of the next year to reach those goals. Of course, you need to reevaluate your marketing plan throughout the year and tweak it as necessary. The social Web is continually changing, and your marketing plan needs to evolve with it in order to be effective.

Using the Content Marketing Strategy Worksheet and Template provided at www.dummies.com/cheatsheet/contentmarketing, you can determine the specific tactics you want to pursue to implement your marketing plan. Without knowing all of the specific aspects of your business, market, target audience, products, and competitors, I can't provide you with a personalized marketing plan, but you can use the information provided throughout this book to create a successful content marketing plan of your own, without hiring an expensive marketing agency to help you.

Cross-Promoting and Interlinking for Greater Success

Chapter 2 explains the importance of creating your core branded online destination as well as surrounding consumers with branded online experiences so they can self-select how they want to interact with your brand. All roads must lead back to your core branded online destination, where you can share more of your amazing content and deepen relationships with your target audience and online influencers. In other words, no one branded online destination should be set free into the World Wide Web and left to struggle to survive on its own. Instead, you need to *interlink* and *cross-promote* your content and conversations to fully integrate your efforts and allow them to feed off one another:

✔ **Cross-promoting content:** When you talk about content that you publish on one of your branded online destinations, you can promote that content on another branded online destination, and vice versa. For example, when you tweet that you published a great blog post or you publish a blog post about an upcoming *Tweetchat* (a live discussion between two or more people via Twitter updates), you're cross-promoting your blog and Twitter content.

✔ **Interlinking content:** When you link to a video you uploaded on Twitter within a blog post or include a link to your SlideShare tab on your Facebook Page, you're interlinking your content. You can also *intralink* your content. For example, in a new blog post, you can link to an older blog post.

As you read about specific types of content marketing throughout this book, you'll discover handy tools to automate cross-promotion and tricks to interlink your content. Both cross-promoting and interlinking your content can increase its exposure by giving people more opportunities to see your content with just the click of a mouse. They can also optimize your search engine efforts because, generally, the more links you have coming into a site, the better your rankings on search engines like Google. Also, cross-promoting and interlinking notifies people that your brand is producing amazing content on more online destinations than the one they're currently looking at.

For example, even though some of your consumers may find your content via a Google search that leads them to your blog, they may prefer to use Twitter. If your Twitter profile is prominently displayed along with an invitation for visitors to follow you on Twitter, consumers might click on the link and start following your tweets. In other words, they can self-select how they want to experience and interact with your brand. So keep in mind that if you don't take the time to cross-promote or interlink your branded online destinations, this kind of opportunity to connect further with consumers over the long-term might not happen.

Do cross-promote and interlink your content when it makes sense to do so. However, be careful not to violate the 80-20 rule; that is, of the time you spend on the social Web, publish quality content 80 percent (or more) of the time and self-promote 20 percent (or less) of the time (see Chapter 1 for more on this topic).

Link Building versus Link Baiting Strategies

Building links is without a doubt an excellent way to boost traffic to your branded online destinations, particularly your core branded online destination, and to increase your Google search results rankings. However, you need to understand the difference between link building and link baiting before you go link crazy! The key to successful linking in content marketing is to achieve a healthy marriage of link building and link baiting.

The following descriptions break down the differences between link building and link baiting:

- ✔ **Link building:** Link building is a long-term content marketing strategy. It is the process of publishing shareworthy content and of building relationships with people online in an effort to boost organic links and traffic to your branded online destinations. For example, your blog posts with content that stands the tests of time and relevancy (often called *pillar* or *evergreen* content) are excellent catalysts for link building — because people want to share great content with their own audiences. They'll link to those blog posts, boosting your incoming links and your audience.

- ✔ **Link baiting:** Link baiting is a short-term content marketing tactic. It is the process of publishing content for the primary purpose of attracting incoming links and boosting traffic. Link bait content is typically written about a hot, real-time topic such as breaking news. The topic may also be a controversial one. In fact, link bait content may not be directly related to your business, but you decide to publish it with the purpose of generating a burst of incoming traffic, with the hope that some of that traffic will stick around and even come back again.

Link baiting helps to attract new visitors who otherwise might not have found your branded online destination. If some of those visitors come back again and like what they find, they may become loyal visitors who share your content and talk about you with their own audiences. The trick to using link bait content successfully is to ensure that your link bait efforts don't frustrate new visitors who want to find more of the same type of content on your site or anger your existing audience who might be confused by irrelevant content.

You can find link bait content ideas a number of ways. Be sure to listen to the ongoing conversations happening across the social Web, and join those about hot topics related to your business. Also, you can use the following resources to actively search for link bait content ideas:

- ✔ **Google Trends:** As shown in Figure 3-1, Google Trends (`www.google.com/trends`) provides real-time lists of hot topics and hot searches.

- ✔ **Twitter trending topics:** At any time, you can find a list of trending topics in Twitter posts in the sidebar at the right of your Twitter profile (you must be logged into your account) or by scrolling across the home page of Twitter.com.

- ✔ **Yahoo! Buzz Index:** The Yahoo! Buzz Index shows the top 20 overall searches around the world on Yahoo! You can also view the top 20 Yahoo! searches in specific categories, such as actors, sports, video games, movies, music, and TV.

Link bait content should enhance your branded online destination rather than detract from it. Keeping your existing, loyal audience happy is essential to your long-term success, so be sure to balance your traffic-generating tactics with your retention strategies.

Figure 3-1:
Google
Trends
shows
real-time
lists of hot
topics and
searches.

Understanding the Do's and Don'ts of Content Marketing

When you venture into the world of content marketing, you're putting your business and brand's reputation on the line. You need to know the laws related to content marketing and publishing as well as the unwritten etiquette that will make you a welcome member of the online community. The worst thing you can do is dive in blindly with no knowledge of the potential legal and ethical repercussions of your actions. Before you publish any content or engage in any online conversations, familiarize yourself with the laws and rules that guide online behavior, as described in this section.

Following the law

You need to know a number of laws outside typical business-related laws when you publish content online. In other words, all the laws that you follow in your traditional and offline marketing initiatives still pertain to the online environment, and some of those are easier to violate online than you might realize. Furthermore, you might not be aware of some laws in your offline marketing efforts that you'll encounter in your content marketing efforts.

This section introduces some of the most common laws that content marketers face. Familiarize yourself with them and follow them! When in doubt, err on the side of caution to protect yourself and your business. Claiming ignorance isn't a valid defense in a court of law.

Copyrights and Fair Use

Copyright law in the United States protects all pieces of original work. Therefore, the person or entity that produced a piece of written content, an image, a piece of audio, a video, and so on is the rightful owner of that piece and owns the copyright to it. By the letter of the law, you can't republish a work without getting permission to do so from the copyright owner. Because content marketing typically includes adding images to blog posts or online articles, adding audio to an original video, and so on, content marketers often violate copyright laws without even realizing it.

Just because you like an image you see on a blog or Web site doesn't mean you can use it legally on your business blog, Web site, or other branded online destination. If that image does not have a copyright license attached to it that allows you to use it free and without getting permission, you can't use it without violating copyright laws.

Owners can apply several types of copyright licenses to their original works. When you find online content that you want to republish in your own content, be aware of the following copyright licenses that you're most likely to encounter:

- **Royalty-free:** You can reuse content that has a royalty-free license attached to it free, but typically you must follow specific guidelines that are set in the license. For example, you may have to notify the owner where the content will be republished or attribute the source in a very specific way within your new content.

- **Rights Managed:** Content that is rights managed requires you to obtain a contract with the owner before you can use it. The contract specifies when, where, and how that piece of content will be republished and the corresponding fee.

- **All Rights Reserved:** Content that has an All Rights Reserved license attached to it means that the owner of that content retains all rights to use that content anywhere and at anytime. It is not available for you to use.

- **Public Domain or Free Content:** Content that is in the public domain or considered free has no copyright attached to it (meaning the owner offers the content for anyone to use freely) or the copyright attached to it expired. You can use this content without seeking permission, providing attribution, or following any other guidelines.

To make it easier for people to allow others to use their original works, Creative Commons evolved as a way to place less-restrictive copyright licenses on those original works. You can visit `http://creative commons.org/licenses` and find out more about applying Creative Commons licenses to your works. Typically, doing so is just a matter of adding a line of text or the appropriate Creative Commons icon to your work. You can see the six Creative Commons license icons in Figure 3-2.

If a Creative Commons license is attached to content that you want to republish on your branded online destinations, you simply need to follow the rules of the license in order to use that content. The six types of Creative Commons licenses are defined as follows:

- **Attribution:** Anyone can republish a work with a Creative Commons Attribution license in any form as long as the original source is cited.

- **Attribution-ShareAlike:** Anyone can republish the work as long as the original source is cited and the new work is licensed under the identical terms of the originally licensed work.

- **Attribution-NoDerivs:** Anyone can republish the work in the exact format as the original work as long as the original source is cited.

- **Attribution-NonCommercial:** Anyone can republish a work with a Creative Commons Attribution-NonCommercial license in any form as long as the source is cited and the work is not used for commercial purposes.

✔ **Attribution-NonCommercial-ShareAlike:** Anyone can republish the work as long as the original source is cited and the new work is licensed under the identical terms of the originally licensed work, and the new work is not used for commercial purposes.

✔ **Attribution-NonCommercial-No Derivs:** Anyone can republish the work in the exact format as the original work as long as the original source is cited and the work is not used for commercial purposes.

In the "Leveraging Design to Enhance Content" section at the end of this chapter, I list a number of Web sites where you can find images and audio content that you can legally republish on your own branded online destinations, free or at a minimum cost.

Copyright law is not something to be taken lightly; however, a gray area of copyright law known as *fair use* offers a bit of leeway in how the law is interpreted and enforced. Fair use allows you to republish content or work owned by another person or entity regardless of the type of copyright license applied to that content or work for educational purposes, to add commentary, for news reporting, or for research. However, fair use is a tricky concept, so it's always best to ensure that you have permission to republish copyrighted material.

Figure 3-2: Each Creative Commons icon stands for a specific type of license.

Libel

Libel is a legal concept defined as any form of writing or published words that are intended to damage another person or entity's reputation. As there are gray areas of copyright laws, there are also gray areas related to libel. For example, forms of satire are not considered to be libelous. However, the best choice when it comes to content marketing is to avoid all forms of negative content that could put your own brand in a negative light, or worse, put you in a position to be sued for libel.

Privacy

Privacy laws are continually evolving, so to be safe, consult with your attorney to ensure that you're in full compliance. At the very least, publish a privacy policy on your Web site, blog, and any other branded online destination where you collect information about your visitors. For example, if you collect personal information through newsletter sign-up forms, behavioral data through Web browser cookies, or financial information through transaction processes, it's essential that you disclose how that information is collected, what it is used for, and if it is shared with any other people, businesses, or entities.

CAN-SPAM Act

The CAN-SPAM Act of 2003 applies to e-mail communications from businesses, particularly marketing-related communications. There are a variety of rules related to how, when, and to whom companies can send e-mail messages. Because many content marketing plans include an e-mail component, such as a newsletter, you need to fully understand the CAN-SPAM Act. You can read the guidelines for businesses at http://business.ftc.gov/documents/bus61-can-spam-act-Compliance-Guide-for-Business.

Reviews, testimonials, and endorsements

The Code of Federal Regulations (CFR) provides laws related to commerce that all businesses must adhere to. Because content marketing often includes the use of reviews, endorsements, and testimonials, it's imperative that you understand Title 16 (Commercial Practices), Part 255 (Guides Concerning Use of Endorsements and Testimonials in Advertising) of the Code of Federal Regulations. You may have to adhere to a number of specific guidelines and forms of disclosure, particularly if you offer free products or compensation in return for reviews — a common practice in content marketing. You can find Title 16, Part 255 in the Electronic Code of Federal Regulations at http://ecfr.gpoaccess.gov/cgi/t/text/text-idx?c=ecfr&tpl=%2Findex.tpl.

Understanding content marketing etiquette and avoiding turn-offs

As a content marketer, you have to adhere to written laws and unwritten rules of etiquette and acceptable behavior. If you break those unwritten rules, you could destroy all of your chances at achieving content marketing or social media marketing success. To help you get started on the right foot, here are some of the most common content marketing turn-offs and etiquette violations:

- **Too much self-promotion:** Stick to the 80-20 rule (discussed in Chapter 1). If you spend too much time talking about yourself and self-promoting rather than engaging with other people, sharing their content, and adding value to the online conversation, people will start to ignore you or remove you from their radar screens entirely.

- **Intentionally or accidentally spamming:** Don't participate in activities that can be labeled as spam. For example, don't leave comments on blog posts that include nothing but links back to your own site, and don't publish blog posts that are nothing more than an ad or marketing piece selling your products. Always try to add value and engage people, and you should be safe.

- **Not attributing sources:** Don't publish content without giving a virtual hat tip to the source that gave you the story idea. For example, if you publish a blog post about a hot topic related to your business that you heard about from another blog or online source, link back to that source within your content. Doing so helps to build relationships and adds to your credibility.

- **Not sounding human:** Content marketing should avoid corporate rhetoric and should never read like a corporate brochure. Instead, content marketing should sound more personable and closer in tone and style to social media marketing than formal communications. No one will want to connect with you and engage with you if you sound like you're reading from a corporate document.

- **Not acknowledging people:** Part of content marketing includes engaging with the people who read or view your content and respond to it. Don't publish content and forget it. You need to be available to respond to comments, answer questions, and so on, or your content marketing efforts will die before they have a chance to drive any indirect or direct results to your business.

- **Sending automated messages:** People are busy, and automated messages clutter inboxes and annoy recipients. For example, don't send an automated self-promotional message to everyone who follows you on Twitter telling them to check out your Web site, blog, Facebook Page, and so on. That's an easy way to make people regret following you.

The more time you spend publishing content and engaging with other people, the more you'll discover about your target audience. Always listen to what they have to say so that you can adjust your content marketing efforts to meet their wants and needs. They're your best source of information for current turn-offs and etiquette expectations. Pay attention and apply what you find out! What is acceptable today may not be tomorrow.

Knowing your words live online for a long time

The content you publish today is likely to be accessible online for a very long time. Even if you publish an article on an article-sharing site, as discussed in Chapter 4, and delete it a year from now, your article may already been quoted on other sites or blogs or even republished on content scraping sites (a form of spam wherein Web site owners republish content found on other sites along with ads in an effort to make money without any effort).

Some content you publish on sites that don't belong to you might be impossible to delete in the future. For example, a social networking site or online forum may not allow accountholders to delete content that is older than a certain number of months or years, even though that old content can still be found in Google searches.

All updates published on public Twitter streams are indexed and archived by the Library of Congress. That means your tweets will outlive you, and they'll probably outlive Twitter, too!

Similarly, comments and posts that you publish on social networking sites like Facebook or LinkedIn or in online forums can be quoted and republished by other users within their own comments and posts. Even if you can delete your original post, the quotation may still be visible in those other users' comments. In other words, you never know where your online content might end up. Therefore, it's critical that you always consider your words and their long-term effect on you, your brand, and your business. When you publish something, you may not be able to take it back!

Did you know that research shows the vast majority of hiring managers view applicants' Facebook, LinkedIn, and Twitter profiles during the interview process? That's why college students are warned against publishing pictures of themselves binge drinking (especially if they're underage at the time) at the weekly fraternity party. People have even been fired from their jobs for things they've published on their personal blogs, Facebook profiles, and Twitter streams (Heather B. Armstrong of Dooce.com is one of the better-known examples). The same concept applies to the content you publish for your business — you never know who is going to see your content (even if you didn't intend them to see it and associate it with your business).

Giving Up Control and Letting Your Content Spread

Content marketing is a powerful marketing tool, but it can reach its full potential only if you're brave enough to give up control of your content and the online conversation related to it. Brand loyalty and brand advocacy can evolve only to a limited extent if consumers aren't given the opportunity to choose how they want to experience a brand and are allowed to interact with it in their own way. If you try to control those experiences, interactions, and conversations, you're severely limiting your business's success.

Many brands have reached unprecedented success by giving up control of the online conversation and allowing their content to spread, while others have learned tough lessons after they mistakenly tried to control the online conversation. You need to make the commitment to allow the conversation and your content to flow in order to gain maximum exposure and growth from your efforts.

Using Creative Commons licenses as a marketing tool

A common mistake in content marketing is to copyright protect your content in a manner that makes it clear you don't want people to republish or share your content with their own audiences. When you publish content online, you can demonstrate your commitment to content marketing and social media marketing by applying a Creative Commons license to that content. If you simply provide attribution to your content (assuming you apply the least restrictive Creative Commons Attribution license), your audience will immediately see that they're welcome to share your content with their own.

Apply a Creative Commons license to your blog posts by including the license notice in your blog's footer and to your online articles, ebooks, videos, and so on. The more content you give wings to and let fly of its own accord across the Web, the more exposure your business will get, the more people will visit your core branded destination (remember, all roads lead back to your core branded destination), the more brand advocates and word-of-mouth marketing you'll get, and the more sales and profits you'll ultimately generate. There's certainly no cheaper way to get the same level of exposure!

Removing the gateway

Another common mistake in content marketing is using a gateway that people must go through in order to access the content. For example, many businesses require that people provide their e-mail addresses in order to access their newsletters, white papers, ebooks, and so on. For maximum exposure, sharing, and conversations, you need to remove those gateways.

Collecting e-mail addresses and hiding your best content behind such a requirement is an old-school concept. Today, the opportunities that you gain by eliminating such gateways and allowing your best content to spread far and wide are significantly greater than the opportunities some e-mail addresses can deliver.

The relationships you can build with people who enjoy your content, respond to it, talk about it, and share it are extremely powerful and far-reaching. Think of it from a different perspective to fully understand this concept. Following are two different marketing options to consider:

- ✔ **Option 1:** Imagine that 100 people are in your store or office and that you provide a piece of useful content for them to discuss with you and with each other, and then imagine that they share and discuss it with their friends, family, and colleagues (or even with strangers). Imagine that they find your content so useful they come back to you for more and tell others to go to you to get the content, too.

- ✔ **Option 2:** Now, imagine that 100 people are in your store or office and that you tell them that you have some amazing content for them, but first they must give you their e-mail addresses. A lot of them will walk away, never to return. Some will give you their e-mail addresses and hope the content you give them is worth handing over their e-mail addresses (a coveted piece of personal information). Others will be happy to get the content and will talk about it with friends and family. They might pass the content on, but if they don't pass it on, other people can't access it without providing their own e-mail addresses. Once the e-mail address is provided, the interaction ends, as there isn't a public place to reconnect to further discuss the content or to find more similar content.

Which scenario sounds like the better option to build a business? There's no competition. A business would be crazy to choose option two, which is severely limiting. Instead of pursuing an exclusive marketing strategy (meaning only some people are invited to the party), pursue an inclusive strategy where everyone is invited to join the party, spread the word, and come back for more at any time. Bottom line, remove the gateway. Let your content spread, and allow people to experience it in their own way in order to give your business the chance for success it deserves.

Using Content as a First Step to Sales

While you read this book and find out more about the specific types of content marketing, you'll discover a wide variety of tactics for implementing content as a direct marketing tool that leads to sales. The trick is to remember that every piece of content you publish online and offline is at the very least an indirect marketing tool. When you develop new content, ask yourself how consumers will interpret that content and if they'll walk away from it with a new awareness of your brand, with piqued interest in how your business can help them, and with the motivation to seek more information or to make a purchase.

A lot of your content will serve the purpose of building relationships and emotional involvement in your brand from consumers' perspectives. You want them to gain a sense of trust and security from your content that extends to how they feel about your brand. That's why it's so important that you focus on publishing amazing, useful, meaningful, and shareworthy content that adds value to your target audience's lives. Much of your content won't precipitate a specific immediate reaction, and that's absolutely fine.

On the other hand, you can apply small tricks to make your content a precursor to sales. For example, you can mention one of your products in a *relevant* blog post and provide a link to your online catalog. You're not directly selling and saying, "buy now," but you are making it easy for people to make a purchase if they want to. Note that if the blog post isn't relevant, it will look like a direct marketing tactic, which may not be welcomed by your audience. Similarly, tweeting coupon codes or mentioning an in-store event on your Facebook Page is perfectly acceptable as long as the tweet or Facebook update is flanked by content that adds value.

While it's important that you stick to the 80-20 rule of content marketing and self-promotion, actively try to find opportunities to offer links to your products and so on when it is appropriate, relevant, and a welcomed addition to your content.

Leveraging Design to Enhance Content

As I mention in Chapter 2, design is an important aspect of your content marketing efforts because the visual appeal of your branded online destinations has a direct effect on consumers' perceptions of your brand. So, be sure to invest time and money into designing branded destinations that accurately reflect your brand promise and position. Fortunately, design doesn't have to cost a fortune. You can find a number of resources to locate affordable designers who can help you create your branded destinations.

As you publish content on your various branded online destinations, you'll need images and possibly audio to enhance your content. For example, images used in blog posts and ebooks can take a boring branded destination or piece of content and turn it into something that is visually appealing, easier to read, and more professional-looking. Following are a number of Web sites offering stock imagery (royalty-free and rights-managed) with Creative Commons licenses and stock audio (royalty-free):

- ✔ **Stock.XCHNG:** At `www.sxc.hu`, Stock.XCHNG is an excellent source both for images you can use freely and for images with a fee attached to them. Be sure to read the specific requirements for an image before you use it to ensure that you're compliant.

- ✔ **morgueFile:** At `http://morguefile.com`, morgueFile offers many images that you can use without providing attribution, but some image owners do request that you e-mail them when you use their images. Be sure to check individual image requirements before you use them.

- ✔ **Picapp:** At `http://picapp.com`, Picapp is a great source for celebrity and newsworthy photos. You can register for a free Picapp account and use images found on the site free, but you do have to adhere to the current requirements posted on the site to do so. For example, ads may be linked to images.

- ✔ **Flickr:** At `www.flickr.com`, Flickr is one of the most popular image-sharing sites. Anyone can set up a free account, upload images to their Flickr account, and tag those images as having specific copyright licenses (whether or not they actually own those images). Therefore, it's important to confirm that the publisher is actually the owner before using an image found on Flickr. You can find images tagged with Creative Commons licenses by visiting `www.flickr.com/creativecommons`.

- ✔ **Dreamstime:** At `www.dreamstime.com`, Dreamstime offers both free images and images with a fee attached to them.

- ✔ **FreeFoto.com:** At `www.freefoto.com`, FreeFoto.com offers over 100,000 images that you can use free as long as you follow the link and attribution requirements for each image as posted on the site.

- ✔ **iStockphoto:** At `www.istockphoto.com`, iStockphoto offers a huge collection of royalty-free images at reasonable prices.

- ✔ **Bigstock:** At `www.bigstockphoto.com`, Bigstock offers a large variety of royalty-free images for as low as $1 each.

- ✔ **Getty Images:** At `www.gettyimages.com`, Getty Images offers rights-managed and royalty-free images, audio, and video. Price tags are typically high because images come from professional photographers who expect to be compensated well when their work is used.

- ✔ **Corbis Images:** At `www.corbisimages.com`, Corbis Images provides royalty-free and rights-managed images in a variety of categories. Like Getty Images, many images have high price tags in order to compensate the owners.

- ✔ **RoyaltyFreeMusic.com:** At `www.royaltyfreemusic.com`, RoyaltyFreeMusic.com offers a variety of music and sound bites for as low as $9.95 for an individual track. You can find royalty-free music, free music, music on hold, production music, and more.

- ✔ **Stockmusic.net:** At `www.stockmusic.net`, Stockmusic.net offers royalty-free music, sound effects, music on hold, and more for as low as $29.95 per track.

Always check the terms related to the copyright license applied to images, audio, or video that you plan to use in your content to ensure that you're compliant. Also, make sure the actual owner of the work provides the license information. For example, images found via a Google search that are identified as having a Creative Commons license attached to them might not actually be owned by the person who published them online. This also happens with Flickr uploads. That amazing, too-good-to-be-true picture of your favorite celebrity that you find tagged with a Creative Commons license on Flickr probably isn't owned by the person who uploaded it with that license. Don't be fooled.

Images and music should enhance your content, not clutter it or detract from it. Don't overload your content with extraneous elements that make it difficult for your audience to digest your content. They're more likely to talk about and share your content with their own audiences if the content is great than if you include some really nice stock photography. Content is always key when it comes to building a business and brand through long-term, sustainable, organic growth via content marketing.

Part II
Marketing with Long-Form Content

In this part . . .

It's time to delve into the most detailed and time-consuming form of content marketing — long-form content marketing. This type of content takes time to create and publish, but it also takes time to consume. That means you need to find out how to produce compelling long-form content that can indirectly promote your business while adding value to people's lives.

Part II introduces you to the tools of long-form content marketing, so you know where to publish it. You also discover how to write effective long-form content and take that content to the next level of success through search engine optimization, syndication, and more.

Chapter 4

Introducing the Tools of Written Long-Form Content Marketing

*T*here is no time like the present to start thinking about the types of content you want to publish to both directly and indirectly promote your business and brand. Much of your decision depends on two factors — your writing abilities and your technical abilities. Fortunately, the tools of online publishing make it easy for even the most technically challenged individuals to become content publishers within minutes. If you know how to use a Web browser, e-mail, and a word-processing application, then your learning curve for most online publishing tools will be short and painless.

The other factor related to pursuing a content marketing plan isn't as easy to master. If you're not comfortable writing more than a few sentences, then long-form content marketing will be more challenging. That's not to say long-form content marketing will be impossible, but you'll need to spend some time polishing your writing skills or find a writer to produce your content. The choice is yours, but don't skip long-form content marketing entirely just because writing isn't your strength. Many successful content marketers freely admit that writing isn't their top skill.

Understanding and Using Long-Form Content Marketing for Your Business

In Chapter 1, I explain that long-form content marketing includes all published content that is more than a few sentences and that offers deep value, such as blog posts, articles, ebooks, press releases, white papers, presentations, videos, podcasts, webinars, and so on. In other words, any content you publish online or offline that takes a person more than a couple of minutes to read, listen to, or view could be considered a form of content marketing when that content is related to a business or brand and provides useful information.

The vast majority of business-related content you publish (even very loosely related content) that's more than a paragraph in length or that takes more than a couple of minutes to read could be considered content marketing.

Most long-form content isn't self-promotional. No one wants to read a 1,000 word marketing pitch. There is a reason infomercials are labeled as such — because to simply call them informational programming would be misleading when they are truthfully just a lengthy commercial.

Your content should not read like a marketing pitch or commercial even if it's intended for direct marketing purposes. While it's acceptable to include a brief promotional message or link within your long-form content, further self-promotion turns your content into an ad or marketing brochure rather than a useful content marketing tactic. There is a fine line between content marketing and advertising. Avoid crossing that line, or your target audience may perceive your content marketing efforts as nothing more than advertising.

The trick to creating successful content is ensuring that it's not about you. Always make sure your content talks more about your target audience than about you. For example, instead of writing a blog post announcing the freeze-and-serve meals available at your restaurant for takeout, write a blog post that explains how to make healthy meals in 30 minutes or less. End the post with a line that says, "If 30 minutes are more than you can spare, you can still eat well without breaking the bank with affordable premade meal solutions. For example, our healthy freeze-and-serve take-out meals are cheaper than dining out but faster than cooking at home." This way, you first provide shareworthy information (refer to Chapter 2 for more on this topic), and second, for convenience (and to make a potential purchase easy), you suggest an appropriate alternative related to your business. In this way, your suggestion is perceived as a welcomed option rather than as an intrusive marketing message.

Most long-form content marketing builds awareness of your business and establishes your brand's position relative to competitors. This type of marketing can help build trust and define you as the go-to person or business on specific topics. Therefore, try to publish long-form content that is well-written and copyrighted with a Creative Commons license (as described in Chapter 3) so your audience can use it and share it with their audiences, thereby exponentially increasing your reach and awareness of your business.

Becoming a Blogger

In the simplest terms, a *blog* is a Web site where the author (called a *blogger*) publishes entries (called *posts*) that are typically displayed in reverse chronological order and stored in dated archives. Some blogging applications allow bloggers to publish *pages* that live outside the post chronology. Posts usually include a comment feature that allows readers to publish their own comments directly beneath the post. Blogs also include sidebar and footer areas where bloggers can display links to their additional branded online destinations and content, ads, and more.

Blogs are very flexible, which enables individual bloggers to set up their blogs exactly the way they want them. Blogs are also highly interactive and an amazing relationship-building tool, thanks to the comment feature and the ability to continually publish fresh content, including links to other relevant content across the social Web. In other words, you can use your business blog to build relationships with potential consumers as well as with other content publishers and online influencers.

Blogging is one of the best options for publishing long-form content. For example, blogs are very search-engine friendly and allow you to create numerous entry points (which live forever in your blog's archives) that search engines can index. People familiar with the social Web are familiar with the pass-along value of blog posts. By spreading links to their own online profiles and through blogging, people quickly share valuable posts with their own audiences. In fact, blogs are probably the best option for a core branded online destination because they are flexible, easy to use, and offer so many ways that you can directly and indirectly promote your business. Therefore, this chapter offers a great deal of information about using a blog for content marketing.

Creating your blog

The first step to becoming a blogger is to create a blog for your business. If you're serious about using a blog to build your business, I highly suggest reading a book like *Blogging All-in-One For Dummies* by Susan Gunelius (Wiley), which offers specific instructions about all the tools and tasks you need to effectively join the blogosphere. Although there's not enough space in this chapter to fully cover the topic of blogging, I do provide some important basics to start you on the path to successful business blogging.

Choosing your tools

Before you can create a blog, you need to decide which blogging application you want to use. The three most popular blogging applications for businesses are WordPress, Blogger, and TypePad. Each offers pros and cons, but I highly recommend the self-hosted version of WordPress (available at www.wordpress.org) to build your business blog. In fact, you can build your entire Web site using the application available at WordPress.org, which makes it very easy to manage your site and make changes on the fly without hiring expensive Web developers and designers to help you. You may still want to hire a freelance designer or developer to ensure that your blog is set up correctly, is professionally designed, and accurately reflects your business and brand. However, with very little technical knowledge or ability, you can manage the ongoing maintenance using the self-hosted WordPress application.

When you choose to use the self-hosted WordPress application from WordPress to create your blog, you must pay for your own Web hosting and your own domain name, but both fees are very affordable. The added flexibility that WordPress offers over other blogging applications makes the small fees related to hosting and domain registration worth it.

The self-hosted WordPress application (often referred to as *WordPress.org* because that is where it can be found for download), is an open source application, which anyone can use. Simply download the WordPress application from WordPress.org and upload it to your Web hosting account. Then you can log into your new WordPress blog account online to create your blog.

Unlike WordPress.com, Blogger.com, and TypePad.com, you *must* obtain your own Web hosting account with a third-party hosting company such as Bluehost.com, GoDaddy.com, or HostGator.com to store your data and serve it to online visitors if you use the WordPress.org application. Doing so sounds harder than it actually is, and a book like *WordPress For Dummies* by Lisa Sabin-Wilson breaks down all the steps for creating your own WordPress site and blog.

WordPress.org users also have the ability to modify their blog designs in any way they want, because they have access to the code used to create those designs. That's a big perk that you're sure to use as you modify your own blog to suit your business' needs. Furthermore, developers create WordPress plug-ins that exponentially enhance the functionality of WordPress.org blogs and Web sites. For example, you can upload WordPress plug-ins to your blog that give your blog posts a search engine optimization (SEO) boost, create contact forms, back up your blog content, add related post links to all your blog posts, and more. The options are always growing as more plug-ins are released, mostly free of charge.

Selecting a layout

When you decide on your blogging application and create an account, you need to choose a layout for your blog. Most blogs are presented in 1-, 2-, or 3-column layout where the largest column takes up about two-thirds of the browser window and one or two smaller columns appear on the right or left or flanking the largest column. Blog posts appear in the largest column, and the one or two sidebars include extra information, links, and so on. Some blogs use a magazine-style layout, such as the one shown in Figure 4-1, which enables you to display a lot of information on the home page of your blog. This layout is popular for blogs that publish new posts frequently throughout the day and want to give new content more exposure on the front page.

Choose the layout that enables you to display your most important information above the fold, meaning visitors don't have to scroll to see it. Depending on how often you publish blog posts and how much extraneous information you want to draw attention to, your blog layout could be magazine, 1-column, 2-column, or 3-column. It's completely up to you.

Figure 4-1:
A magazine layout displays snippets of many blog posts on the home page.

You can always change your blog layout at anytime, so don't feel like you have to commit to a layout forever. Just try to retain brand consistency in terms of color, header design (like the masthead of a newspaper, your blog's header spans across the top of every page and at the very least should include your logo), and so on. This way, even if the layout changes, return visitors will still know they've made it to the right place. You never want to confuse your audience by not meeting their expectations!

If you choose WordPress as your blogging application, you can find many resources online with premade themes to give your blog a unique look. There are three types of WordPress themes: free, premium, and custom. Free themes are exactly what you would think. They are offered free for anyone to use. Premium themes come with a price tag (typically $50–$100 for a single-use license) and can be modified to give your blog a unique look than free themes can provide. Custom themes are the most expensive (typically over $1,000). They are designed from the ground up specifically for the site they're built for.

I recommend using a premium theme that offers free support and has a reputation for being well coded. Following are a number of sites where you can find free and premium WordPress themes:

- ✔ **eBlogTemplates.com:** Offers a wide variety of free themes. (www.eblogtemplates.com)

- ✔ **FreeWordPressThemes.com:** Offers free themes handpicked for usability. (www.freewordpressthemes.com)

- ✔ **WordPress Themes:** Offers thousands of free themes that are easy to search by category. (www.wpthemesfree.com)

- ✔ **StudioPress:** Offers the popular Genesis premium theme, also called a framework. (www.studiopress.com)

- ✔ **iThemes:** Offers a variety of premium themes. (http://ithemes.com)

- ✔ **WooThemes:** Offers free and premium themes. (www.woothemes.com)

- ✔ **Templatic:** Offers both free and premium themes. (http://templatic.com)

- ✔ **DIYthemes:** Offers the popular Thesis premium theme framework. (http://diythemes.com)

- ✔ **Elegant Themes:** Offers a number of premium themes. (www.elegantthemes.com)

Designing your blog

When you know which blogging application and layout you want to use on your blog, you need to put the pieces together and design your branded online destination. Fortunately, blogging applications make the design process easy, but you can enlist the help of a professional designer or developer to make your blog work exactly the way you want it to. This is one of the few investments that you'll need to make as part of your content marketing plan, so invest wisely. For example, work with a developer to fully integrate your online storefront with your blog and Web site so that consumers will find the experience seamless and easy to navigate. This investment will deliver long-term returns because it makes the buying process easier. As mentioned in Chapter 2, design is an important part of your content marketing strategy. Don't skimp!

At the very least, your business blog should prominently display your logo and links to your other branded online destinations, a well-written About page, integration with your Web site, a contact form, and easy-to-read content. You need to make sure your theme works well and your content is displayed neatly. For example, using a small font that is difficult to read damages the user experience on your blog and means fewer repeat visitors.

Some design problems are easy to notice and fix, while others are less obvious or more challenging. For example, if you don't know the coding languages used to create your blog, Cascading Style Sheets (CSS), and HyperText Markup Language (HTML), you may need a designer or developer to help you.

Publishing content to your blog

You can publish content to your blog several ways, and you should use all of them. For example, create pages (if your blogging application allows it) that provide static information about your business and publish posts to share your thoughts, breaking news, useful information, advice, and tips. Publish helpful links, videos, and so on within your posts and in your blog's sidebar. The space is there; use it to directly and indirectly market your business!

Don't be afraid to get creative with the content you publish on your blog. Although writing blog posts is a form of long-form content marketing, you can also republish your short-form marketing content on your blog. For example, display images from your Flickr profile in your blog's sidebar or publish your Twitter posts in your blog's sidebar. Both options are ways you can cross-promote your content and further deliver useful information to your audience.

 The most popular blogs are updated frequently — as often as several times per day. To ensure your blog is persistently in front of your audience, try to publish new content at least three times per week. The more the better, but if you publish less frequently, it's easy to be forgotten. Remember, the online audience is fickle and quick to replace publishers who aren't meeting their expectations.

Furthermore, try to keep your blog posts succinct. While blogging is a form of long-form content marketing, the information you deliver via your blog should be concise and easy for readers to skim through to determine if they want to read it in more detail. A good word count target for blog posts is 500–800 words, but more or less is fine as long as your post is interesting and conveys valuable information. If one of your posts gets to be longer than 800 words, consider breaking it up into a series (which is also a great use of tease marketing). Also, be sure to use headings, lists, and images, as appropriate, to break up text-heavy posts.

Using comments to generate conversations

After you publish a blog post, don't abandon it. If people submit comments to your blog posts, respond to them! One of the primary advantages of content marketing is the ability to build relationships with your target audience because relationships typically lead to sales, brand loyalty, brand advocacy, and increased business. Your chance to build relationships is lost if you ignore your audience. If a person leaves a comment on one of your blog posts, it's safe to assume that person is engaged in your content and open to hearing from you. You wouldn't ignore that person if you were in a face-to-face situation, so don't ignore them online!

Be careful of spam comments and comments that are submitted simply to incite arguments. Moderate comments submitted to your blog to ensure they aren't spam, don't include links to offensive Web sites, and don't include offensive language. While you want to allow free speech, your blog is *yours*, which means you can delete or edit comments that might damage the user experience on your blog and your reputation. However, that doesn't mean you can simply delete negative comments about your business on your blog. Chances are if a disgruntled customer submits a complaint on your blog and you delete it, that person will not go away quietly. Don't try to hide your mistakes. Instead, discuss the issue with the customer either through private e-mail or by responding professionally to negative comments. Always consider the source and craft your response accordingly. You can find more tips about maintaining your online reputation and responding to negative comments about your business in Chapter 16.

Comments don't happen only on your blog though. You should also take time to read other blogs and submit comments on posts that interest you. Be sure to use the same name in the name field of blog comment forms and include your Web site (or blog) URL in the URL field in every comment you submit to any blog. This useful SEO trick can increase links to your branded online destination as well as traffic. If people like your comment, they just might click on the link to see what else you have to say!

Making it easy to share blog content

If you're taking the time to write shareworthy content on your blog, then you should also take the time to make it very easy for people to share that content with their own audiences on Twitter, Facebook, LinkedIn, Digg, StumbleUpon, and any other online profile or destination they choose. If you use WordPress as your blogging application, then you're in luck. A number of plug-ins make it easy to automatically add social Web sharing links and buttons to your blog posts. Even if you don't use WordPress, many tools can help you add some social sharing links to your blog posts in Blogger and TypePad. However, because I recommend WordPress.org, following are a number of WordPress tools and plug-ins that enable you to make sharing a snap for your audience:

- **TweetMeme Retweet Button:** Add the extremely popular Retweet button so people can tweet a link to your blog post in their Twitter streams (`http://wordpress.org/extend/plugins/tweetmeme`).

- **Facebook Share (New) Button:** Add a Facebook Share button so people can easily share a link to your blog post in their Facebook updates (`http://wordpress.org/extend/plugins/facebook-share-new/screenshots`).

- **ShareThis:** Add links to share your blog post on a wide variety of sites (`http://wordpress.org/extend/plugins/share-this`). Similar plug-ins include AddThis (`http://wordpress.org/extend/plugins/addthis`) and Sociable 3.0 (`http://wordpress.org/extend/plugins/sociable-30`).

Make sure visitors have the ability to easily share every post on your blog in order to boost exposure and traffic to those posts. It costs nothing, takes a few minutes to set up, and can have a significant effect on the performance of your blog posts in terms of directly and indirectly marketing your business.

Leveraging feeds and subscriptions

RSS (Really Simple Syndication) is the most commonly used Web feed format, which is the technology used to standardize Web content so people can read it via e-mail or feed reader.

Some companies actually aggregate Web feeds (including blog feeds) and make them available as part of larger content packages, which are sold to companies, Web sites, news organizations, and more.

You should set up your blog's feed using a tool like FeedBurner (`www.feed burner.com`) and prominently display an invitation for visitors to your blog to subscribe to receive your feed content via e-mail or feed reader. Subscribers receive an e-mail message with your new blog content on a daily basis, so they can keep up with your content without having to continually visit your blog looking for new content. Some people prefer to aggregate the feeds of the blogs they enjoy and access all those feeds in one place using a feed reader like Google Reader. You should invite people to subscribe to your blog via feed reader or e-mail so that they can choose how they want to receive and consume your content. Figure 4-2 shows an example of a feed subscription invitation in a blog's sidebar.

You can also use feeds to cross-promote your content. For example, you can publish the feed content from other blogs you write or enjoy in your blog's sidebar or footer using the RSS widget provided in WordPress. You can also feed your blog content to your Twitter, Facebook, or LinkedIn updates, and vice versa, using a tool like Twitterfeed (`www.twitterfeed.com`) and the tools built into Facebook and LinkedIn. Check out the feeds displayed in a blog footer as shown in Figure 4-3 to see how it works.

Figure 4-2:
Prominently
display
your blog's
feed
subscription.

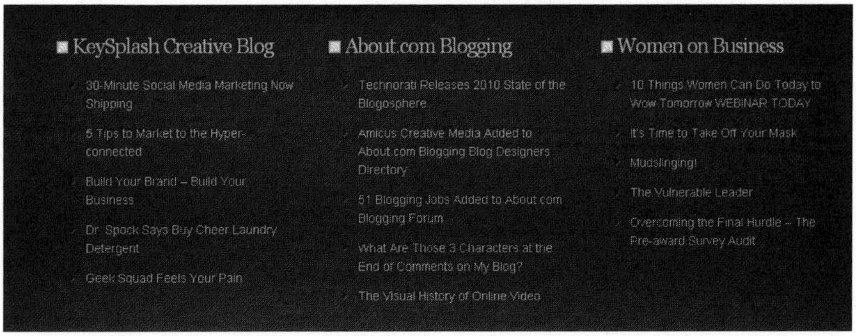

Figure 4-3:
Cross-
promote
your content
by publish-
ing feeds
from your
other blogs
and social
profiles on
your blog.

■ KeySplash Creative Blog	■ About.com Blogging	■ Women on Business
30-Minute Social Media Marketing Now Shipping	Technorati Releases 2010 State of the Blogosphere	10 Things Women Can Do Today to Wow Tomorrow WEBINAR TODAY
5 Tips to Market to the Hyper-connected	Amicus Creative Media Added to About.com Blogging Blog Designers Directory	It's Time to Take Off Your Mask
Build Your Brand – Build Your Business	51 Blogging Jobs Added to About.com Blogging Forum	Mudslinging!
Dr. Spock Says Buy Cheer Laundry Detergent	What Are Those 3 Characters at the End of Comments on My Blog?	The Vulnerable Leader
Geek Squad Feels Your Pain	The Visual History of Online Video	Overcoming the Final Hurdle – The Pre-award Survey Audit

Feeds can do more to help you promote your varied content than just making it easy for people to know when you publish new blog content. Be creative with your feeds and let them automatically cross-promote your content.

Promoting your blog

As shown in the previous section, you can feed your blog content to your online profiles to give your blog posts more exposure. You should also include a link to your blog in your online profile biographies, in your e-mail signature, in your forum signatures, on your business card, on your letterhead and invoices, and anywhere else you can think of. This is particularly important if your business blog is your core branded online destination.

Other promotional opportunities include guest blogging (discussed in the next section), feeding your blog updates to LinkedIn groups that allow the News feature (read more about LinkedIn groups in Chapter 8), and syndicating your blog content through companies like Newstex (`www.newstex.com`) and Demand Studios Blog Distribution Network (`www.demandstudios.com/freelance-work/bloggers.html`). In other words, include a link to your blog anywhere and everywhere you can!

Furthermore, do some keyword research and write blog posts with SEO in mind (as discussed in Chapter 7). Applying simple SEO tactics to your blog posts can help drive organic search traffic to your blog that can last for a long time!

Being a guest blogger

Guest blogging is a popular blog promotional tactic that you can use to build awareness of and traffic to your business blog. You can do guest blogging in two ways. You can either write blog posts as a guest writer for other blogs or publish blog posts by guest writers on your blog. Both options can help you build relationships with other bloggers and increase traffic to your blog.

For example, when other bloggers write guest posts on your blog, they are likely to share it with their audience of followers who might not already be reading your blog. On the flip side, when you write guest blog posts for other blogs, your content gets in front of new audiences who might like what you have to say and follow you back to your own blog to read and further interact with you.

Conducting blogger outreach

The first step to writing guest blog posts for other blogs is doing your research. You need to find blogs whose existing readers match your target audience. Conduct a Google Blog search (http://blogsearch.google.com) to find blogs about topics related to your business. Read your competitors' blogs and follow links from people who submit comments to your competitors' posts to see if they write blogs related to your business.

When you find blogs related to your business, check the popularity of those blogs using sites like Compete (www.compete.com) and Alexa (www.alexa.com) to get a better understanding of traffic patterns. Also, you can look for advertising information on those blogs. Because advertisers typically want to know information about traffic and audience demographics before they pay for ad space, some bloggers publish that information in the advertising section of their blogs.

When you find blogs that you want to write guest posts for, begin to leave comments and join the conversations happening on those blogs so that you get on the bloggers' radar screens. Follow the bloggers on Twitter and connect with them on their various online profiles. This is particularly important for highly successful bloggers who get many inquiries each day. When you've established a relationship or at least gotten on a blogger's radar screen, send an e-mail asking if you can submit a guest post. Explain that the post will be original content for that blog only and mention the topic so that the blogger understands your content will be useful to that blogger's audience.

Don't harass bloggers and don't send generic messages to them, or you'll be accused of blog blasting. Instead, send personalized e-mail messages that demonstrate the value you can deliver to the bloggers' audience, and make it clear that your guest post won't be self-promotional.

Finding guest blogging opportunities

You can find guest blogging opportunities by searching Google for keyword phrases such as *guest blog submission* or *write for us,* but that can be time-consuming and hit or miss in terms of getting positive responses. To find more guest blogging opportunities, you can join a site such as MyBlogGuest (www.myblogguest.com), which makes it easy for guest bloggers to find blogs that are actively accepting guest blog posts. Alternatively, you can check the About.com Blogging Forum, which includes a folder where calls for guest bloggers are often published (http://forums.about.com/n/pfx/forum.aspx?nav=messages&webtag=ab-weblogs&lgnF=y).

Tricks to make guest blogging work for you

For your guest blogging efforts to be successful, you need to choose blogs to write for that can enable you to get in front of your target audience. That means you need to do your research first. Next, you need to follow the suggestions provided earlier in this section related to effectively reaching out to bloggers for whom you'd like to write guest posts, and finally, you need to write amazing, shareworthy content in your guest blog posts.

Be sure to include a brief bio at the end of your guest blog posts with a link back to your blog and Web site. Just make sure your bio is short (two to three sentences) and isn't written in a self-promotional tone. You don't want your post to be ruined when people get to the end of it and find themselves bombarded with marketing messages that leave a negative last impression of you and your business.

Writing Articles and Contributing to Web Sites

A number of article publishing Web sites allow you to publish your content free, providing another way for your target audience to engage with your brand. You can also reach out to Web sites that accept contributors and pitch your content for inclusion on those sites. Article publishing and Web site content contributions are typically a bit more formal in tone and formatting than blog content, so you need to approach this form of long-form content marketing with that in mind.

Finding article and content publishing sites

Some article publishing sites allow anyone to create an account and publish content, while others have an application process that you need to pass before you can publish content. Always read the fine print before you join a site to ensure that the manner in which content is published and used on those sites matches your content marketing goals.

Following are a variety of article publishing sites that you can research:

- ✔ **EzineArticles.com:** Free article publishing site (`http://ezine articles.com`).
- ✔ **ArticleDashboard.com:** Free article publishing site (`www.article dashboard.com`).
- ✔ **GoArticles.com:** Free article publishing site (`www.goarticles.com`).
- ✔ **HubPages:** Free social content publishing site (`http://hubpages.com`).
- ✔ **Squidoo:** Free content publishing site (`www.squidoo.com`).
- ✔ **Associated Content:** Members can publish approved content for free or for payment (`www.associatedcontent.com`).

You can find more article publishing sites by conducting a Google search using a keyword phrase such as *article directories, article publishing sites,* or *sites like ezinearticles.com.*

Writing articles for the Web

When you write articles for the Web, you need to consider more than simply conveying useful information. Many article submission sites and sites that accept contributors have specific guidelines you have to follow or your content won't be published. Always search for writers' guidelines on sites you plan to submit articles or content to, and follow them to the letter.

You should also be sure to write with SEO in mind, because many article directory sites are very search-friendly. To get maximum exposure for your articles, you need to be sure that people can find them. It can also help to write your articles in HTML so that you can be confident they are published exactly how you want them to look.

You can learn basic HTML on a site like Dave's Site (`www.davesite.com/webstation/html`) or w3schools.com (`www.w3schools.com/HTML/default.asp`).

Finally, take some time to read other articles that have already been published on sites where you want to submit your content and be sure to format your articles similarly to other articles related to your topic that perform well. Many article publishing sites allow you to sort content by topic or view popular articles. Find out what top performers are doing on each site, and then write and format your articles similarly.

Republishing and retooling

When you're submitting content to article publishing sites, you need to remember that those sites aren't your own branded online destinations. Therefore, your content appears alongside content from a lot of different people and businesses. Make sure the sites you choose match your brand promise, but also make sure your efforts match the site where your content will appear.

For example, article directory sites are perfect places to retool and republish your existing content. As long as you don't republish the exact same article in more than one place, you can derive benefits from it. A content marketing trick is to *repurpose* your content so that it's not exactly the same but conveys similar concepts on multiple sites. Save your hard work and efforts for crafting original, amazing content on your own branded online destinations, and use repurposed or retooled content on article directory sites as a supplement to your online presence.

Promoting your articles

Articles are perfect for supplementing your content marketing efforts, but I don't recommend leading with them. For example, instead of linking to your articles on article directories, link to similar content on your blog or other branded online destination. Articles should serve a primary purpose of capturing the attention of people who might not find your content otherwise and directing them (through a link within your content) to your core branded online destination where they can discover more about you, read more of your amazing content, and further interact with you.

With that said, it's my recommendation that you don't spend time promoting your content on article directories. Instead, let those articles pick up extraneous traffic and send it your way, but don't drive traffic to those articles. It's far more beneficial to spend your time driving people to your branded online destinations. That's why article directories are the perfect place for your repurposed content.

Authoring Ebooks

Ebooks are a highly popular form of long-form content marketing. They can deliver a lot of information in an easy-to-read, easy-to-share, and easy-to-produce manner. It seems like ebooks are available on about any topic you can think of, but the well-written, authoritative ebooks stand far above the rest in terms of popularity and pass-along value. Furthermore, the promotional opportunities are plentiful.

Choosing an ebook topic

When you decide to write an ebook as part of your content marketing plan, you need to choose a topic that is directly related to your business. An ebook isn't a direct marketing tool. On the contrary, an ebook should be highly informational or educational with little or no direct marketing messages included. In fact, the most effective ebooks in terms of content marketing success include little more in terms of direct marketing messages than a line of copy at the beginning or end that says, "for more information contact us at XYZ or check out our blog at ABC.com." If the information is useful enough, that ebook will drive interest, conversations, and traffic without a direct and repeated request.

Consider writing about a topic that you're passionate about or that you receive a lot of questions about. Either approach ensures that your ebook will be interesting and useful. Always put your target audience first. While you might have marketing message you'd like to deliver, if your ebook doesn't meet your audience's wants and needs, your message will be ignored. The content of the ebook in terms of its consumer appeal should be your top priority. The trick is ensuring that you can link that ebook topic back to your business in some way so that readers are likely to look to you for more information and great content.

Considering length

Ebooks should be fairly short. If you type your ebook draft in a word processing program like Microsoft Word, set your margins to one inch, your font to 12-point Times New Roman, and your line spacing to double space. Your target length should be approximately 20 pages or 5,000 words. Of course, the most important thing is that your ebook is concise, clear, and informative. Don't agonize over length. Just make sure that your ebook is long enough to be useful, and you'll be okay.

You don't want your ebook to be just a few pages, or it's not an ebook at all. It's a long article. On the other hand, you don't want your ebook to be too long, or you run the risk of rambling and losing readers before they finish (or before they even start) reading. Write with the 20-page or 5,000-word target in mind for best results.

Writing your ebook

Your ebook should be written like a short book. That means you need a title, copyright page, table of contents, and chapters. You need to write original content and cite sources for information that isn't your own original content. Get started by determining what you want readers to walk away understanding after they read your ebook. When you determine that end goal, you can create an outline that shows how you're going to get there throughout your ebook's chapters.

Make sure you use headings, lists, callouts, and images in your ebook. Many people read ebooks online, so it's important that yours is easy to scan on a computer screen. Remember, ebooks should be short and easy to read. Your tone and style should be less formal than a research paper or encyclopedia but more formal than a blog post or Facebook conversation. You need to demonstrate your expertise in your ebook or no one will read it, but you also need to seem human and accessible or no one will read it. Try to find a balance between exuding authority and exuding arrogance and your ebook will have a greater chance for success.

When you're done writing your ebook and think it's perfect, show it to colleagues, friends, family, and even existing customers to get their feedback. Their suggestions are likely to make your ebook even better and you might even be surprised at the spelling and grammatical errors they find. Always have someone else proofread your own work. You're too close to it and you'll miss typos and other errors no matter how many times you read it.

Designing your ebook

When your ebook is written, it's time to make it look great. Design can really give an ebook a boost, because great design makes an ebook look more professional and makes it easier to read. Following are ten ebook design suggestions that can help you develop a better final product:

✔ Format your ebook in a landscape orientation since many people read ebooks online.

✔ Use a font size and type that's easy to read both online and offline such as Georgia or Verdana with a size no smaller than 14 points.

✔ Use a white background with black text for the body of the ebook to ensure maximum readability online and offline.

✔ Test your ebook on different monitors and in printed form to ensure that the colors and layout look good everywhere people might view them.

✔ Use Web-friendly colors and fonts.

✔ Use a lot of white space for maximum readability.

✔ Use images to break up long blocks of text.

✔ Invest in royalty-free images that readers are not likely to have seen on other Web sites, blogs, or ebooks.

✔ Save your ebook in PDF format so that it's easy (and free) for people to download, print, and share.

✔ Hire a designer to make sure your ebook looks great and is saved optimally for download and sharing.

No matter how great your content is, if your ebook looks terrible, is difficult to view, or impossible to download, no one will read it. Don't waste the time and effort writing your ebook by trying to design it on the cheap.

Making it easy to share your ebook

One of the best things you can do to ensure that your ebook is a successful component of your content marketing plan is to remove the gateway and allow anyone to access it (refer to Chapter 3 for information on removing gateways). Second, publish your ebook with a Creative Commons Attribution license (refer to Chapter 3 for more on Creative Common licenses) so that anyone can share it, republish it, and use it in their own work as long as they cite you as the owner and source. You can include information on your copyright page that explains the Creative Commons Attribution license and even request that attribution be provided in a specific manner, such as a link to your Web site or core branded destination.

Make sure that your ebook includes a footer so that your name and Web site link are displayed at the bottom of every page. This way, even readers see only a single page of your ebook, your name and URL will be available to them.

Publish the link to view and download your ebook on your core branded online destination along with a message that describes the Creative Commons Attribution license and make it clear that readers are welcome to share the content with their own audiences. Many people skip the copyright page, so you want to be certain they understand they can pass along your ebook freely. The goal is for your ebook to get maximum exposure, so you want everyone to understand the Creative Commons Attribution license and what it means to them.

Promoting your ebook

After your ebook is uploaded to your Web site and core branded destination and is available for the world to see, it's time to start spreading the word about the ebook:

1. Begin by publishing a blog post about your ebook and be sure to include a link to read or download the PDF file along with a note assuring readers that it's okay to share the PDF file with their own audiences.

2. Use a service like bit.ly (`http://bit.ly`) to create a trackable link that goes to the page where your ebook can be found online. Tweet that link along with a note about your ebook and share it on Facebook, LinkedIn, and on all your other online profiles and destinations.

3. Include links to your ebook in your forum signatures, e-mail signature, and business card. You can even upload your ebook to SlideShare (discussed in the "Publishing Presentations" section, later in this chapter) or make it available through Amazon's Kindle eReader device using the Amazon Digital Text Platform (`https://dtp.amazon.com/mn/signin?ie=UTF8&ld=AZEbooksMakeM`). The key is getting your ebook included in Amazon searches, which can really increase exposure for your ebook, you, and your business!

To offer your ebook on the Kindle, you do have to put a price tag on it, but you can use the lowest price, $0.99, and offer some of your content for free preview.

Bottom line, if you take the time to write and design a great ebook that your target audience is likely to find very useful, don't be afraid to shout it to the world!

Writing Press Releases

Press releases are different from other forms of content marketing because they should not include marketing language at all. Instead, press releases should be written in a journalistic style and about truly newsworthy events that are likely to be of interest to wide audiences. Try to make your business newsworthy so that you can create press releases to indirectly market your business. You can turn a lot of events related to your business into news. For example, events such as launching a new product or Web site, taking on a new client, attending an event, hosting a training session, or hiring a new employee could all be turned into newsworthy press releases.

In order to use press releases as a content marketing tool, you need to learn the correct way to write press releases and how and where to publish them online in order to generate exposure for you and your business.

Writing and formatting press releases

Press releases should be written in the following way:

1. Start by writing a headline that explains the news being released and includes your company name.

2. Lead with the town, state, and date for the release.

3. Quickly get to the point of your news release by addressing the who, why, when, where, what, and how questions of journalism.

   The key is to write so that all the critical information about your release can be communicated within the first paragraph.

4. Include supporting details and quotes from you or key individuals related to the press release.

5. End with a boilerplate paragraph about your company that includes your Web site URL and a contact name, an address, a phone number, and an e-mail address for media inquiries.

Press releases should be written in the third-person style and should not include any kind of promotional messages. They should be completely factual and devoid of hype. Write press releases with a target word count of no more than 500 words. Try to write with keywords in mind, particularly within the first 250 words of your press release and within any links used in your press release. If the sites where you upload your press release allow you to include keyword tags, be sure to do so to maximize the number of people who can find your release in searches.

Distributing press releases

There was a time when press releases could be distributed only through large wire services used by news organizations. Today, you can distribute press releases through a wide variety of services and Web sites offering varying costs and reach. Following are a number of options to choose from:

✔ **PR Newswire:** Varied price levels with different distribution for each (www.prnewswire.com). Small business packages are available.

- ✔ **PRWeb:** Different price levels for different types of distribution (`www.prweb.com`).
- ✔ **Free Press Release:** Offers free and paid distribution options (`www.free-press-release.com`).
- ✔ **openPR:** Offers free press release publishing (`www.openpr.com`).
- ✔ **PR.com:** Offers free and paid press release publishing (`www.pr.com`).
- ✔ **Small Business Trends:** Offers free press release publishing (`www.smallbiztrends.com`).
- ✔ **WomenOnBusiness.com:** Offers free press release publishing (`www.womenonbusiness.com/submit-a-press-release`).

It's perfectly acceptable to submit your press release to multiple sites and services. Just be aware of the costs and overlap in distribution audience to ensure that you don't spend more money than necessary to reach the same people.

Promoting your press releases

Press releases aren't necessarily content that you can promote. Instead, press releases are a supplement to your content marketing strategy that allows you to get your name, URL, and information in front of audiences who might not see it otherwise. Be sure to publish your press releases on your own Web site and blog, and link to them from your Twitter, Facebook, and LinkedIn profiles and branded destinations to share your news with your existing audience. If you belong to groups on Facebook, LinkedIn, and so on whose members might find value in your news, share the link in those groups, too. Some of those people might even share your news further with their own audiences.

Don't spend time promoting your press releases that can be found on distribution sites and services. Instead, drive that traffic to the version on your own Web site or blog where they just might click around to read more of your fine content.

Writing White Papers

White papers are different from blogs, articles, press releases, and other content because they are usually based on extensive research. For example, a marketing company that researches consumers' responses to ads in online video may write a white paper explaining their research, analyzing the results, and offering their conclusions, opinions, and suggestions. Less research-intensive content is better suited for an ebook that appeals to a broader audience.

Analyzing what a white paper is and how best to use it

White papers are an excellent form of content marketing for highly technical companies and businesses that have complex topics to discuss and educate their audiences about. For example, an accountant could write a white paper about a new tax law and its impact on taxpayers' lives.

Think of it this way: If the content you want to write would be better suited to an academic or professional journal than a trade magazine, it should be a white paper. White papers typically include charts, graphs, footnotes, bibliographies, quotes, and so on. Sources are checked and rechecked, and the final product is something that readers can rely on for its accuracy and authority.

Promoting a white paper

You can promote your white paper across your branded online destinations. For example, write about it on your blog, tweet a link to it, mention it on Facebook and LinkedIn, share it with groups you belong to, and so on.

White papers take a lot of time and effort to write, and you should be proud to share it with the world.

You can also share your white paper with other bloggers and Web sites whose audiences will find your research valuable. Many bloggers and site owners will be happy to add a link to your white paper to their resource lists, publish a post about it, or interview you about it. A white paper can be extremely useful to specific audiences, so target niche blogs whose readers match those specific audiences. You might be surprised at how willing those bloggers are to share your work.

You can also get creative in promoting your white papers. Of course, you can include a link in your newsletters or e-mails, but you can also create a video that offers a few key snippets or findings from your white paper along with a link to read the complete white paper. You could hold a webinar or Tweetchat to discuss the major findings in the white paper. The opportunities are limited only by your creative thinking!

Publishing Presentations

SlideShare (www.slideshare.net) is a tool that enables you to upload your PowerPoint, OpenOffice, or PDF presentations to your own branded channel. After you upload your presentation, people can easily view, print, download, share, and embed your presentations into their Web sites or blogs. SlideShare makes it easy for you to share your sales presentations, training presentations, and more with a broad audience, and because people can embed and share your uploaded presentations, the pass-along value is huge.

Understanding the value of sharing your presentations

At first glance, you might think sharing your presentations is like giving away all your trade secrets, but that's not the case at all. Imagine being able to pitch your sales presentation in a room filled with hundreds or thousands of people who've already expressed interest in what you're going to present to them. That's exactly what you get when you publish that same sales presentation on SlideShare; however, instead of pitching a room full of people, you're pitching a global audience via the Web. That's an opportunity businesses would be crazy to miss!

You might be tempted to upload your presentations to SlideShare but not enable the functions that allow people to print, download, share, or embed those presentations elsewhere online. Doing so significantly limits the exposure and reach of your presentations. Remember, content marketing works from the sharing and word-of-mouth marketing that your amazing content elicits. Don't stop your content from doing what it was meant to do. Instead, remove the gateway and let it spread for maximum success.

Using SlideShare

You can create a free account with SlideShare, customize your own SlideShare channel, and begin uploading presentations immediately. Be sure to create a complete profile, including links to your core branded online destination, and make your profile public so that people can find your content. You can see an example of a free SlideShare page in Figure 4-4. When you upload presentations, make sure you set them up so people can print, download, share, and embed them.

Figure 4-4:
A free
SlideShare
page can
look very
professional.

SlideShare does offer professional packages with price tags attached to them. Paid accountholders get access to analytics and can remove ads from their videos and channels. I recommend starting with a free account and upgrading to a professional account in the future if SlideShare becomes a vital component of your content marketing strategy.

Promoting your presentations

Of course, you should blog about your presentations when you upload them (be sure to embed them in your blog post), and share links to them on Twitter, Facebook, LinkedIn, and so on. You can even add a SlideShare tab on your Facebook Page and a SlideShare widget on your blog to further promote your presentations.

When you upload presentations to SlideShare, be sure to name them with keywords in mind and include a description and tags that are keyword rich to boost the number of people who find your presentations through SlideShare searches. SlideShare also enables you to include a text transcript of your presentation, which is great for SEO — use it! You can even create collections of presentations and join groups on SlideShare, which can give your presentations more exposure.

Chapter 5

Using Video, Audio, Online Events, and E-Mail for Long-Form Content Marketing

*E*ven if you're not a natural writer, you can use long-form content marketing to build your brand and your business. Video, screencasts, audio, podcasts, events, and e-mail can all be forms of content marketing when they are used to indirectly promote your business. Of course, you never want to cross the line that divides content marketing from ads and commercials. This chapter shows you how to create varied types of long-form content that will add value to consumers' lives and engage them with your brand.

Don't limit yourself when it comes to long-form content marketing. If you create any content that provides deep value and a new way for consumers to experience your brand, then let that content play its part in your content marketing plan. Remember, if you build it, they won't necessarily come. Make sure your content is out there for the world to see, share, and talk about!

Creating Videos

Online video continues to grow in popularity with billions of videos viewed every month by people around the world. Video used as a form of content marketing should be informative, entertaining, or educational rather than self-promotional. That's what makes video content shareworthy and encourages people to view it. If you simply publish commercials and infomercials, the value of your online video content plummets. Remember, content marketing is about enhancing user experiences and engaging audiences, not interrupting them. Ads interrupt, while useful or entertaining content engages. Be useful.

Online video has propelled businesses and unknown entertainers to success and superstardom. Video-sharing sites enable people to not only view your video content but also comment on it, share it, and embed it on their own blogs and Web sites. When you create your own channel on a video-publishing site like YouTube (www.youtube.com), you create another branded online destination where people who prefer to watch videos rather than read text can engage with you. And if you're lucky enough to catch lightening in a bottle and publish a video that goes viral and spreads across the Internet, get ready for more exposure and success than you've ever dreamed of.

Knowing what kind of videos to create

Creating videos takes more planning and time than typing a blog post or Twitter update. You need to decide what you're going to talk about, prepare your backdrop, make sure you say everything correctly, and edit your video for clarity, sound, and more. It's not a quick tactic, but if you create good videos that entertain or educate people (refer to the story of Gary Vaynerchuk in Chapter 1), you can draw a large audience of viewers. For online video to work, you need to commit to creating good videos consistently. A single video published on your YouTube channel doesn't make a successful content marketing effort.

But what will people be interested in and want to watch and learn about? The first thing you need to do is research. Search for other videos about your business or by your competitors. See what they're doing and find out what types of videos get a lot of views and comments. Think about what kind of value you can add to your audience through video. Following are a number of suggestions for video content:

- ✔ Demonstrate how to use a product.

- ✔ Show people how to perform a specific task related to your business or products.

- ✔ Interview customers who can share their own experiences related to your line of business.

- ✔ Interview an expert related to your business.

- ✔ Capture behind-the-scenes footage of your employees in your office or store so that your audience gets to know the people behind the business.

- ✔ Offer commentary on news or current events related to your industry.

- ✔ Answer questions submitted by your viewers or customers.

- ✔ Film company events such as trade shows, seminars, parties, and company baseball games to provide more insight into your business and the people who work there.

As long as you're personable and passionate about the subject of your videos, your efforts won't go unnoticed. Spend less time worrying about what to talk about in your videos and more time just talking about what's on your mind and what your customers tell you is important to them. Your desire to offer valuable information or entertain your audience rather than simply advertising your business and products will shine through.

Finding tools to create and upload videos

Before you can become an online video publisher, you need to get the tools necessary to create and upload professional-looking videos. You don't need to create Academy Award-worthy videos, but you don't want your videos to look like an elementary school project either. The quality should match your brand promise while staying affordable.

To film your videos, you need a video camera and microphone. Many popular online video publishers use a simple webcam and microphone connected to their computers to film their videos. If you own a Mac, the webcam and microphone built into your Mac work just fine. If you want something more portable, you can purchase a Flip video camera for under $200. The more you spend on a video camera, the better the quality, so it's up to you to decide what you need to create your videos.

You also need a tool to upload your videos to your computer (most new computers have built-in USB ports where you can hook up your video camera and directly upload your videos to your computer) and a tool to edit your videos. Many video editing software programs are available, including the free editors Windows Movie Maker for PC and iMovie for Mac.

When your video is uploaded to your computer, you can also add music, voice-overs, images, and more (refer to Chapter 3 for a list of places you can go to find music and images that you can use without violating copyright laws). It's also a good idea to have an image-editing program such as Adobe Photoshop or the free editing programs available at www.picnik.com, www.getpaint.net, or www.gimp.org to modify images in your videos.

When your video is finalized, you need to upload it to the Web. You can choose from many video publishing and sharing sites. Some of the most popular options are as follows:

✔ www.youtube.com

✔ www.tubemogul.com

✔ www.dailymotion.com

✔ www.blip.tv

✔ www.vimeo.com

✔ www.viddler.com

You can upload your video to one or more sites in an effort to give it maximum exposure. (TubeMogul allows you to upload your video once and make it available on a variety of other sites, providing you have an account with those other sites.) Some of these sites allow you to create your own branded video channel, which I highly recommend. It's just one more way to create a branded online destination where you can further surround your audience with branded experiences from which they can self-select how to interact with your brand.

Uploading videos for maximum sharing and discussion

To increase pass-along value and views, when you upload a video to a video-publishing site, make sure anyone can view the video, share it, and embed it in other Web sites and blogs. Also, to boost search traffic, if the site allows you to add a description and tags, use them and be sure to describe and tag your video with keywords in mind.

You may also have the option to add annotations and transcripts to your video content, which you should do in order to give your video content another search engine optimization (SEO) boost. Take the time to name your videos clearly and accurately, and if it's appropriate to add keywords to the title without sounding like you're trying to arbitrarily stuff keywords into the title, use them.

When you create your videos, your goal is for people to view, share, and embed them in their own sites. Therefore, be sure to include your Web site or core branded online destination at the beginning and end of your video content so that, no matter where they find your video online, viewers know who created it and where they can find out more.

Creating a YouTube channel

YouTube is by far the most popular video-publishing site. For free, you can create your own branded YouTube channel where you can upload all your video content (as long as each video is under 15 minutes). To create your own YouTube channel, you need to have a YouTube account. If you don't already have a YouTube account, visit www.youtube.com to create one and then follow these instructions to create your YouTube channel:

1. **Log into your YouTube account and click your username in the top-right corner of the screen.**

   A drop-down list appears, as shown in Figure 5-1.

2. **In the drop-down list, click the My Channel link to open the Channel Settings page, as shown in Figure 5-2.**

3. **To configure your channel settings, click the tabs and links to name your channel, enter your profile information and customize your channel color scheme.**

Within a few minutes, you can have your own branded YouTube channel ready to start uploading videos, similar to the one shown in Figure 5-3.

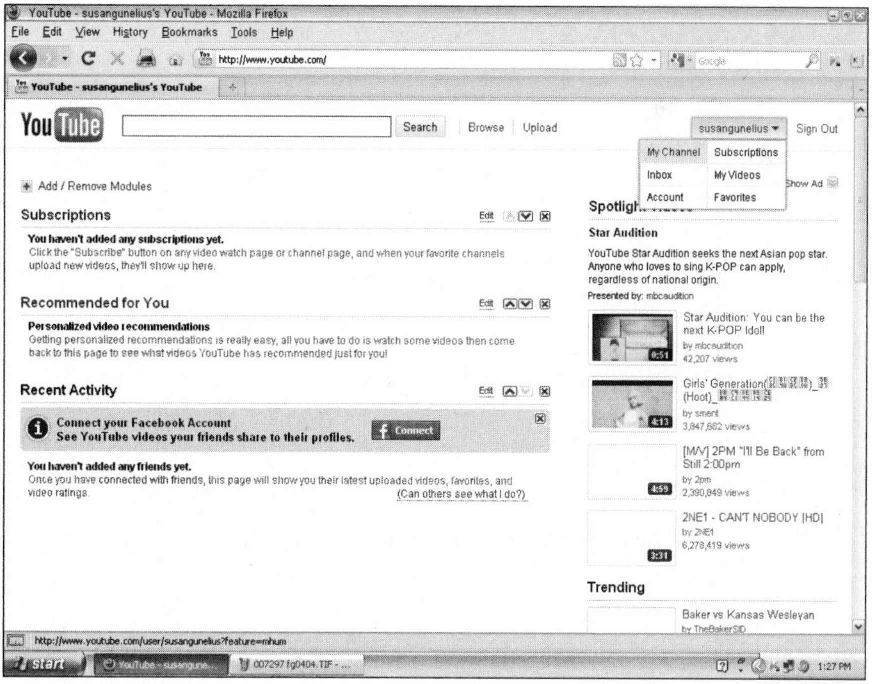

Figure 5-1: Click the My Channel link to view and configure your YouTube channel.

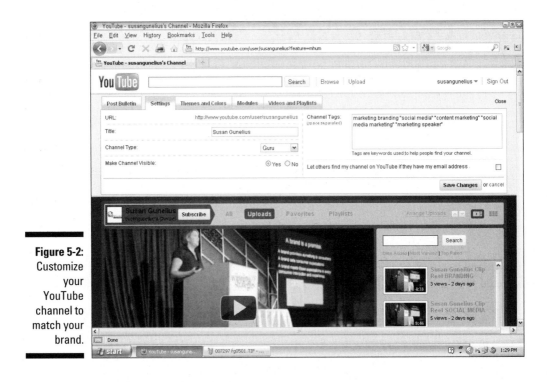

Figure 5-2:
Customize
your
YouTube
channel to
match your
brand.

Figure 5-3:
A branded
YouTube
channel
stands out
and looks
great.

Make sure you configure your channel settings to be as public as possible and enable all forms of discussion and sharing for maximum exposure.

Creating screencasts

Another form of online video is the *screencast,* which is simply a video of your computer screen with audio. Screencasts are used most often to provide tutorials showing viewers how to accomplish a task online or on their computers. For example, a technical training company might create a screencast for e-mail beginners that shows them how to create an e-mail message. The screencast "films" the computer screen as the task is executed. Audio, such as a person's voice explaining what is happening on screen, can be added to the screencast to create a useful tutorial.

Many Web developers use screencasts very effectively to indirectly promote their businesses. For example, if a WordPress theme designer creates screencasts showing people how to use and customize their themes and how to accomplish common tasks, that information is very useful to users who aren't proficient in WordPress design. If some of those screencasts cover WordPress tasks that aren't dependent on the theme, those screencasts could be useful to an even wider audience. People will find value in those screencasts. They'll talk about them, share them with other people, and drive more awareness and traffic to the designer's site, which could lead to increased sales.

Many screencast applications are available, ranging in price from free to hundreds of dollars. Here are some popular options:

- ✔ **CamStudio:** Free and very popular open source screencast application available at `http://camstudio.org`.

- ✔ **Screencast-o-Matic:** A Web-based application that provides both a free and a paid option available at `www.screencast-o-matic.com`.

- ✔ **Jing:** You can find both a free and paid version of Jing at TechSmith at `www.techsmith.com/jing`.

- ✔ **Camtasia Studio:** From TechSmith, Camtasia Studio is one of the most popular and feature-rich screencast applications with a price tag to match. PC and Mac versions are available at `www.techsmith.com/camtasia.asp` and `www.techsmith.com/camtasiamac`.

- ✔ **ScreenFlow:** This is a Mac-only application that is feature-rich but with a lower price tag than Camtasia Studio. It is available at `www.telestream.net/screen-flow`.

Depending on the type of business you own, screencasts could be a great addition to your content marketing plan. Just be sure to include your name and Web site or core branded online destination at the beginning and end of your screencast to ensure that viewers know who created it and how to get more information from you no matter where they find it.

Promoting your videos

Your online video content can be a great addition to your Web site and blog because it adds visual and audio appeal to a text-heavy branded destination. Publish a blog post announcing your new video content and embed your video into your post. Add it to your blog's sidebar and publish it on a special page on your Web site. You can also tweet a link to your video, add it to your Facebook profile and Page, mention it on LinkedIn, in groups and forums you belong to, and so on.

The popularity of online videos makes it clear that people like video content. Don't be afraid to share yours. You can even add a line to your e-mail signature that says, "Check out the latest on ABC Company TV" with a link to your YouTube channel.

Another easy way to boost organic search traffic to your online video content on your YouTube channel is to create playlists, which allow you to select multiple videos and display them as individual videos on your YouTube channel *and* within separate playlists. For example, if you've published a series of videos about the same topic, put them together in a playlist. You can promote the link to the playlist as well as the links to individual videos. When people click on the playlist link, they'll automatically view the videos in that playlist sequentially. Also, playlists are indexed separately from individual videos, which means that people conducting keyword searches related to your content have two ways to find your videos.

Using Audio and Podcasts

You can record and publish audio on your Web site or blog anytime you want. You can also create a podcast, which is an audio recording that you publish using an RSS feed that allows people to subscribe to receive new updates of the podcast via their preferred podcast services.

Podcasts are different from online radio because they aren't broadcast at a specific time and place. Instead, people can access and download podcasts anytime after they're published, and people can listen to them anytime they want and as many times as they want. You can even create your own online talk show podcast to promote your business through content marketing using the easy-to-use tools available to you on the Web.

You can use audio content to promote your business just as you use video content. In other words, the goal is to create useful audio content that people want to listen to, talk about, and share. With the popularity of portable MP3 players such as iPods, people can download audio content and podcasts and listen to that content in more places than ever. For example, many people listen to audio content during their daily commute to and from work or while exercising. When you think about it that way, your audio content can deliver branded experiences that other forms of content can't.

Choosing a topic

When you decide that you want to create audio content or a podcast to help market your business, you need to pick your topic. Because audio content requires you to do a lot of talking, you need to pick a topic that you're passionate about and know a great deal about. The topic should be relevant to your business and important to your target audience. If it's not relevant to your business, it won't do much to indirectly promote your brand, products, and services. Instead, any correlations you try to draw between your irrelevant content and business will cause confusion among your target audience.

Similarly, if your audio content isn't useful or entertaining to that audience, it won't help you promote your business. Finally, your audio or podcast content needs to add value to your target audience, or it won't get shared and talked about among the right people. For example, if you own a wine store and your audio content becomes popular among a teen audience, that audience can't buy your products, and your content won't help you reach your marketing goals. Make sure your audio content topic is appropriate for your target audience.

Spend some time searching for podcasts related to your business to find out what topics are popular and where there are gaps in coverage. You can model your format after popular podcasts, but you have to bring something new, different, or extra to the table in order to attract listeners.

Finding tools to create and share audio and podcasts

Creating audio content and podcasts isn't difficult. Depending on the type of audio content you plan to create, your equipment needs may vary. For example, if you plan to simply record audio content and upload it directly to your blog, you need a microphone connected to your computer. If you plan to join an online talk show provider Web site to record and publish your audio content, you might only need a telephone to record your content.

If you want to record your audio content locally and publish it yourself, then Audacity (`http://sourceforge.net/projects/audacity`) or GarageBand (`www.apple.com/ilife/garageband`) are excellent, free audio-recording programs.

If you want to use a service or Web site to upload your audio content and make it available for sharing, listening, distributing, and possible download from iTunes, then you can try one of the following resources to record and publish your content:

- ✔ **BlogTalkRadio:** At `www.blogtalkradio.com`, BlogTalkRadio is a very popular site where you can host your own online talk show using your phone. It's a very social site. People can call in and participate in your show, publish written comments about your show, and more. You can upload your show to iTunes and even create your own branded show page free. However, free options are limited in terms of the length of your show and the number of callers you can have at one time. Check the current account offerings to ensure the features match your needs and budget.

- ✔ **Blubrry:** At `www.blubrry.com`, Blubrry enables you to create your podcast and upload it to Blubrry for hosting and creating an RSS feed so that you can upload your content to iTunes. If you prefer, you can use a separate Web host for your audio content and simply make your post available through Blubrry as another way for people to find it. The latter option requires more technical knowledge than the former.

- ✔ **Podbean.com:** At `www.podbean.com`, Podbean.com is another site that offers hosting of audio content. If Podbean.com hosts your audio content, that content is also available on iTunes and is easily integrated into some of your other branded online destinations, such as your blog or Facebook Page.

Promoting your audio and podcast content

To promote your audio and podcast content, one of the first steps you take is to make sure it's available through several distribution points. For example, publish your audio content on BlogTalkRadio or Blubrry and make sure it's also available on iTunes. Blog about it, include a page with your audio content on your Web site, add it to your Facebook profile and Page, and so on. The more places people can find and listen to your audio content, the better.

In addition, you should mention new audio content anytime you publish it by tweeting a link to it, updating your Facebook and LinkedIn profiles with it, sharing it on social bookmarking sites like Digg and StumbleUpon, adding the link to your e-mail signature, telling people about it in forums you belong to, and talking about it in your newsletter. You might even be able to license your audio content through a licensed syndication company like Newstex (www.newstex.com) to get in front of professional audiences off the Internet.

Holding Online Events

In-person events are expensive, but online events are far more affordable and growing in popularity. They're also a great form of content marketing! For example, webinars, virtual trade shows, and live streaming are all viable forms of content marketing that don't have to cost a fortune but that can generate a lot of buzz about your business, which just might lead to sales. In fact, you can even partner with other companies and organizations to hold live events for wider appeal, greater exposure, and better results.

Live events take a lot of planning and advance promotion to be successful, so it's not typically one of the first content marketing opportunities that businesses pursue. However, live events are something you should keep in mind for the future or at least be willing to dive into when the right time and opportunity arise.

Hosting webinars

The term *webinar* is the fusion of the words *web* and *seminar*. Webinars are online seminars, training sessions, or presentations that anyone can hold from their homes or offices using their computers and possibly a webcam and microphone. Webinars can be very popular, particularly if they offer noteworthy information free.

If you use webinars for content marketing, then offer them free in order to increase interest, word-of-mouth marketing, and attendance.

You can choose from a number of Web conferencing providers to host your webinar. Each provider offers slightly different features at very different prices. Some of the most popular options are as follows:

- ✔ **GoToMeeting:** At www.gotomeeting.com/fec/webinar, GoToMeeting is owned by Citrix and requires you pay a monthly fee to host your webinars. A free trial is available.

- ✔ **WebEx:** At www.webex.com, WebEx is owned by Cisco and requires you pay a monthly fee to host your webinars. That fee also includes mobile access. A free trial is available.

- ✔ **Adobe Connect:** At www.adobe.com/products/acrobatconnectpro, Adobe Connect requires that you pay a monthly or annual fee to host your webinars, but a free trial is available and a pay-per-use option is provided for individuals and small businesses.

✔ **Yugma:** At www.yugma.com, Yugma is a popular, free Web-conferencing solution. Paid packages are also available with more options.

✔ **Dimdim:** At www.dimdim.com, Dimdim is another popular, free Web-conferencing solution. A paid version with additional features is also available.

When you choose a webinar provider, make sure the provider offers event management services. If you host a large, critical event, you may want to invest in these services to ensure that everything runs smoothly before, during, and after your event. This isn't essential, but it's good to know the option is available if you want it in the future. Also, make sure you can cancel or change the date and time of your event at any time, and make sure the provider archives your webinar content so that it can be viewed after the event by people who missed it.

Participating in virtual trade shows and events

Virtual trade shows and events are growing in popularity as the cost of in-person trade show and event participation continues to rise. Virtual trade shows are live events, so to be successful, they require a great deal of promotion in advance to get the word out and boost attendance. That's one of the reasons why it's a good idea to join a virtual trade show related to your business or hold your own along with complementary businesses that can help you spread the word about it.

A number of virtual trade show event-planning and management companies (such as INXPO at www.inxpo.com) enable you to hold your own virtual trade show. Here are some options:

✔ www.goexhibit.com

✔ www.clickexpo.co.uk

✔ http://6connex.com

✔ www.itradefair.com

✔ www.unisfair.com

When choosing a virtual trade show service, be sure to compare price, support, customization, publicity, reporting, and analytics offerings as well as attendance and participation capacity to ensure that you choose the right solution for your business and audience.

Live streaming events

If your business holds interesting or entertaining live events, then streaming those events live on the Internet can be a great way to provide another branded experience to consumers who can't be there in person. For example, a DJ business could live stream parties or a band could live stream concerts. You can even live stream your attendance at events (with permission, of course) such as award ceremonies, seminars, and more.

The trick to successful live streaming events is to make sure that they're useful or meaningful to your target audience and that the technology you use for live streaming works very well. Furthermore, you need to commit to promoting your live streaming event heavily in order to attract attendees.

You can use a number of tools to live stream your events such as Livestream at www.livestream.com and Ustream's Watershed at https://water shed.ustream.tv. Make sure you have good video and audio equipment as well as good lighting, and be sure to choose a provider to host your live stream that can meet the viewing demands of your event. The last thing you want is for your audience to visit your live stream online and find out they can't view it!

Promoting your online events

As mentioned throughout this section, online events require a great deal of promotion to be successful. Because they're usually one-time events, if you don't get people to attend, your event won't help you. Online events deliver content once, but the goal is for people to like the content enough that they talk about it with their audiences and come back for future virtual events or go to your other branded online destinations.

With that in mind, it's critical that your Web site URL and core branded online destination are prominently displayed during your virtual event. You want the content you're delivering through your event to drive people to your other branded destinations where you can further engage them and build relationships with them. The virtual event is just the first step in a larger part of your content marketing plan. It's the dangling carrot.

To promote your online events, you need to blog about them; tweet about them; mention them on your Facebook profile, groups, and Page; talk about them on your LinkedIn profile and groups; talk about them in your audio and video content; and ask other online influencers with whom you've developed relationships to help you spread the word. Publishing guest blog posts on blogs where the target audience for your event spends time is another excellent tactic to promote your online events. Finally, use the event promotion tools in Facebook and LinkedIn to further spread the word.

Be sure to mention your event everywhere you can and don't be afraid to tie an exclusive offer to event attendance to boost the pre-event buzz. For example, offer a discount on a future purchase to attendees. Just make sure that your offering is good enough to actually move people to action, or it won't help you.

Integrating E-Mail Marketing into Your Content Marketing Efforts

Throughout this chapter, I often reference using e-mail newsletters or e-mail signatures to promote your content marketing efforts. It's important to integrate your offline and online content marketing tactics, so including both in your e-mail messages is a simple first step. If you send a lot of e-mail messages, then including links to your amazing content or branded online destinations in your e-mail signature is a nonintrusive way to indirectly market that content.

Don't overload your e-mail signature with links. Pick two or three of your most important links and change them as necessary to stay fresh and relevant.

If you don't already have an e-mail marketing campaign such as a newsletter or sales campaign that you send on a continual basis to a group of people, you should start to think about creating one. E-mail marketing is a perfect complement to your online content marketing efforts because it gives you more opportunities to get your content in front of your target audience through an experience they might prefer. Add an e-mail sign-up form in your blog's sidebar and on your other branded online destinations. Make it easy to sign up and be sure to explain in the sign-up form that e-mails will include a variety of special offers and convenient access to truly useful information, tips, tutorials, and more.

In order to adhere to the CAN-SPAM Act (refer to Chapter 3 for more information), people on your e-mail marketing list should have opted in to receive information from you, which means they like experiencing your brand through e-mail. To deliver e-mails that add value, look at them as an extension of your content marketing plan rather than just simply as a sales tool. You might be surprised how much click-through and response rates increase when you start sending useful, meaningful information messages to your e-mail marketing list.

Choosing an e-mail marketing tool

When you're ready to start sending e-mail campaigns, you should look into using an e-mail marketing provider that can automate processes for you, authenticate your e-mail for greater deliverability, and make sending bulk e-mails incredibly easy. Most e-mail marketing providers also enable you to easily customize e-mail templates so that your e-mails are branded for your business and look great. To see what can be done, take a look at the customized and branded e-mail created with MailChimp shown in Figure 5-4.

Following are some of the most popular and reasonably priced e-mail marketing providers:

- **MailChimp:** At www.mailchimp.com, you can execute your e-mail marketing free if you meet certain limitations, and the video tutorials are great.

- **Emma:** At http://myemma.com, Emma is a popular choice with affordable plans.

- **Constant Contact:** At www.constantcontact.com, you can use the free trial to test the features of Constant Contact before you commit to paying the fee.

- **VerticalResponse:** At www.verticalresponse.com, VerticalResponse is very popular, and a free trial is available.

Figure 5-4: Customization is easy when you use an e-mail marketing tool.

Some of the features to compare when shopping for an e-mail marketing service include price, number of e-mails you can send, e-mail list size limits, authentication services, tracking and reporting, and e-mail branding and customization.

Creating content marketing e-mail messages

For e-mail to be a form of content marketing rather than direct response marketing that leads to sales, you need to think of it as a newsletter that encourages people to click through to read more on your branded online destinations without feeling like they're being bombarded with sales messages. This means you need to lead with your best content and make sure you follow the 80-20 rule (discussed in Chapter 1) where no more than 20 percent of your content is self-promotional.

Your content marketing e-mail messages should hype the various share-worthy content that you have published online, but it should also have its own pass-along value. Be sure to include easy links or buttons for recipients to share content from the newsletter on their social networking profiles or Twitter, and make sure they can forward the e-mail to people within their own networks who might like to read it.

Bottom line, you have two primary goals when using e-mail as a form of content marketing — to drive recipients to your branded online destinations through your e-mail content marketing efforts and to produce e-mails that have their own pass-along value. By keeping those two goals in mind as you create your e-mail messages for content marketing purposes, you'll have more success in developing content that your audience wants to read, share, and talk about thereby indirectly marketing your brand and business, too.

Chapter 6

Writing in Long Form for the Web

- -

In This Chapter

▶ Choosing your style and voice

▶ Writing shareworthy content

▶ Knowing when to follow and break grammar rules

▶ Formatting tips

▶ Finding more tools for long-form writing

- -

*L*ong-form content marketing requires planning and skills. Unlike short-form and conversational content marketing, long-form content marketing is intrinsically more detailed and comprehensive than any other type of content marketing. In other words, creating compelling long-form content for marketing purposes can't be done haphazardly.

Publishing long-form content that's written poorly isn't going to help your business. This chapter shows you how to write long-form content that accurately reflects your brand promise, giving it the opportunity to promote your business positively.

Finding Your Style and Voice

Chapter 1 discusses the fundamental steps of branding: consistency, persistence, and restraint. When you follow these steps to build your personal or business brand, consumers develop perceptions of your brand and expectations of what your brand can deliver with each interaction. Those perceptions and expectations promise something to consumers, and that brand promise defines your brand in consumers' minds and positions your brand against competitors.

Your long-form writing content must accurately reflect the brand promise or you risk not meeting consumer expectations for your brand. When a brand fails to meet consumer expectations, consumers turn away from the brand. Therefore, it's essential that the style and voice you use in your long-form content are consistent representations of your brand promise.

Your *style* and *voice* are how you express yourself in your long-form content. Just as you speak differently to your boss than to a child, you also need to use a specific style and voice for your long-form content that's appropriate for your brand and audience. The goal is to create content using a consistent voice that matches consumers' expectations for your brand.

Create long-form content using the voice and style that you'd use when speaking to your target audience in a face-to-face conversation. Again, you need to achieve brand consistency across all consumer touch points, and that includes your long-form content used for marketing purposes.

For example, if you own a retail business selling children's toys but write a blog that sounds like a doctoral thesis, then that style doesn't match the expectations consumers probably have for a children's toy brand. In other words, your content has to match your brand promise and so does your style and voice. Following are examples to illustrate the disparity between style and voice and consumers' expectations for a brand:

- ✔ **Children's brand style and voice disparity:** "After analyzing the performance of the newly launched ABC Baby product, our research revealed a discrepancy between the manufacturers's documented battery life expectancy and true performance."

- ✔ **Children's brand style and voice consistency:** "When we tried the new ABC Baby toy, the battery died a lot faster than the ads claim."

Clearly, the second version better matches style, voice, brand, and audience expectations. Before you begin creating your long-form content, you need to choose the best style and voice.

Making Your Long-Form Content Shareworthy

When you're writing your long-form content, have a goal of creating content that people will want to share with their own audiences. In other words, try to create amazing, shareworthy long-form content that can spread much wider than your own branded online destinations.

Shareworthy content is meaningful and useful content. To create shareworthy content, you need to understand what is meaningful and useful to your target audience. Therefore, you must take the time to listen to your target audience online, hear what gets them talking and sharing, and then create that kind of content. You need to give them the content they want or they won't read it, talk about it, or share it. You can create what you feel is best content in the world, but if it's not the content that your target audience wants and needs, you won't build your brand or your business.

You can apply the "Four Rights of Advertising" to your content marketing efforts to ensure you're creating shareworthy content. The Four Rights of Advertising are

> Deliver the *right* message to the *right* audience at the *right* time in the *right* place.

To be shareworthy, your long-form content has to deliver the information and messages that your target audiences want and need. Keep in mind, audiences consist of different segments; the right message for one segment might not be the right message for another. While your content marketing efforts grow, you can expand your messaging to meet the needs and wants of diverse audience segments, but to get started, focus on your core target audience. Make sure you're delivering amazing content that audiences want and need where the audience spends time online. If you're successful in getting your content in front of the right people, the chances of your content being shared grow exponentially.

Realistically, not every piece of long-form content you create will be shareworthy, and that's okay. Just make sure that you offer shareworthy content frequently enough to keep your audience interested in what you have to say. Every audience is different, so there isn't a specific rule of thumb to follow when it comes to how frequently you publish shareworthy content. However, a shareworthy piece of content doesn't have to be a 20-page ebook. Even a 300-word blog post could be shareworthy. Remember, *what* you say makes a piece of content shareworthy, not the number of words you use.

Try to create at least one truly amazing piece of content each week. A well-thought blog post offering ten tips can really benefit your audience. A 3-minute video can explain a concept your audience wants to understand better. Of course, the more shareworthy content you create, the better. Your success can only grow by publishing shareworthy content.

Following and Breaking Formal Writing Rules

When using content for marketing purposes, you're allowed to break some writing rules because content created for content marketing should more closely align with rules of copywriting than rules of formal writing. I'm not saying don't pay attention to grammar and spelling. You need to write well, but you don't have to write formally.

The rules of copywriting tell you to match your style and voice to your audience. The same holds true for long-form content marketing. You should create long-form content using the same style, voice, and grammar that you use when you're speaking directly to your target audience. For example, one-sentence paragraphs and sentence fragments are acceptable. Contractions and colloquialisms are welcome and expected. Depending on your audience and their expectations for your brand, slang might even fit into your long-form content.

However, don't read this section and think you can completely disregard the rules of grammar and spelling. You still need to keep those rules in mind, but you don't have to follow them to the letter. Just as you ignore some grammar rules when you speak, you can do so in long-form content writing when doing so enhances your content in your readers' minds.

The most important thing is to create content written in a way that your target audience wants. Just as you must match your style and voice to your audience's expectations, you also have to match your sentence structure and words. When in doubt, write with your audience's expectations as your top priority and grammar second. As with all copywriting and marketing message creation, the audience comes first.

Formatting Long-Form Content

When it comes to creating long-form content for the Web, you need to think about more than just *what* you say and *how* you say it. You also need to consider how the content will *look* on a computer monitor. Because more and more people are accessing Web content via smart phones and e-readers, you also need to think about how your content will look on mobile devices. Long blocks of text aren't going to entice anyone to read them. You need to ensure your long-form content is inviting and easy to read.

You can use a number of tricks to break up text-heavy Web pages, which are often the result of writing long-form content. The following list describes several options:

- ✔ **Short paragraphs:** Write short paragraphs for long-form content. A one-sentence paragraph is perfectly acceptable on the Web because shorter paragraphs offer more white space. Long blocks of text in long paragraphs are overwhelming to visitors, whereas short paragraphs make scanning content easier, which might entice people to read more or share that content.

- ✔ **Color:** Use color sparingly. If you go overboard with color, visitors won't know where to look. Using color to draw attention to specific parts of your content can make long-form reading less intimidating.

- ✔ **Fonts:** Choose fonts that are easy to read onscreen, such as Verdana or Georgia. Also, consider using different fonts for headings and callouts to make them stand out. Different fonts can draw attention to certain parts of your content or simply break up long blocks of text.

✔ **Headings:** Some content management systems, such as WordPress and Blogger, allow you to use formatting tools to create headings within your content quickly and easily. If your publishing tool doesn't offer easy-to-use formatting tools, you can still create headings by altering fonts (as described in the preceding bullet).

✔ **Images:** Inserting images into your text is a great way to add visual appeal to your long-form content and break up text to provide visual relief. Before using images you don't own, review the information on copyrights and fair use that I discuss in Chapter 3.

If your publishing tool inserts HTML heading tags into your online content to apply heading styles (such as in WordPress), take advantage of the tags. Search engines like Google give the text within heading tags more weight than plain text when ranking keyword search results.

Figure 6-1 shows how long-form content can look overwhelming when it appears in long blocks of text with no relief. Comparatively, Figure 6-2 shows content where some of the tricks in the preceding list break up those long text blocks.

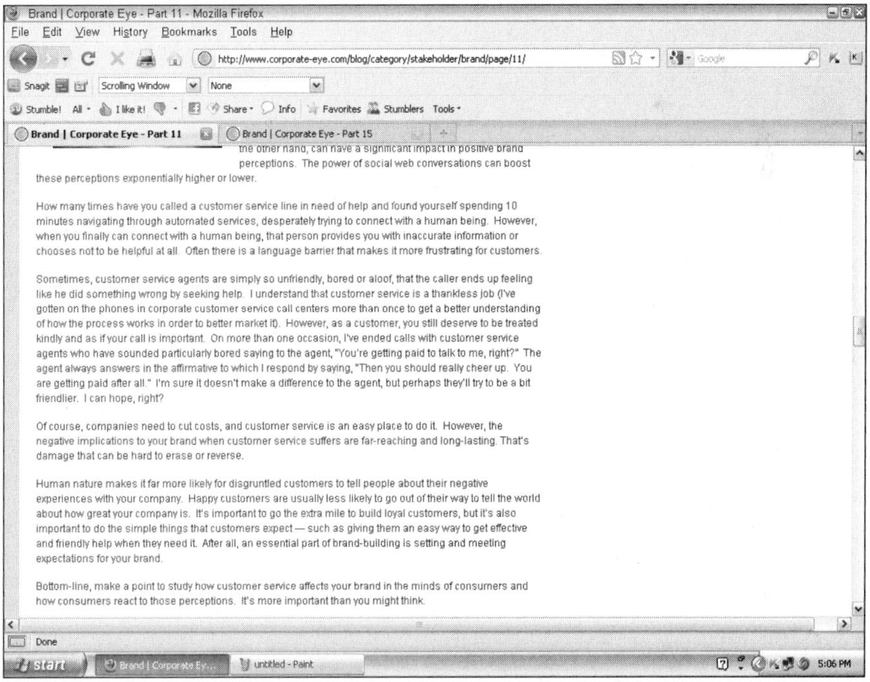

Figure 6-1: Long blocks of text are difficult to read online.

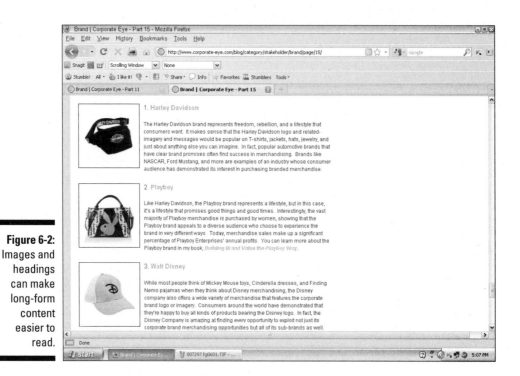

Figure 6-2:
Images and headings can make long-form content easier to read.

WARNING!

Avoid using too many formatting tricks in a single piece of long-form content. Too much formatting can mitigate your efforts and actually make your content more difficult to read. Instead, err on the side of caution and aim to enhance your content with formatting rather than usurp the actual content with excessive formatting.

Finding More Tools for Long-Form Web Writing and Content Marketing

Chapters 4 and 5 describe a variety of tools for creating and publishing long-form content to promote your brand and business directly and indirectly. At times, you might need additional tools to make creating, publishing, and sharing that content easier. The tools suggested in this section help you do more with long-form content without breaking the budget.

New tools are released all the time, so the suggestions here aren't exhaustive. Don't be afraid to test new tools (particularly, free tools) to determine whether they can help you reach your long-form content marketing objectives.

PDFs

Often, long-form content is best published and shared in PDF format. Usually, ebooks are published in PDF format because PDF files can be opened by anyone who downloads the free Adobe Reader tool from Adobe (`http://get.adobe.com/reader`). Additionally, you can protect your PDF files by saving them in a manner that prevents others from editing them.

If you offer content online in PDF format, make sure you include a link for people to download the free Adobe Reader tool so they can open your PDF file on their computers.

You can download a number of free PDF creator tools. I recommend downloading PDFCreator from Sourceforge.net (`http://sourceforge.net/projects/pdfcreator`) for Windows users. PDFCreator is easy to use and works very well. For the most features and options, invest in feature-rich software, such as Adobe Acrobat (`www.adobe.com/products/acrobatstandard.html`), to create PDF files.

Screen shots

Taking screen shots is a great way to enhance long-form content, particularly for tutorials or step-by-step instructions that demonstrate how to complete a task using a computer. For example, an ebook that teaches readers how to create holiday cards using specific software would be much better if the designer includes screen shots of the steps the reader has to follow.

Be sure to follow copyright laws, which I describe in Chapter 3, before you publish screen shots in your content.

Figure 6-3 shows a piece of long-form content that includes a screen shot to demonstrate how these types of images can enhance content to make it visually and contextually appealing.

Figure 6-3:
Screen shots can clarify content and add visual appeal.

You can capture a screenshot by following these steps:

1. **Set up the screen the way you want it.**

2. **(Windows) Press the Ctrl+Print Screen keys to capture the entire screen; to capture just the active window, press the Alt+Print Screen keys. (Mac) Press Command+Shift+3 to capture the entire screen; press Command+Shift+4, and then space, and then click a window to capture just a window.**

   This copies an image of the screen to the Windows Clipboard. On a Mac, the image is saved as a file on the desktop.

3. **(Windows) Open an image editor, such as Photoshop or Paint.**

4. **(Windows) Press Ctrl+V to paste the image of the screen into the editor. (Mac) Open the image file from the desktop.**

5. **Edit the image if desired, and then save it.**

While it's easy to capture a screen shot using this method, you're limited with what you can capture using that method. For a small investment, you can get a tool like Snagit from TechSmith (www.techsmith.com/snagit/default.asp) to capture screen shots in a variety of ways, save screen shots in a multitude of formats, enhance screen shots, and much more.

File-uploading tools and apps

Sometimes you create a piece of long-form content that becomes a huge file. Simply zipping the file doesn't compress it enough for you to publish it online, e-mail it to anyone, or share it with other people. Fortunately, tools can help you upload, publish, e-mail, and share large files without spending a lot of money.

Following are several tools with varied price tags that enable you to work with large files effectively:

- **File sharing and sending tools:** If you create a very large file and need to send it to another person, you can do so without worrying about file attachment sizes in e-mail by using a tool like YouSendIt (https://www.yousendit.com) or StuffIt (www.stuffit.com/win-home.html). Both offer free services and paid services that provide more features and options.

- **FTP tools:** If you need to upload a very large file to publish on your Web site or blog or make that file available via a link from your Facebook, Twitter, or other branded online destinations, then you might need to use an FTP tool. FTP is an acronym for File Transfer Protocol, which refers to the process of copying a file from one host to another over the Internet. You can find many free FTP tools, such as FileZilla (http://filezilla-project.org) and Core FTP (http://coreftp.com).

Document collaboration

Sometimes you need to create a document and work on it with people located in a different office, city, state, or country than you. Similarly, there might be times when you need to work on a document from multiple computers that aren't networked. An easy way to enable multiple people to collaborate on the same document or for you to access a document from various computers without carrying a copy of your file with you is to use a document collaboration tool, such as those offered free through Google Docs (http://docs.google.com).

Google Docs allows you to work on word processing documents, spreadsheets, presentations, drawings, and forms anytime and anywhere. It's a powerful tool that you can use in a variety of ways to create and enhance your long-form content.

Skype and interview recorders

Interviews are excellent for long-form content marketing. You can interview experts and customers to create meaningful, useful, and shareworthy long-form content. Using a free online calling tool, such as Skype (`www.skype.com`), you can talk to people around the world (as long as they create a free Skype account). Using a Skype call recorder, you can record the audio and video of the interview (if the interviewee has a microphone and Webcam connected to his computer), and publish the interview online.

Following are several tools that you can use to record interviews:

- ✔ **Call Recorder for Mac:** Available at `www.ecamm.com/mac/callrecorder`, this is my preferred tool for recording audio and video of Skype calls. It's inexpensive, very easy to use, and works very well.

- ✔ **Total Recorder:** Available at `http://totalrecorder.com`, this tool is a good option for Windows users, but to record video, you have to pay a higher price for a more feature-rich version.

- ✔ **Pamela Call Recorder:** Available at `http://shop.skype.com/extras/productivity/pamela-call-recorder`, the free Pamela Call Recorder Skype Extra is a great choice for recording audio only of Skype calls.

Always ask permission to record audio or video of an interview of any kind before you do so. It is illegal to record phone calls in many states and countries without obtaining permission.

Testing new tools

The tools suggested in the preceding sections are just a few options to help you create the best long-form content possible to market your business and brand. Don't be afraid to test other tools you learn about while you're creating and sharing your long-form content. Frequently, new WordPress plug-ins and Twitter apps launch that can improve your long-form content or simply make the process of creating, publishing, and sharing that content quicker or easier. Read blogs like About.com Blogging (`http://weblogs.about.com`) and the Junta42 blog (`http://blog.junta42.com/`) to keep up with new tools for content marketing and the wider content industry.

Chapter 7

Taking Long-Form Web Content to the Next Level

In This Chapter

▶ Using search engine optimization

▶ Building relationships

▶ Syndicating content

*Y*our online content is an excellent tool for building your brand, driving word-of-mouth marketing, and developing relationships with consumers. If you take the time to write with search engine optimization in mind, you'll increase the potential for more people to find your content via keyword searches on such sites as Google, Yahoo!, and Bing.

This chapter shows you many of the basic do's and don'ts of search engine optimization (SEO) as well as how content syndication can increase the exposure of your content and get it in front of audiences that you might not reach on your own.

Using Search Engine Optimization

Search engine optimization (SEO) is the process of creating online content and Web pages that maximize traffic from search engines. When Internet users want to find information about something, they typically visit their preferred search engine (for most people, that site is Google) and type related keywords into the search box. The search engine uses a proprietary algorithm to deliver a list of related links for that query based on the Web pages it has indexed.

Therefore, if your content is written with the specific keywords that people are likely to use when they search for the type of information you offer, you have a better chance of seeing a link to your content in those search results. If your content appears in the top 10 results for your targeted keywords, you've hit the jackpot in terms of driving traffic to your content via search engines, and that's where search engine optimization techniques can help you.

Search engines are continually updating their algorithms in an effort to deliver the most relevant results to keyword queries. Because those algorithms are proprietary, no one knows exactly how they work. Many search engine optimization experts spend a lot of time analyzing search trends to dissect the right and wrong ways to create content that ranks well in keyword searches.

However, as you can imagine, search engines don't want people to trick the system. Many people use search engine optimization techniques for spam purposes. I discuss some of these activities later in this chapter to help you understand why people use them and why you should avoid them.

Search engines want the best and most relevant content to rank highest in search results. Bottom-line, search engine optimization tricks are constantly evolving, and there is no single recipe for success.

Researching keywords

You can apply search engine optimization techniques to all your long-form content marketing efforts, but before you can write with search engine optimization in mind, you need to find out what keywords to target in your content. That's where keyword research comes into play.

Fortunately, you can use a number of tools to conduct keyword research and discover which words to target in your content. Some tools are free and others require that you pay a fee to use them. The best route is to start with a free tool. Later, if you want to get very serious with keyword research, you can pay for a more comprehensive tool.

Google offers two free tools that can help you conduct keyword research:

 ✔ **Google AdWords Traffic Estimator Tool:** Available at `https://adwords.google.com/select/TrafficEstimatorSandbox`, the Google AdWords Traffic Estimator Tool shows traffic estimates for the keywords you enter into the search box, as shown in Figure 7-1.

 ✔ **Google AdWords Keyword Tool:** Available at `https://adwords.google.com/select/KeywordToolExternal?defaultView=2`, the Google AdWords Keyword Tool allows you to enter a keyword or phrase and see a list of related keywords along with the amount of global and local monthly searches for those keywords, as shown in Figure 7-2. Be sure to click the Column button on the right above the keyword results list to reveal all available columns. Using that data, you can determine how popular keywords are and target those that best match your business while delivering a good amount of search activity.

Figure 7-1:
Type your
keywords
into the
search box
to get traffic
estimates.

Figure 7-2:
The Google
AdWords
Keyword
Tool helps
you learn
the popular-
ity of related
keywords.

If you have a Google AdWords account, log into your account so you can see the full list of related keywords generated by the Google AdWords Keyword Tool, and be sure to click the Advanced Options button for both Google AdWords tools to access additional functionality.

Two of the best keyword research tools that come with a price tag are

- ✔ **Wordtracker:** Available at www.wordtracker.com, Wordtracker is one of the best keyword research tools, offering a wealth of information for in-depth keyword analysis.

- ✔ **Keyword Discovery:** Available at www.keyworddiscovery.com, Keyword Discovery offers similar options to Wordtracker.

You can sign up for free trials with Wordtracker and Keyword Discovery and compare the results before you commit to paying for one.

You can also conduct keyword research on sites that offer Web analytics, such as your blog. A free tool like Google Analytics (www.google.com/analytics) enables you to find out which keywords visitors to your content used to find it via search engines, which adds another layer of data to your keyword research.

Going after the long-tail

As the Web gets more and more crowded, the search engine optimization world has ventured into the process of going after the *long-tail* — searches for very specific keywords — to increase targeted traffic to Web sites. These highly focused keywords are likely to drive fewer searches and less traffic, but that traffic will be very targeted.

People who use very specific search keywords (most frequently, two- or three-word phrases) know exactly what they're looking for. Instead of targeting broad keywords with a lot of competition for visitors with extremely diverse needs, long-tail search optimization aims to target narrow keywords with less competition for visitors with very specific needs.

For example, if you own a business that offers supplies that auto detailers use, you could target keyword phrases like *auto detailing supplies, auto detailing equipment,* or *auto detailing products*. Each of these options is more focused. The phrases will deliver fewer visitors, but those visitors are far more likely to be interested in your content. Visitors who might find your site from a broad keyword search on *autos* or even *auto detailing,* likely want to get their own cars detailed, not purchase supplies for their auto detailing businesses.

The trick is to focus on keywords that deliver a decent amount of traffic but not so much traffic that there is likely to be a large amount of competition for that traffic. For example, if you own an auto detailing business, the keyword *autos* would have too much traffic to be useful because the keyword is too broad. You'd have to compete with far too many sites for that traffic, and companies with deep pockets likely own those sites. On the other hand, if you focus on keywords that generate very few searches, you won't get much traffic from them at all. To find success, you need to find the happy medium between keywords that are too broad and keywords that are too narrow.

Applying search engine optimization techniques

After you choose your keywords, you need to write your content using search engine optimization techniques so your content has a chance to rank higher in search results for those keywords than content on other Web sites. This section shows you easy ways to seamlessly integrate search engine optimization techniques into your long-form content without making your content read like a piece that was written specifically for keyword density purposes.

Many Web sites churn out content for the sole purpose of creating keyword-dense content that ranks high in search engine results. Much of this content lacks quality and doesn't add value to readers' lives in a meaningful way. Remember, to grow your brand and business, quality should always be a top priority for your content.

Following are many of those tricks and suggestions, but remember, search engine algorithms change all the time. Therefore, be sure to read the SEO resources listed later in this chapter to keep up on trends. To remember the following fundamental search engine optimization techniques, think of the acronym TALKS, which stands for Title, Alt-tags, Links, Keywords, Subtitles:

- ✔ **Title:** Use keywords in the title of your content. Typically, titles are weighted more heavily in search engine algorithms than body text.

- ✔ **Alt-tags:** Alt-tags (alternative text tags) are indexed in search engine algorithms, so you should use them for all images you publish alone or as part of other content. An *alt-tag* is a piece of HTML code that appears onscreen when an image can't load in a Web browser.

✔ **Links:** Use keywords in and around linked text in your content. Search engines give linked text and the text around links more weight in ranking than non-linked text. Also, work to increase the number of incoming links to your content. You can read more about the importance of getting incoming links later in this chapter.

✔ **Keywords:** Focus on a single keyword phrase of two or three words for each piece of content. Use it at least two or three times in the first paragraph of your content and as many times as you can within your content without keyword stuffing (discussed in the next section). Also, be sure to include your keyword in the final paragraph of your content.

✔ **Subtitles and headings:** If you can use HTML heading tags in your content, include subtitles and headings throughout your long-form content and apply heading tags to them. Include your keywords in your subtitle and headings when you can. Content in heading tags is given more weight by search engines than regular paragraphs.

Be careful that you don't fall into the trap of writing for search engines rather than writing for your audience. In other words, search engine optimization should complement your amazing, shareworthy content, not detract from it.

Avoiding search engine optimization mistakes

You need to avoid a number of search engine optimization "don'ts." These mistakes can damage the user experience of your content or get you labeled as a spammer. Search engines try to deliver fair and relevant results. If you try to trick search engines into thinking your content is something that it's not, you could be banned from search engine results entirely. If you want your brand and business to grow, a search engine ban would be fatal.

Following are some of the biggest SEO mistakes to avoid at all costs:

✔ **Keyword stuffing:** Repeating your targeted keywords in your content several times is recommended for search engine optimization, but stuffing your content full of your keywords can do more harm than good. Search engines view keyword stuffing as a spam technique, and your content will be flagged as such if you're caught publishing more keywords than useful content. For example, don't include a long list of varied permutations your keywords at the bottom of your Web page, in the sidebar, or anywhere else on your Web site.

✔ **Content scraping:** The content you publish should not be published elsewhere online. Even if you are the original author, republished content can be considered spam.

✔ **No original content:** Make sure your content appears on Web pages that offer far more original content than ads, links, or other content that adds no value to the user experience.

✔ **Hidden keywords or links:** Hiding keywords and links in your content in a very small font or a font color that blends into the Web page background on which they appear is a red flag to search engines, and your content will be marked as spam if you're caught.

✔ **Too many links:** Similar to using too many keywords in your content, you can be labeled a spammer if you publish too many links in your content. Even if you're not labeled a spammer, too many links can damage the user experience with your content. Try to use no more than one link for every 125 words of content.

✔ **Paid text links:** Search engines count the number of incoming links to a Web page as a positive indication that the content on that page is good (or no one would link to it). Therefore, paid text links can be viewed as a spam technique because they artificially inflate the perceived popularity of a Web page. Both the site that pays for a text link and the site that publishes it can be banned from Google search results completely if they're caught.

✔ **Duplicate content:** While *content scraping* refers to republishing content on multiple sites, *duplicate content* refers to publishing the same content on multiple pages within the same Web site. Make sure the content on each page of your Web sites is unique.

If your content or Web site is banned from search engines, such as Google, being indexed again is nearly impossible. You do not want to lose search traffic to your content, so be sure to avoid all the SEO mistakes in the preceding list no matter how tempting they might be. The long-term risks do not outweigh the short-term benefits.

Finding search engine optimization help

Search engine optimization techniques are constantly evolving because search engine ranking algorithms change. Therefore, you need to keep up with the trends and best practices that search engine optimization experts recommend. What works today might not work tomorrow.

Following are several very useful sites where you can continually learn about search engine optimization from professionals who work in the discipline every day:

✔ **SEOmoz (www.seomoz.org):** This site offers both free access and paid membership to numerous resources that detail — and teach — search engine optimization.

✔ **Search Engine Journal (www.searchenginejournal.com):** This site contains articles written by search engine experts.

✔ **Search Engine Land (www.searchengineland.com):** This site provides access to free resources, or you can pay for a membership to access more information and benefits.

✔ **Search Engine Roundtable (www.seoroundtable.com):** This site features conversations happening on SEO forums across the Web.

Building Relationships and Opening the Doors for Dialogue

One of the best ways to increase search engine traffic to your content is to spend time building relationships and engaging in conversations with people across the Web. By taking the time to build a band of loyal brand advocates who will talk about your content and share your content, you'll develop a growing number of incoming links to your content over time, and those incoming links are valuable in the world of search engine optimization.

As discussed earlier in this chapter, search engines rank content with a lot of incoming links higher in search results than content with few incoming links under the assumption that content with a lot of incoming links must be good or no one would link to it. Therefore, the more incoming links you can get to your content, particularly incoming links from authoritative Web sites, the better in terms of boosting the search engine rankings for that content.

Before you try to get more incoming links to your content, you should find out how many incoming links you have. The quickest way to get a good idea of how many incoming links a specific Web page has is to visit www.google.com and type **link:www.*yourblogname.com*** into the search box (replace *yourblogname.com* with the specific domain for the Web page where your content is published). Press Enter and a list of incoming links is returned to you. You can do the same thing on Yahoo! by visiting www.yahoo.com and typing **linkdomain:www.*yourblogname.com*** into the search box (again, substitute your domain for *yourblogname.com*).

If you have a free Google account, you can use Google Analytics (www.google.com/analytics) or Google Webmaster Tools (www.google.com/webmasters/tools) to get more information about sites you own or manage.

After you know how to calculate incoming links to a Web page, you can start working to build more of them. Of course, the best way to get incoming links is to write shareworthy content, but fortunately, you can promote your content in many ways to boost those incoming links even more.

Following are several free ways that can help you get more incoming links to your content:

- ✔ **Communicating:** Leave comments on other blogs and participate in discussions in online forums and groups whose audiences are likely to be interested in your content. Include a link to your content in your signature.

- ✔ **Promoting:** Announce when you publish new content and provide a link for quick access on Twitter, Facebook, LinkedIn, and other social media sites you use.

- ✔ **Bookmarking:** Use social bookmarking sites, such as StumbleUpon and Digg to share your content with a wider audience.

- ✔ **Interlinking:** Write original content for multiple sites and interlink that content.

- ✔ **Link baiting:** Write content about hot, trending topics in an attempt to attract some of the search traffic and links related to those topics. You can find trending Twitter topics scroll across the home page of Twitter and check Google Trends for daily trending search topics (www.google.com/trends).

- ✔ **Requesting:** If you write a particularly unique piece of content, don't be afraid to e-mail your friends and peers, connect with them via Twitter or other social media sites, and ask them to share your content with their own audiences.

If people respond to your requests and communications and then link to your content, be prepared to reciprocate if they ask you to share or link to their content.

The time you take building relationships across the Web audience offers more exposure for your content and helps with search engine optimization, which means more search traffic. Bottom line: Relationship building should be a top priority in your content marketing plan.

Syndicating Content for Broader Exposure

Clearly, getting more exposure for your content is essential if you want to build your brand and business through content marketing. In other words, your content needs to get in front of as many people as possible. Syndication is an easy way to achieve broader exposure without much time or effort on your part.

Just as news organizations syndicate columns or programs across multiple newspapers or networks, content publishers can syndicate their content through multiple distributors to get that content in front of more people.

Some content syndication opportunities you might be able to use if your content is available in an RSS (Really Simple Syndication) feed format are

- ✔ **Free:** Content is republished, typically online, without payment.
- ✔ **Ad-supported:** Content is republished, typically online, with the possibility of payment through an ad revenue-sharing agreement.
- ✔ **Licensed:** Content is republished, typically offline or via closed systems, such as corporate and university libraries, with the author receiving royalty payments when his or her content is accessed by end users.

You can find content syndication opportunities for a variety of online content. For example, the Demand Studios Blog Distribution Network (www.demandstudios.com/blogger-application.html) enables bloggers to syndicate their content online for broader exposure but without payment. Alternately, Newstex (www.newstex.com) offers licensed syndication through offline distributors with royalty payments to the creators of blog, Twitter, video, and other content with an RSS feed.

Each content syndication opportunity is unique, so take the time to evaluate the exposure potential, including where your content will be republished and who will have access to it, as well as the earning potential to ensure the opportunity will help you meet your content marketing objectives.

Many of the most well-known Web sites syndicate their content to other sites or through offline distributors. For example, the Associated Press syndicates its content to multiple news sites. Top blogs like Gawker and Engadget license their content for syndication through Newstex so that content is distributed through such companies as LexisNexis and Thomson Reuters.

Syndication has been around for a long time, but online publishers are only just beginning to recognize the potential that syndication has in terms of exposure. If you truly want to build your business and brand through content marketing, then you need to be willing to give up some control and let that content spread as far and wide as possible. Syndication is just one tool in your toolbox that you can use to make that happen.

Part III
Marketing with Short-Form Content

The 5th Wave   By Rich Tennant

"I can tell by your résumé that you're very experienced in short-form content marketing."

In this part . . .

The best content marketing strategy includes diverse types of content creation and distribution. Short-form content offers a quick way for you to create content and for people to consume that content. Part III shows you everything you need to know to start using short-form content marketing to build your brand and business.

Chapter 8 introduces you to the various tools available to help you create, publish, and distribute short-form content. If writing isn't your strength, don't worry. Short-form content can come in the form of photos and infographics, too.

Take some time to read Chapters 10 and 11 to improve your short-form content writing and marketing skills. These chapters provide a variety of tips, tricks, and tools that can help you take your short-form content marketing efforts to the next level of success.

Chapter 8

Introducing the Tools of Short-Form Content Marketing

. . . .

In This Chapter

▶ Understanding and using short-form content marketing for your business

▶ Publishing with Facebook

▶ Networking with LinkedIn

▶ Using other social networking tools

. . . .

*F*or many people, short-form content marketing is less intimidating than long-form content marketing. Perhaps you feel less overwhelmed by the idea of publishing short content to market your business. You can always extend your content marketing plan to include long-form content marketing in the future.

This chapter shows you how to get started using free and inexpensive tools so you can publish short-form content that helps build your brand and your business. Whether you want to publish words, images, or even links, you can use those activities for promotion, and this chapter shows you where and how to do it.

Understanding What Short-Form Marketing Is

Short-form content marketing encompasses all published content that includes no more than a few sentences and communicates useful information. Twitter updates, Facebook updates, LinkedIn updates, and images are typical examples of short-form content. In other words, any original content that you publish online or offline that takes just a minute or so for a person to read, listen to, or view is a form of content marketing when that content relates to a business or brand and provides useful information.

The distinction that separates short-form content marketing from other forms of content marketing is the length required for consumption and the originality and value-add of that content. For example, a Twitter update that provides a useful tip or reference is a form of short-form content marketing because it offers meaningful information.

To determine whether your short-form content is effective, ask, "Does my content offer original, useful, and meaningful information to my target audience?" If the answer is yes, then you've created a piece of short-form content that could effectively market your business and brand.

Short-form content marketing should not be 100 percent self-promotional. Simply hyping your products and services isn't short-form content marketing — that's advertising and promotion. Instead, you need to prioritize adding value and providing useful information above self-promotion in your short-form content marketing efforts or you won't see the positive results you want and need.

Publishing with Facebook

Facebook is the most popular social networking tool in the world with over 350 million users. You can create a personal Facebook profile, a Facebook Page for your brand or business, and a Facebook group and use them for focused content publishing, conversations, and sharing. After you create a Facebook account, you can publish updates, comment on other people's content, share links, upload images and videos, send private messages, and more. A wide variety of Facebook apps extends the capabilities of Facebook, and the tool is constantly growing and evolving.

To discover all the technical aspects of Facebook, read *Facebook For Dummies* by Leah Pearlman and Carolyn Abram or visit the Facebook Help Center at www.facebook.com/help/?ref=pf.

You can use Facebook for short-form content marketing by publishing original content through your Facebook Page, profile, and group updates. You can also publish original images and videos on Facebook or republish content from your other branded online destinations, such as videos from your YouTube channel, images from your Flickr account, or presentations from your SlideShare account.

Setting up your Facebook profile

When you create an account on Facebook at www.facebook.com, you are creating your personal Facebook profile. This is your main presence on Facebook, and it is where you publish your biography, updates, images, and more. You can *friend* other Facebook users by sending them friend requests. When a friend accepts your request (or you accept a request sent to you), then you are connected to that person, which means you can view his profile, send him private messages, and publish comments on his Wall.

For short-form content marketing purposes, you should set your Facebook profile to be public, which means anyone can see it without having to be friends with you first.

The majority of your short-form content marketing efforts on your Facebook profile will occur through your Facebook Wall where you publish short updates, which can include links and images. Your friends can also comment on your Facebook updates, which is a form of conversational content marketing (see Chapter 13). Figure 8-1 shows a Facebook Wall.

Keep in mind that your Facebook profile is your *personal* space on Facebook. Your business or brand is represented by a Facebook Page, which is discussed later in this chapter. Therefore, your Facebook profile can and should include information about your business, but it should not be *only* about your company. This is the place on Facebook where you conduct networking most similar to how you network with people in a face-to-face setting. Through the short-form content you publish in your Facebook updates, you can establish yourself as an expert in your field and offer useful information that your friends can learn from and share.

Figure 8-1:
Facebook
profile
updates
offer a place
to publish
original
short-form
content.

Log into your Facebook account, and visit www.facebook.com/username to create a personalized URL for your Facebook profile to make it easier to promote and for people to find. You can also create a personalized URL for your business or brand's Facebook Page here, but 25 people have to *like* (that is, add) the page before you can set a personalized URL for the page.

Facebook offers the perfect online destination for you to build relationships because it's the closest thing to face-to-face networking. Just as you would behave in a certain way and discuss specific topics in a face-to-face networking setting, so should you behave and discuss topics on Facebook. Again, offer content that accurately reflects your brand image and promise, so your Facebook profile becomes one more branded online destination where your target audience can connect with you and experience your brand.

Finding people to friend on Facebook

When you create your Facebook profile, you need to find people to friend to expand your network and give your content more exposure. You can find people to connect with on Facebook a number of ways. For example, after you have some friend connections, you can look through their lists of friends to find more people to connect with. After you join groups, you can look through group member lists to find people to friend.

You can also use a variety of search tools within Facebook to find people to send friend requests to. Visit the following URLs to find people:

- ✔ **Friends Search:** Log into your Facebook account and visit www.facebook.com/srch.php. You can search for people by name, by e-mail, by company name (to find people who have identified themselves in their Facebook profiles as past or present employees of a specific company), or school (to find people who have identified themselves in their Facebook profiles as having attended a specific high school or college).

- ✔ **Find Friends:** Log into your Facebook account and visit www.facebook.com/find-friends?ref=pf. You can search for people in your e-mail address book, by last name, in your instant messaging contact list, or (if you're logged into your Facebook account), scroll to the bottom of the page and look through the list of suggested people to friend.

If a Facebook user's profile is private, you can't view it unless you're friends with that person. However, even if a user's profile is private, you can send a friend request to him or her.

Don't be afraid to send friend requests to people who you think you'd be interested in connecting with and who you think would be interested in the content you publish on Facebook. Recipients can always decline your requests, so there is no harm in sending them.

Feeding your blog content to your Facebook profile

You can promote your long-form content marketing through short-form content marketing efforts on your Facebook profile by automatically publishing links to your new blog posts on your Wall. One of the easiest ways to do this is to use a handy application called Twitterfeed (www.twitterfeed.com). Simply create a free Twitterfeed account, paste your blog's RSS feed URL into the designated text box, and connect your blog to your Facebook account. (You can also connect your blog to your Twitter account this way.) In a day or so, an update will automatically publish on your Facebook Wall with a link to your newest blog post whenever you publish new content on your blog.

You can also use a Facebook app, such as NetworkedBlogs (available through the Facebook Applications Directory), which you can access when you're logged into Facebook at www.facebook.com/?ref=home#!/apps/directory.php?app_type=0&category=100.

It's imperative that your Facebook profile updates include original short-form content that is useful and meaningful to your target audience. Don't let your Facebook updates be only automated updates from your blog. Instead, take the time to publish original tips, opinions, answers to questions, and more to ensure Facebook is an effective short-form content marketing tool for your business.

Setting up a Facebook Page

A Facebook Page (see Figure 8-2) can be created for a business, brand, organization, or celebrity. You must have a Facebook profile before you can create your business' Facebook Page. When you create your business' Facebook Page, you are the administrator of that page, and you can publish updates, upload photos, add videos, and more to that page. You can also send updates directly to anyone who *likes* (adds) your page (although recipients can't respond to those messages and can opt out of receiving them). As the administrator, you get access to a variety of statistics related to your page's performance.

Facebook Pages are always public, and can be viewed by anyone regardless of whether or not they have a Facebook account. Any Facebook user can like your Facebook Page. After a user likes your page, he or she can publish comments on your page's Wall and participate in conversations.

To create a Facebook Page, follow these steps:

1. **Visit `www.facebook.com/pages/create.php`, as shown in Figure 8-3.**

   Here you can select the type of page you're creating, give your page a name, and accept the legal terms.

2. **Click the Create Official Page button.**

   Next, you need to customize your page.

3. **Upload an image to represent your page, enter information about your business, and enter your Web site URL.**

   Click the Publish button to make your page available online.

Figure 8-3:
You can create a Facebook Page for your business in minutes.

A Facebook Page is, by default, already online as soon as it is created. If you don't want anyone to accidentally find your page, you can take it offline to edit it before you make it live. Just go to Edit Page⇨Manage Permissions and make sure the check box next to Page Visibility Only Admins Can See This Page is selected. When you're ready to show your Facebook Page to the world, return to that settings page and uncheck the Page Visibility check box.

After your Facebook Page is live, take some time to publish some original content to it. No one will like your page if you don't publish interesting content. Then, send messages to your Facebook friends asking them to like your page and begin promoting it through your other online branded destinations.

Don't forget to set up a personalized URL for your Facebook Page (log into your Facebook account and visit www.facebook.com/*username*) after 25 people like it. It's much easier to promote your Facebook Page using a customized URL, and it's easier for people to remember and find it.

Knowing what to publish on Facebook

When you use Facebook for short-form content marketing purposes, keep in mind that the content you publish has to add value to your target audience's lives. Amazing, shareworthy content motivates readers to share it with their audiences, engage in conversation with you, and discuss it with others.

Primarily, Facebook is a networking tool; therefore, you have a lot of leniency in the type of content you publish on your Facebook Page or profile. Just make sure your updates offer a good balance of original content, conversations (see Chapter 13), and sharing. Part of your short-form content marketing success through Facebook is dependent on your willingness to acknowledge the work of others and reciprocate sharing. In other words, you need to talk about others, not just yourself, and you need to give more than you receive.

Your short-form content could consist of your opinions, discount offers, useful tips, answers to questions, analysis of trends, warnings, and much more. Keep track of your updates that generate the most comments, *likes* (adds), and sharing, and then create more of that type of content. In other words, you need to listen to your Facebook friends and connections. Their behaviors and conversations can teach you a lot and help you identify your future content initiatives. You can even publish a Facebook update where you ask your connections what kind of content they want from you. Give them a chance to get involved and tell you what they want!

Joining Facebook groups

Any Facebook user can create a Facebook group. You can log into your Facebook account and visit `www.facebook.com/groups` to create your own group. Typically, groups are created to allow smaller groups of people to discuss specific topics.

Some groups let anyone become a member, some are invitation only, and others let anyone request to join, but the request has to be approved. The group's content can be set to Private (so only group members can see it) or Public (so anyone can see it).

As a member of a Facebook group, you can join conversations, publish updates, share content, and more. Join Facebook groups that are likely to have members that are interested in your business, products, and services. Look for niche groups whose members are as closely aligned to your target audience as possible. Although niche groups are likely to have fewer members than broad topic groups, those members are likely to be more interested in your business and content.

When you join a Facebook group, make sure you behave in a manner that makes you a welcomed member and participant. Avoid self-promotion. Instead, publish your amazing short-form content that truly adds value to the conversations happening among group members. If you take the time to build your reputation as a knowledgeable and trustworthy member, others are likely to follow you beyond the group where you can further build your relationships with them and deliver more of your content.

You can join up to 300 Facebook groups.

Facebook groups offer a fantastic way to build relationships with people and indirectly market your business through content. You can join or leave groups at anytime, so start searching for groups and join some! To search for groups on Facebook, simply log into your Facebook account and type your chosen keywords into the search box at the top of the page. Click the See More Results link at the bottom of the list that pops up to open the results page. On the results page, click the Groups link in the left sidebar to narrow your results to include groups only. Scroll through the results and click through to view groups of interest to you.

It's important to review the members and activities in groups before you join. You want to spend time in groups that are very active with many members publishing updates and participating in conversations. A group with just a few members, with no activity, or with activity by just a few members won't deliver the results you need based on your time investment in publishing short-form content.

Using Facebook apps

A number of Facebook apps can help you with short-form content marketing initiatives. NetworkedBlogs (available through the Facebook Applications Directory at `www.facebook.com/apps/directory.php`) is a great app to help promote your long-form content via your Facebook profile. Other apps that help you cross-promote your content include the My LinkedIn Profile app, which enables you to publish your LinkedIn profile as a tab on your Facebook Page or profile, and the Eventbrite app, which allows you to publicize events (such as long-form content Webinars), sell tickets, and keep track of responses to event invitations.

The Promotions Facebook app is another great option, which allows you to create branded promotions and run them on your Facebook page. These promotions could include contests, quizzes, and more. You can tie promotions into your original short-form content, too!

To find out more about the various Facebook apps (new apps are launched frequently), search through the Facebook Applications Directory. You can search by keyword or category, you can view featured applications, and if you're logged into your Facebook account, you can view some of the applications your friends are using.

Participating appropriately on Facebook for your brand

An easy test to use to ensure the content you publish on Facebook gives an accurate and consistent representation of your brand is to ask yourself if your mother, boss, or other authority figure of your choice would approve of it. If the answer is yes, then that content is probably suitable for publishing on your Facebook Page or profile, or in Facebook groups. Next, ask yourself whether that content benefits your target audience and offers a positive example of what consumers can expect from your brand and business. If the answer is yes, then that content is appropriate for your brand.

For example, don't publish pictures of yourself doing shots at your friend's wedding on your Facebook profile if you use that profile for business and short-form content marketing purposes. Similarly, don't participate in conversations that don't provide a positive reflection of you, your brand, and your business. Although your friends might be arguing and using colorful language about the results of the latest football game, you should avoid such conversations on Facebook where existing and potential customers and business partners might see.

Furthermore, the applications you use on Facebook can have a negative effect on your brand. Mafia Wars might be a fun Facebook application, but is it appropriate for your brand image? Games are entertaining, but they can hurt your brand and cause people to turn away from your content and your business. Err on the side of caution and only use Facebook apps that enhance your brand rather than detract from it.

Networking with LinkedIn

LinkedIn is the social networking tool for career-oriented people and business purposes. With over 85 million users, you have an opportunity to market your business with short form content on LinkedIn. However, it's important to understand that LinkedIn is more private than Facebook. That's because you must have a relationship with someone in order to send a connection request to him or her.

For example, you must have worked in the same company (as defined in your LinkedIn profiles), know that person's e-mail address (which must be associated with their LinkedIn account), or attended the same school (as defined in your LinkedIn profiles). If you don't have a prior relationship, you are supposed to request an introduction through a mutual LinkedIn connection.

Despite the closed nature of LinkedIn, it can be a great place for content marketing, particularly for business-to-business companies because the site is the social networking tool for business people.

For more information and specific instructions to use LinkedIn, read *LinkedIn For Dummies,* by Joel Elad, or visit the LinkedIn Learning Center at `http://learn.linkedin.com`.

Creating your LinkedIn profile

The first step to use LinkedIn for short-form content marketing is to create your LinkedIn profile, which is your personal space on LinkedIn. Simply visit `www.linkedin.com` and enter your name, e-mail address, and a password into the sign-up form fields. Click the Join Now button to create your LinkedIn account.

Next, you need to take some time to make your LinkedIn profile shine by adding a photo and inputting your personal information, work experience, Web site links, and so on. Lead with your strengths, and make sure the first thing people see on your profile is the most important information to build your brand and business. You can view a LinkedIn profile in Figure 8-4 for reference.

Make sure you set your LinkedIn profile to public, so people don't have to be connected with you in order to view it. Potentially, this gives your profile maximum exposure.

After you publish your profile, publish updates, and are actively participating on LinkedIn, you can add more to your profile, such as recommendations, which I discuss in the upcoming "Getting and giving recommendations" section.

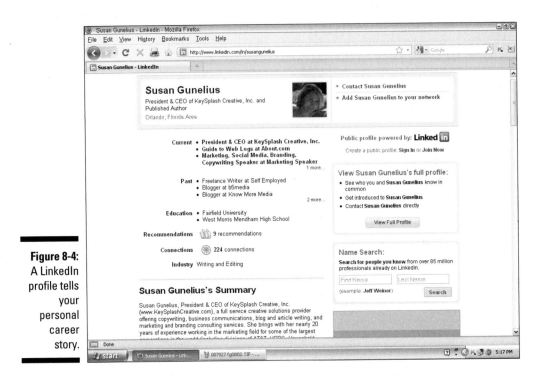

Figure 8-4:
A LinkedIn
profile tells
your
personal
career
story.

Feeding your blog and Twitter content to LinkedIn

LinkedIn makes it easy for you to cross-promote your long-form blog content by setting up the Blog Link application, which automatically publishes an update on your LinkedIn profile with a link to your new blog posts. Simply visit www.linkedin.com/opensocialInstallation/preview?_ch_panel_id=1&_applicationId=1500 and follow the instructions provided to import your blog's feed to your LinkedIn profile.

You can also feed your short-form Twitter content to your LinkedIn profile by joining your LinkedIn and Twitter accounts. Note that your LinkedIn profile must be set to public and your tweets must not be set as private in order to join your accounts. Simply log into your LinkedIn account and visit the Edit Profile page. Click the Add Twitter Account link and verify your Twitter account information. Your Twitter updates will begin publishing to your LinkedIn profile.

You can also publish your LinkedIn updates on your Twitter feed by selecting the check box next to the Twitter icon (you can find the Twitter icon beneath the update text box) before you click the Share button and publish your update on your LinkedIn profile. The first time you check this box, you need to verify your Twitter account information.

Finding people to connect with on LinkedIn

LinkedIn is more closed than Facebook, so it can be a bit more challenging to find and connect with people that you haven't worked with, gone to school with, or known well. However, you can find people on LinkedIn using some built-in search tools and some creative tricks.

First, you can use the Find People search tool by logging into your account and visiting www.linkedin.com/search/fpsearch?trk=tab_pro. Here you can enter keywords to find people outside your network and narrow your search results by location, industry, interests, and much more.

If the Find People search tool doesn't deliver the results you want, you can try using the Advanced People Search at www.linkedin.com/search?trk=tab_pro. With this tool, you can apply very detailed search criteria, such as job function and seniority.

You can also find LinkedIn users by looking at your connections' connections and searching through members of groups that you belong to.

Getting and giving recommendations

A unique aspect of LinkedIn is the recommendations feature. You can write recommendations for anyone you're connected with on LinkedIn, and that recommendation is published within that person's LinkedIn profile if he or she accepts it. You can also ask your connections to write recommendations about you.

Recommendations are a great way to boost your credibility. Many hiring managers read LinkedIn recommendations when they're researching new employees because recommendations are like testimonials. Therefore, recommendations can work to your advantage in terms of building your brand reputation, too. Customer testimonials are a proven, powerful word-of-mouth marketing tool.

To write a recommendation for another LinkedIn user or request a recommendation from one of your LinkedIn connections, log into your LinkedIn account and hover your mouse on the Profile link in the top navigation bar to display a drop-down list of links. From that list, click the Recommendations link to open your recommendations management page. From this page, you can view the recommendations you've sent and received. You can also search for users and create recommendations for them or request recommendations from other people.

Recommendations are typically a two-way street, meaning if someone writes a recommendation for you, it's usually expected that you'll write one in return if you have something positive to say about the other person. Similarly, if you write a recommendation for another person, that other person should probably write a recommendation of you in return (assuming he or she has something good to say about you).

You might wonder how giving and getting recommendations is considered a form of short-form content marketing. In simplest terms, the recommendations you write and receive are direct representations of your brand and business. They help to indirectly market your business, build brand awareness and brand trust, and increase exposure because those recommendations are published in your profile (if they're made about you), in the other person's profile (if you recommend that person), and in both your LinkedIn update stream and the other person's LinkedIn update stream.

Answering questions

LinkedIn Answers is an incredible opportunity for you to market your business through short-form content. Just visit www.linkedin.com/answers?trk=hb_ft_answers, shown in Figure 8-5, to see what you can do with LinkedIn Answers.

You can ask a question on LinkedIn Answers or answer questions. The answering part presents a significant opportunity for short-form content marketing. You can browse for questions by category and answer those where you can offer insight or help. Answering questions is a great way to boost your online exposure, build relationships with people, and earn a reputation as an expert in your field.

If you spend time answering a lot of questions and provide the best possible answers to those questions, your reputation as an expert could be recognized and you might find yourself featured as an expert in a category on the LinkedIn Answers home page. That means even more exposure for you and more people who will see your short-form content via LinkedIn Answers.

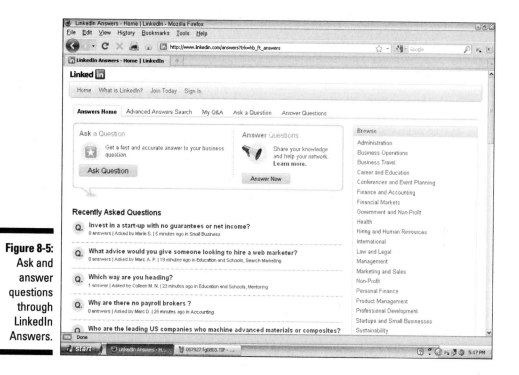

Figure 8-5:
Ask and answer questions through LinkedIn Answers.

Joining and participating in groups

LinkedIn groups give users a chance to delve deeper into niche topics that are important to them. You can create LinkedIn groups and join up to 50 groups with a free LinkedIn account. Some groups are private and others are open to anyone on LinkedIn to join.

You can send private messages to other members of groups you join regardless of whether your profile is connected to theirs on LinkedIn.

You can find groups by keyword, category, and language in the LinkedIn Groups Directory, which you can access by logging into your LinkedIn account and clicking the Groups link in the top navigation bar. A sub-navigation bar appears where you can click the Groups Directory link to search for groups. You can also click the Groups You May Like link to find a list of groups that match your LinkedIn profile and activities. If you want to start your own group, just click the Create a Group link and follow the instructions provided.

After you join a group, you can begin publishing your original short-form content updates to the group. Just make sure that your content is relevant and interesting to group members. Make sure you listen to existing conversations and offer information that matches the audience's wants and needs. If the group offers the News feature, you can feed your blog to the group so an update publishes each time you publish a new blog post.

Using LinkedIn apps

You can add a variety of LinkedIn apps, such as the Blog Link app mentioned earlier in this chapter, to your profile to add functionality and enhance your content. Remember, applications should support your brand promise and not detract from the user experience on your profile. With that in mind, following are several LinkedIn apps that you can try to aid in your short-form content marketing efforts via your LinkedIn profile:

- **Behance:** Use this app to add an image gallery or portfolio to your LinkedIn profile (www.linkedin.com/opensocialInstallation/preview?_ch_panel_id=1&_applicationId=104096).

- **Box.net:** Let anyone who visits your LinkedIn profile download your documents or enable other people to contribute to your shared documents (www.linkedin.com/opensocialInstallation/preview?_ch_panel_id=1&_applicationId=1300).

- **Google Presentations:** Share your Google documents in your LinkedIn profile (www.linkedin.com/opensocialInstallation/preview?_ch_panel_id=1&_applicationId=1400).

- **SlideShare:** Share your presentations and documents from your SlideShare profile in your LinkedIn profile (www.linkedin.com/opensocialInstallation/preview?_ch_panel_id=1&_applicationId=1200).

- **WordPress:** Syndicate the feed from your WordPress blog to your LinkedIn profile updates (www.linkedin.com/opensocialInstallation/preview?_ch_panel_id=1&_applicationId=2200).

Depending on the type of brand or business you want to market through your LinkedIn profile, some of these applications are likely to be more beneficial to you. As long as the applications you use help you deliver meaningful content to your connections, you can feel confident adding them to your LinkedIn profile.

Creating a company profile page

If you have a registered, company-owned domain name (for example, my company e-mail address is susan@keysplashcreative.com), not just a common e-mail domain like gmail.com, hotmail.com, and so on, you can create a profile page for your company on LinkedIn. Company pages allow you to present your brand, products, services, and people to the 85 million LinkedIn users.

If you don't have a company e-mail address, you can create a LinkedIn group for your company instead.

When LinkedIn users opt to follow your company page, they receive notifications via network updates or e-mail when you publish news and information to your company page. With a free LinkedIn account, you can create a satisfactory LinkedIn company page that allows you to create another engaging branded online destination. You can even access analytics about your company page's followers and other company pages they follow.

A company page consists of four tabs that enable you to determine what content you want to highlight, how to provide information to specific audience segments and visitors, and more. The four tabs that make up a company page on LinkedIn are

- ✔ **Overview:** The Overview tab is the landing page for your company profile on LinkedIn. This is where you introduce your brand and business. On this page, visitors can see everyone in their network who works at your company as well as your company's blog posts and Twitter feeds if you configure them to publish on your company page.

- ✔ **Careers:** The Careers tab displays any job postings you've published on LinkedIn. If you pay for an upgraded Silver of Gold Careers Page, you can add information about your company culture, feature your best employees, and customize your messages to specific audience segments.

- ✔ **Products and Services:** The Products and Services tab is where you can showcase and promote your products and services. Visitors to this tab not only find out about your products and services, but they can also see how many of their network connections recommend your products and services and read those recommendations. (Don't worry, you control which recommendations publish on your company page.) This customer testimonial section of a company profile page is very powerful. Furthermore, this tab is viewer-aware. You can set up five audience segments based on industry, job function, seniority, geography, or company size and display different information to visitors based on their LinkedIn profile characteristics.

✔ **Analytics:** The Analytics tab is only visible to you or the person designated as the administrator of your company page. Here you can access
information related to who your company page followers are and what
other company pages they follow.

You can send recommendation requests within your company page. When
you receive recommendations, make sure you respond to them to create a
dialogue with customers.

You can create your company profile page on LinkedIn at anytime by
following these steps:

1. **Log into your LinkedIn account and click the Companies link in the
   top navigation bar of your profile home page.**

   This opens the Companies Home page shown in Figure 8-6.

2. **Click the Add a Company link in the upper right of the page.**

   The Add a Company page opens, as shown in Figure 8-7.

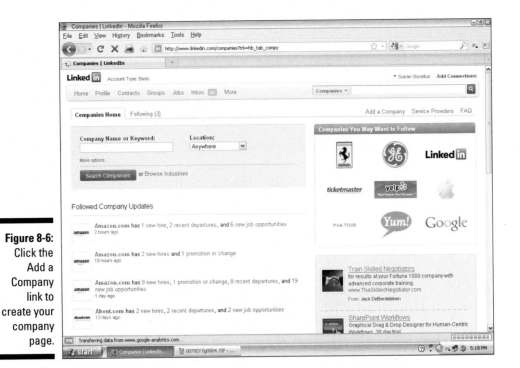

Figure 8-6:
Click the
Add a
Company
link to
create your
company
page.

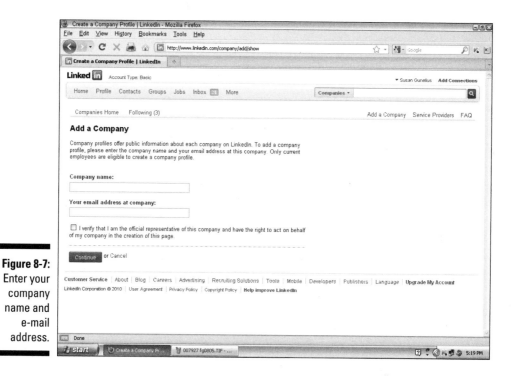

If your company e-mail address is associated with your LinkedIn profile, the Create a Company page appears where you can enter your company information. If your company e-mail address is not already associated with your LinkedIn profile, a confirmation e-mail is sent to you at that e-mail address.

3. **Click the link in the confirmation e-mail to log into your LinkedIn account (using your current primary account e-mail address) to confirm your new company e-mail address and add it to your account.**

4. **After you enter the information that you want to include on your company page, click Create a Company to publish your page.**

LinkedIn users can find your company page in a variety of ways. You can add a Follow Us on LinkedIn button (or link) to your company Web site, blog, e-mail signature, and anywhere else that you can think of. LinkedIn users can find links to your company page on your employees' LinkedIn profiles through notifications they receive when one of their connections recommends one of your products or services on your company page or when they see one of your published job listings in a job search, the Jobs You May Be Interested In section of their profiles, or the Companies You May Be Interested in Following section.

Company pages can be an excellent opportunity for short-form content marketing. Remember, LinkedIn users who follow your company page receive updates whenever you publish new information, so it's a good idea to keep your company page fresh, so it appears on followers' radar screens frequently. It's just one more way you can spark interest and conversations, build relationships, and raise brand awareness and word-of-mouth marketing through content.

Finding More Social Networking Options

Most people think of the most popular sites when they think of social networking, but there are many opportunities for short-form content marketing through less popular or niche social networking sites. You can even create your own social network! The key to success is to avoid spreading yourself too thin. You don't want to risk the quality of your content for quantity.

If you'd like to create your own social networking site, Ning (`www.ning.com`) is an excellent choice, although you're required to pay a fee to create a network on Ning. It's nice to have complete control over your social network, but you need to consider whether the required fee outweighs those benefits before you commit to using the site.

Other popular social networking sites include Bebo (`www.bebo.com`), MySpace (`www.myspace.com`), and Google Buzz (`www.google.com/buzz`). You can also find many smaller social networking sites that cater to more focused audience segments. A few options include Entrepreneur Connect for small business owners and entrepreneurs (`http://econnect.entrepreneur.com`), orkut which is very popular among people in India and Brazil (`www.orkut.com`), Last.fm for music lovers (`www.last.fm`), and BlackPlanet for African Americans (`www.blackplanet.com`).

You can find a great list of social networking sites on Wikipedia (`http://en.wikipedia.org/wiki/List_of_social_networking_websites`). Keep in mind this list is compiled by individuals and is not guaranteed to be accurate. You need to visit individual sites of interest to you and confirm the accuracy of information provided by Wikipedia, but the list is a great starting point in your search for niche social networking sites for your short-form content marketing efforts.

In other words, niche social networking sites attract people of a specific location, age, gender, life stage, race, religion, occupation, and more. You can find a social networking site for just about everyone, so it's very likely that niche audiences are interacting on these smaller social networking sites and are the perfect match for your short-form content.

Chapter 9

Using Twitter and Creative Ideas for Short-Form Content Marketing

· ·

In This Chapter

▶ Microblogging with Twitter

▶ Uploading images and photos

▶ Using widgets

▶ Creating animated gifs and infographics

· ·

*T*he Internet provides a wide variety of tools and opportunities for effective content marketing. The key to success is being brave enough to try new things, tweak, and try again. You also need to be creative and continually look for new ways to publish, share, and promote your amazing content.

This chapter shows you why and how to use Twitter for content marketing. Believe it or not, you can create original content that successfully markets your business in the 140-characters or fewer that Twitter allows. You also find out how to use more creative ways to build your brand and business with content, including images, social bookmarking, infographics, buttons, and animated gifs. You're only limited by your creativity when it comes to content marketing.

Microblogging with Twitter

Microblogging is a term used to define short-form blogging. Most microblogging tools offer features that are much more limited than traditional blogging tools. The purpose of microblogging is to publish quick updates that take just a minute to create and consume. For people who find writing challenging, microblogging is a great alternative.

Microblogging alternatives

You can find a number of tools that enable you to publish short updates. Each site offers slightly different features, such as the ability to publish images or videos. Similarly, some sites allow you to publish longer updates than others, and the conversation functions differ from one site to another. Therefore, the suggested Twitter alternatives that follow are included because they provide similar purposes in terms of publishing shorter updates than you're likely to see on a blog.

If Twitter isn't for you, look at other short-form content marketing tools, such as Tumblr (`www.tumblr.com`), Plurk (`www.plurk.com`), or Jaiku (`www.jaiku.com`).

Twitter (`www.twitter.com`) is one of the first tools many businesses turn to when they get started with short-form content marketing through microblogging. Not only is Twitter the "it" social media tool these days, but it's also free and extremely easy to use. Just create a free account and start publishing updates (called *tweets*) of 140-characters or less. Your Twitter updates appear in reverse chronological order in your Twitter stream, which publishes on your Twitter profile, like the one shown in Figure 9-1.

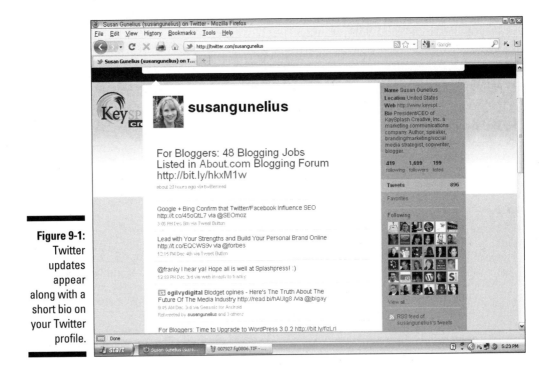

Figure 9-1:
Twitter updates appear along with a short bio on your Twitter profile.

While Twitter is the most popular microblogging tool, others are available. (See the sidebar, "Microblogging alternatives.") Because of its popularity, this section focuses on using Twitter for your short-form content marketing activities.

Creating your Twitter profile

The first step to using Twitter for short-form content marketing is to create your Twitter account by completing the form at `https://twitter.com/signup`. As you can see in Figure 9-2, to create a Twitter account, you provide the name that you want to appear on your profile, the username you want to appear in your Twitter profile URL, a password, and your e-mail address.

Just read and agree to the Twitter terms of service, and click the Create My Account button. You now have a Twitter account and a generic profile page. However, your profile doesn't say anything about you to demonstrate who you are. It's time to add some details to your profile, so it includes a link to your Web site and information about you, your business, and maybe even your tweets. This information appears in the right column on your public Twitter profile (refer to Figure 9-1), and it's your chance to demonstrate why visitors should read your content and follow you for future updates.

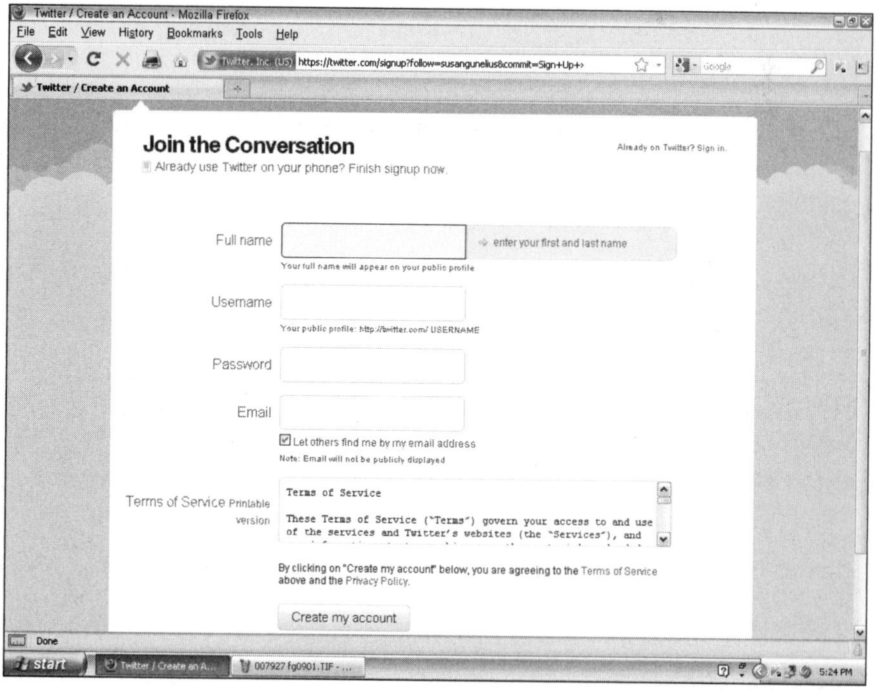

Figure 9-2: Enter the required information to create your free Twitter account.

To create or update your profile, follow these steps:

1. **Log into your Twitter account and click the drop-down arrow next to your name in the upper-right corner. Then click the Settings link in the drop-down list to view your account settings.**

   This opens the Account page of your profile.

2. **Click Profile in the blue secondary navigation bar to open your profile page, as shown in Figure 9-3.**

   On this page, you can add a picture, your name, location, link, and bio to personalize your Twitter profile.

3. **Click the Change Image link and then click the Browse button to find your image. Select your image and click the Open button.**

4. **In the appropriate text boxes, enter your name, Web site URL, and bio.**

5. **Click the Save button when you're done creating or updating your profile.**

You could use your business or brand logo as the image for your Twitter profile, but a picture of you makes your tweets seem personable rather than automated corporate rhetoric. Save the logo for your background design as discussed in the next section.

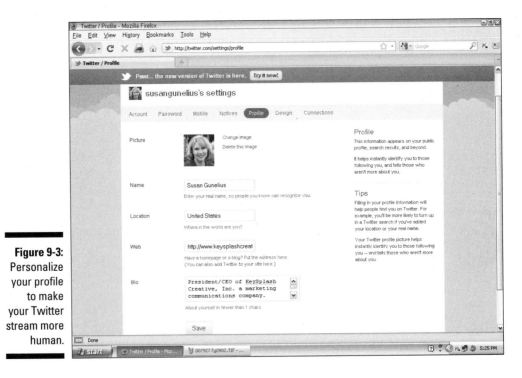

Figure 9-3: Personalize your profile to make your Twitter stream more human.

A personalized Twitter profile makes your short-form content seem more personable. Your audience is more likely to develop an emotional connection with you if your profile is personalized, which is imperative to building relationships with them that will lead to brand loyalty and advocacy.

Branding your Twitter destination

The design of your Twitter profile should also be branded, so visitors have a visual connection to your brand promise in addition to the messages and content you publish. If you click the Settings link in the drop-down list below your name in the upper right corner of your Twitter profile when you're logged into your account, you can access the settings navigation bar shown in Figure 9-3 where you can select the Design link to modify your Twitter profile background with a standard image.

A generic image isn't enough. Instead, you should click the Change Design Colors and Change Background Image buttons to match your Twitter profile landing page to your brand. Don't worry if you don't have an image to use for your background and don't know how to create one. Many Twitter background design tools and designers offer free or inexpensive backgrounds. Following are some Twitter background resources:

- ✔ **Social Identities:** At www.custombackgroundsfortwitter.com, you can find free Twitter backgrounds or pay a reasonable fee for a custom Twitter background design.

- ✔ **TwitrBackgrounds.com:** At www.twitrbackgrounds.com, you can find free Twitter backgrounds, or for a fee, you can personalize a background with up to four of your own images. You can upload your images and preview your background before you pay for it. You can also pay for a custom background.

- ✔ **TwitBacks:** At www.twitbacks.com, you can set up a free account and choose a background to which you can add your photo, bio, logo, social media profile links, and more.

While visiting other profiles on Twitter, you'll see the difference a personalized or custom Twitter background can make in positioning a brand and setting audience expectations for the content that is published on a Twitter stream. Spending a few minutes or a small fee to get a personalized or custom Twitter background is definitely worth it when it comes to using Twitter as a short-form content marketing tool.

Understanding Twitter terminology

Before you dive into short-form content marketing with Twitter, you need to understand some terminology that is unique to Twitter. It's safe to say that you won't hear words like *tweet* or *retweet* except in relation to Twitter. If you understand the terminology of the tool you're using for short-form content marketing, you can leverage the power of Twitter to build your brand and business.

Following are some of the most common Twitter terms:

- **Tweet:** An update published on a Twitter profile feed. Tweets are limited to 140 characters or less.

- **Retweet (RT):** When a Twitter user shares a tweet published by another Twitter user with his own followers, his shared update is a *retweet*. Retweet can also be a verb, as in, "I retweeted that link."

- **Twitter stream:** An archive of tweets in a Twitter profile that publishes in reverse chronological order.

- **Twitter profile:** A Twitter accountholder's personal space that includes a bio, tweets, direct messages, and related information.

- **Direct message (DM):** A private message shared between Twitter users that only the sender and recipient can view through their Twitter accounts. Direct messages can be sent only to people who already follow you.

- **@reply:** Pronounced "at reply," an *@reply* is a direct response or message to another Twitter user published within a user's Twitter stream preceded by *@username* (where *username* is replaced with the other user's Twitter ID). An @reply within a tweet is considered a mention of another user.

- **Hashtag:** To help Twitter users find tweets of interest to them, users include keywords preceded by the # symbol, such as #contentmarketing.

- **Follow:** If you like another user's tweets, you can click the Follow button on her profile, so her tweets appear within your stream of tweets published by people you follow. Those Twitter profiles appear in your list of people you follow and in the other person's list of people who follow them.

- **Twitter app:** Third parties create applications to enhance the functionality of Twitter.

- **URL shortener:** A service that enables you to enter a long URL that's shortened to save space in a tweet. Some URL shorteners enable you to shorten URLs and track clicks, too.

When using Twitter, you'll find that these terms make more sense. Scroll through some Twitter streams of other users to get an idea of how @replies, retweets, hashtags, and URL shorteners are used, particularly by your competitors, to get some ideas for your own Twitter activities.

Finding people to follow on Twitter

An important aspect of effectively using Twitter for content marketing purposes is to build your list of quality followers. The first step to attracting followers is publishing amazing content on Twitter. Quality followers who will actively engage with you and retweet your content won't follow you if your content is uninteresting. You find out more regarding what to tweet about later in this chapter.

Additionally, you need to find and follow interesting people who tweet about your business and are in some way interesting to (or part of) your target audience. Because Twitter is very much a social media marketing tool, a good portion of your Twitter activities will incorporate social media marketing strategies and tactics. That means engaging with other users, building relationships, and building your band of brand advocates is extremely important because it directly affects your ability to use Twitter for content marketing.

The people you follow and build relationships with on Twitter should include existing customers, target customers, industry experts, and online influencers. In other words, as part of your social media marketing activities, you should try to get on the radar screens of people who have influence with your target audience across the social Web. Your target audience listens to, seeks information from, and trusts these people. If you can develop relationships with key online influencers, your content can get in front of an audience who can spread the information and make it that much more credible simply because of their reputations.

Online influencers typically have many followers who actively interact with them and share their content.

Now you need to go out and find the people to follow on Twitter for your content marketing purposes. Following are a number of Twitter tools, tricks, and apps that can help you find people to follow who would be interested in your business, products, services, and content:

✔ **Twitter Advanced Search:** At `http://search.twitter.com/advanced`, you can type in specific keywords related to your business or that your target audience is likely to use. You can search for tweets including specific keywords, locations, and more.

✔ **Hashtags:** Search for specific hashtags related to your business on Twitter.

✔ **Follow Others' Followers:** Visit your competitors' Twitter profiles and check out whom they follow and who's following them.

✔ **Local Twitter Apps:** Use Twitter apps that enable you to find people based on their locations. This is particularly useful for businesses that operate in specific areas. Try Nearby Tweets (`http://nearbytweets.com`), ChirpCity (`http://chirpcity.com`), Localtweeps (`http://localtweeps.com`), TwellowHood (`www.twellow.com/twellowhood`), LocaFollow (`www.locafollow.com`), and GeoChirp (`www.geochirp.com`).

✔ **Expertise and Interest Twitter Apps:** Use Twitter apps that enable you to find people based on areas of expertise or interest. Try ExecTweets (`www.exectweets.com`), Listorious (`http://listorious.com`), and WeFollow (`www.wefollow.com`), or use Muck Rack (`http://muckrack.com`) to find journalists in your area.

Bottom line, your content marketing efforts will go unnoticed unless you take the time to follow the right people. If your content is great, then you're likely to see a lot of the people who you follow on Twitter reciprocate and follow you in return.

Following Twitter etiquette

The last thing you want to do is destroy your content marketing efforts by breaking one of the unwritten rules of social media and Twitter. When you publish more content and gain more followers, your business and brand will gain more exposure and grow. Social media users, including Twitter users, can be a critical group that might not overlook mistakes or lapses of judgment.

Don't put yourself in the position of undoing the progress your content marketing work has provided by forgetting your Twitter manners. As long as you're honest and not overly self-promotional, you should be okay. Following are a variety of unwritten rules of Twitter etiquette that you must follow at all times to become and stay a welcomed member of the Twitter community:

✔ **Keep private information private:** Don't tweet information on your public Twitter stream that invades someone's privacy. Instead, use the direct messaging feature for private conversations.

✔ **Reveal your sources:** Don't publish tweets that make it appear content you're publishing or tweeting was created by you if it was not. Appropriately attribute sources using the @reply or retweet features.

✔ **Keep it clean:** Avoid using obscenities or tweeting and sharing content that is not a positive reflection of your brand image and promise.

✔ **Avoid automated services:** It's acceptable to feed your blog content to your Twitter stream, but don't let your Twitter profile rely completely on automated updates and features. For Twitter to be considered a content marketing tool, you need to publish original content in your tweets. Furthermore, don't use automated follow tools that automatically add hundreds or thousands of followers to your Twitter profile, which could cause your profile to be flagged as spam and deleted.

✔ **Avoid negativity:** It might be tempting to publish tweets with your complaints or problems, and it might be tempting to participate in arguments on Twitter. However, you should avoid these temptations because they can damage your brand reputation.

Think before you tweet.

Always act with common sense when you publish online content and use Twitter as a content marketing tool. If your Twitter stream is public, and it should be if you're using Twitter as a content marketing tool, then you must make sure that your tweets accurately reflect your brand promise. Your tweets live online for a long time. In fact, the Library of Congress archives all public tweets and Google indexes them for search results, so they'll always be available somewhere. Don't risk your brand reputation by tweeting inappropriate updates. The damage those negative tweets can do is extremely difficult to undo.

Knowing what to tweet about

You must publish interesting and useful tweets or no one will want to follow you, share your content, or engage with you. But what should you tweet about? That's a very common question, particularly from people who want to use Twitter as a content marketing tool.

The important thing to remember is that Twitter is a tool that incorporates social media marketing, short-form content marketing, and conversational content marketing. If you take the time to ensure your Twitter stream offers a good balance of all three marketing types, you'll be positioned for success. That means you need to publish original content, share others' content, engage with other users, and build relationships with other users. If you're not doing all of those activities, then the results you'll experience from your Twitter efforts will not reach full potential.

Before you follow anyone on Twitter, take some time to publish a number of tweets over the course of several days. This way, when other users receive notification that you're following them, they can view your Twitter stream and see that you offer valuable content, which makes them more likely to follow you in return.

In terms of short-form content marketing activities, you need to tweet original content that adds value to your audience's lives. Long-form content marketing allows you to create content that is very detailed and truly tells the complete story that you want to share. However, short-form content marketing gives you just a sentence or two to get a piece of valuable information across to an audience that moves quickly. With that in mind, your short-form content marketing tweets must be succinct, attention getting, and communicate something that's immediately meaningful to your target audience when they see it.

Following are ten simple tweet suggestions that you can use for short-form content marketing:

- ✔ **Discounts:** Offer a discount code, promotion, or sale information to consumers.
- ✔ **Tips:** Offer tips to using your products.
- ✔ **Warnings:** Provide warnings about things to avoid with your products or in your industry.
- ✔ **Directions:** Publish directions (this could be in multiple tweets) that show people how to accomplish a specific task.
- ✔ **Announcements:** Tweet new or exciting happenings in your business.
- ✔ **Opinions:** Offer your opinion on trends or industry news.
- ✔ **Answers:** Publish answers to questions you receive. You can even use a tool like Formspring (`www.formspring.me`) to solicit questions.
- ✔ **Solve problems:** Provide resolutions to common problems related to your products or industry.
- ✔ **Recommendations:** Establish yourself as an expert in your field by recommending products, services, and more (even those beyond your offerings) that can help consumers.
- ✔ **Clear up confusion:** If information related to your business or industry is inaccurate or causing confusion, publish tweets that provide accurate, easy-to-understand information.

At the core of your Twitter stream should be a consistent message that matches your brand promise. Followers will expect a specific type of content from you in terms of reliability and quality, and your tweet's original content drives your brand promise. Stay true to your brand and provide interesting content that people want to read, and you'll succeed.

How to get more retweets

One of the goals of using Twitter for short-term content marketing is providing content that is interesting enough to your target audience that they want to retweet it. In other words, your Twitter content should be shareworthy, so it spreads beyond your social Web reach. To that end, you can take a few steps to make your tweets more retweetable.

First, give your links the importance they deserve within your tweets. If your tweet is nearly 140 characters and the link is at the very end of that tweet, when someone retweets it, the link could be truncated. That's because a retweet typically includes the original publisher's @username at the beginning of the retweet. For the @username to fit into the 140-character or fewer limit, the end of your original message might have to be cut.

You do not want your tweeted links to disappear or you won't get the traffic to those links that you want. Imagine that the link leads people to your Web site to take advantage of a special discount. If people retweet your update and the link to your sale is cut off, those retweets won't be as useful to you as they could have been with your link. Therefore, make sure your tweets are written in a manner that ensures the most important information, such as a link, isn't truncated in retweets.

You also need to understand your existing and prospective followers, so you provide content that they want and need, and are likely to retweet. Use a URL shortener (described in the next section) that enables you to track clicks, so you know which content is generating the most retweets. The trick is to provide more of the same kind of content to your audience.

It's also important that you use social media marketing and conversational content marketing tactics to engage with your followers, retweet their content, and build relationships with them via direct messages and @replies. By networking with your followers, you'll get to know them better. People are likely to look more closely at your content and retweet it when they know who you are and what to expect from you and your tweets.

Finally, don't give up. Building a Twitter following, particularly quality followers who actively retweet your content, takes time. Keep tweeting useful content, and in time, your followers will start retweeting it.

Using URL shorteners

URL shorteners are essential for Twitter users, because they make it easy to turn lengthy URLs into URLs that are approximately 20 characters (the length varies slightly from one URL shortener to another). When you only have 140 characters to work with, you don't want half of those characters to consist of a lengthy URL.

Most URL shorteners are free to use. You simply have to create an account or link your Twitter account to the URL shortener tool. Then, you can copy the long URL you want to include in your tweet and paste it into the URL shortener tool. With the click of a button, your URL is transformed into a short version, which you can copy and paste into your tweet.

Some URL shorteners allow you to track the number of clicks on the URL, and some allow you to customize the link. The most popular URL shorteners include

- **bit.ly:** At `http://bit.ly`, you can customize your shortened URL and track clicks. You don't have to register for an account to use bit.ly, but you don't get access to statistics unless you create a free account.

- **Ow.ly:** At `http://ow.ly/url/shorten-url`, you can shorten URLs for free and without an account. If you do create a free account, you can connect your account with Twitter and HootSuite (a third party Twitter app for Twitter organization and management).

- **Snipurl:** At `http://snipurl.com/site/index`, Snipurl (also called Snurl or Snipr) enables you to shorten and customize URLs. You can also track and manage your shortened URLs (called *snips*) if you create a free account. A handy toolbar makes it easy to snip a URL at anytime.

- **TinyURL:** At `http://tinyurl.com`, you can shorten and customize URLs free without creating an account.

Most Twitter users expect tweets to include shortened URLs, and shortening URLs has become a Twitter standard. In fact, a lengthy URL in a tweet might raise a red flag that you're new to Twitter or don't care about widely accepted best practices.

Finding helpful Twitter apps

Earlier in this chapter, I described several Twitter apps that can help you find people to follow. Those apps can also help you find hot topics and create useful content that is timely. Twitter apps come and go, so you never know what new tool will pop up that you want to try or what old tool that you love might shutdown.

Most Twitter apps are offered free, so the people who develop and maintain them might not do so forever. Therefore, don't become overly dependent on a Twitter app. Make sure you can live without it, because your favorite Twitter app might disappear one day.

Twitter apps can help you stay organized, automate tasks for you, help you promote your business, and so much more. Following are some of the Twitter apps I recommend you check out because they each offer something that can help boost a short-form content marketing plan:

- **TweetDeck:** Organize your Twitter followers and manage your Twitter activities more efficiently (`www.tweetdeck.com`).

- ✔ **monitter:** Keep track of what is being said about your business and brand on Twitter (`http://monitter.com`).

- ✔ **Twitterfeed:** Automatically publish your new blog posts in your Twitter stream (`http://twitterfeed.com`).

- ✔ **twtQpon:** Create coupons and share them with your Twitter followers (`http://twtqpon.com`).

- ✔ **SocialOomph:** Write tweets and schedule them to publish, track tweets, extend your Twitter profile, and more, with a free or paid account (`www.socialoomph.com`).

- ✔ **TwitLonger:** Publish tweets over140 characters (`http://www.twitlonger.com/index.php/main_new`).

- ✔ **BubbleTweet.com:** Create short video messages that appear when someone views your Twitter profile (`http://www.bubbletweet.com`).

- ✔ **CoTweet:** Create one Twitter account for your business that multiple employees can access and tweet from using individual login profiles (`https://cotweet.com`).

The best part of using Twitter apps is that none of them can destroy your Twitter profile and you can stop using them at any time. You have complete flexibility in terms of the apps you choose to use, so don't be afraid to experiment.

Participating in live tweets

Live tweeting an event is a great way to share useful information with your Twitter followers. A *live tweet* happens when you attend an event, which could be a training session, presentation, trade show, and so on, and publish tweets during the event to report what you see and hear in real time. It's a great way to deliver instant information that is likely to be of interest to your audience, and to build up your retweets. That's because live tweets are usually meaningful and helpful to people.

You can promote your live tweet in advance, so your followers know they can listen in on the event at the time you tell them. Live tweets are particularly successful when you tweet from events that are expensive to attend (such as a seminar lead by a well-known figure) or offer coveted information.

Even though live tweets happen in real time, your followers can still access your tweets from an event after the fact. Get creative when it comes to ensuring your live tweets live beyond the actual event and spread further than your followers by ensuring the tweets you publish include valuable content. Consider turning them into a blog post or other piece of long-form content to get more exposure from your efforts.

Bottom line, the best content marketing strategies are fully integrated with your overall marketing plan. That means your short-form content marketing efforts on Twitter should not exist in a silo. Instead, think about how you can cross-promote your content marketing efforts and repurpose that content to give it more chances to build your brand and business.

Uploading Photos and Images

Short-form content used for marketing purposes doesn't have to be limited to text. You can also use photos and images for short-form content marketing. For example, an interior design business can publish portfolio photos and before and after pictures. Similarly, a restaurant can publish photos of menu items, and a hotel can publish photos of rooms. The options vary and just about any business can use them.

Photos and images can show off your products or they can help to give your brand a personal touch. By taking pictures of your office, employees, company picnic, and so on, you can give your business a personality that helps build relationships with consumers.

You can also create original images, such as graphs, charts, drawings, designs, and so on, that represent your business or tell a story of some kind. Any original image that provides useful information to your target audience is a form of short-form content marketing.

Understanding copyright licenses

In Chapter 3, you find out about the types of copyright licenses that can apply to your original content, including images. For content marketing purposes, you should protect your original content with a Creative Commons Attribution license. This gives your content the maximum exposure potential because people can freely share and republish your content as long as they cite you as the owner and creator of that work.

You can apply a Creative Commons Attribution license to any work you create. All of the information you need can be found in Chapter 3 and at www.creativecommons.org.

 If possible, include a caption or note with your photos or images identifying them as copyrighted under a Creative Commons Attribution license. For example, if space allows, you can include a full citation that says, "© *year* by *Your Company Name or URL;* Copyright holder is licensing this under the Creative Commons License, Attribution 3.0 (http://creativecommons.org/licenses/by/3.0/us)."

The key to short-form content marketing success is publishing content that people want to share and talk about. If you restrict use of your content, you also restrict the exposure that content can get. For maximum exposure, use a Creative Commons Attribution license and let your short-form content spread as far as possible.

Finding sites to upload and share photos

You can upload your photos and images to your Web site or blog, but you can open up more opportunities for sharing and conversation by uploading those photos and images to image-sharing sites. These sites allow people to upload image files, include descriptions, and make it easy for those images to be shared further with 1-click Twitter-sharing, Facebook-sharing, and more. They also make it easy for people to comment on images and connect with other people. In other words, image-sharing sites are a different type of social Web site that offer great opportunities for short-form content marketing.

The trick is to upload useful and interesting images, and take time to create titles, keywords, and descriptions that help people find those images in onsite searches as well as image searches on search engines like Google.

Cross-promote the images you upload on image-sharing sites by tweeting them, sharing them on Facebook, including them in blog posts, and so on.

Following are some of the most popular image uploading and sharing sites to get you started with using images for short-form content marketing:

- ✔ **Flickr:** Flickr (www.flickr.com) is owned by Yahoo! and is one of the most popular image uploading and sharing sites. You can create a free account and start uploading images immediately.

- ✔ **Picasa and Picasa Web Albums:** Picasa and Picasa Web Albums (www.picasa.google.com and www.picasaweb.google.com) are owned by Google. You can download the Picasa image-editing tool, and upload and share your images in your own Picasa Web album.

- ✔ **Photobucket:** Photobucket (www.photobucket.com) offers free image uploading and sharing features with easy sharing on Twitter, Facebook, and MySpace.

Many small and large companies and brands use Flickr as a short-form content marketing tool. Check out Dell's Flickr page (www.flickr.com/photos/dellphotos), shown in Figure 9-4, for inspiration.

Figure 9-4:
Dell
publishes
images
of new
products
and events
on its Flickr
page.

When you upload images to image-sharing sites, be sure to apply the appropriate copyright license to your images and use keywords in the title, tags, and description to boost search traffic.

Reviewing Other Short-Form Content Marketing Tools

You have more ways to create and publish short-form content for marketing purposes than you might realize. Any original content that you publish online could be considered a form of content marketing if it's useful to your target audience. If that content can be consumed within a minute or two, it could be considered a form of short-form marketing.

Content marketing opportunities are limited only by your ability to think out-of-the-box. This section introduces you to a number of other ways you can market your business using short-form content that hasn't been discussed in this chapter and Chapter 8. Of course, this list isn't all-inclusive, and new opportunities arise all the time. Think like a publisher rather than a marketer and seek new ways to get your amazing, shareworthy content in front of your target audience of people who are likely to be interested in it.

Creating animated gifs

Animated gifs can be used to create noticeable banner ads or short-form content marketing. Imagine a cartoonist who creates an animated gif of a cartoon strip, or a hair salon that creates an animated gif to show the before and after of a haircut. An animated gif can bring static images to life or offer a snippet of video content automatically rather than requiring a person to click a video link or player.

Animated gifs have long been associated with banner ads and the viral sharing of funny moments in films or humorous compilations of images and text. However, with a bit of planning, they can be a great way to communicate content quickly and visually.

Many image editing and Web design software programs can create animated gifs, but a great way to get started is to use a free online tool. The following list provides several popular options, which you can test to see which best meets your needs and technical skills (they're all easy to use though):

- ✔ **Gickr.com:** At `http://gickr.com`, you can make animated gifs that include up to 10 images, alter the speed and size of your animated gif, embed it into other Web sites, and save it to your computer easily. You can also make animated gifs from YouTube videos and Flickr images.

- ✔ **Imator:** At `http://imator.com`, you can use a drag-and-drop system to create animated gifs in typical display ad sizes, which you can download to your computer.

- ✔ **Picasion:** At `http://picasion.com`, you can make animated gifs that include up to 10 images, alter the speed of your animated gif, embed it into other Web sites, and save it to your computer easily.

- ✔ **GIFup.com:** At `www.gifup.com`, you can use a drag-and-drop system to create animated gifs and save them to your computer.

After you determine whether creating animated gifs is something you want to use for short-form marketing purposes, you can invest in purchasing and learning how to use a software program to do so with more functionality and customization options. Alternately, a free design program like GIMP (`www.gimp.org`) can enable you to get the job done.

Using widgets

Buttons and badges can be used simply to cross-promote your content marketing efforts, as discussed in Chapter 15, but also, they can be used to broaden the exposure for your short-form content marketing. For example, you can publish a Twitter widget in your blog's sidebar that displays your most recent tweets, as shown in Figure 9-5.

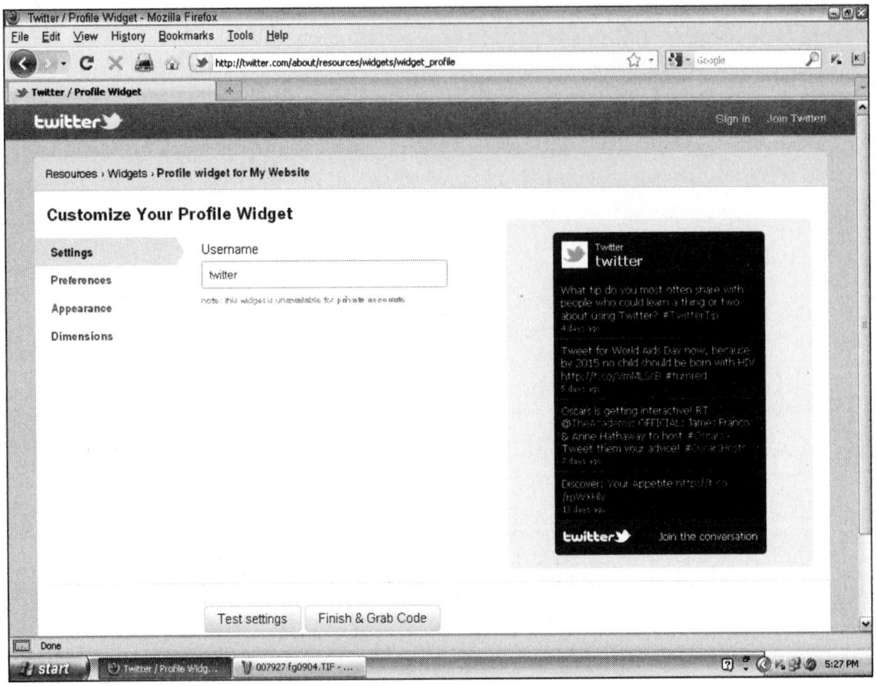

Figure 9-5:
Republish
your
short-form
content
from Twitter
in your
blog's side-
bar with
a Twitter
widget.

To create your own Twitter widget, visit `http://twitter.com/about/resources/widgets/widget_profile`, provide the information requested in the form and customize your widget by selecting options from those provided. Then, simply copy and paste the HTML code provided into your blog's sidebar, Web site, or other site where you'd like to publish it to give your short-form Twitter content more exposure.

Similarly, you can create slideshows from your uploaded images on Flickr, and then click the Share link from that slideshow to access the code needed to embed the slideshow on another Web site or blog.

Be careful not to republish the same content multiple times on the same site. For example, if your Twitter stream consists primarily of your automated blog feed updates, republishing that content in your blog's sidebar as a Twitter widget won't help the user experience on your blog. In fact, it could hurt it. Use that real estate for new, valuable content and information or start publishing more meaningful, original content on your Twitter stream so the widget adds value to your blog.

The key is to find ways to make sure your content is seen by as many people as possible. You can achieve that by promoting your content, but making it available through more of your branded online destinations is quick to set up and gives your audience easy access to experience your content in multiple ways.

Developing infographics

An *infographic* is a concise visual representation of a lot of information. For example, if you own a classic car dealership, it might be interesting to your customers if you develop an infographic that tells the story of the history of the Ford Mustang convertible. If you own a residential cleaning business that focuses on using eco-friendly products, then an infographic that describes the damage that chemical cleaners cause across the world to animals and the environment could be a great marketing tool that people find meaningful and want to share and talk about.

Figure 9-6 shows an infographic created by Infographic Labs (`http://infographiclabs.com`) that depicts a visual guide to SEO. This type of infographic could be an excellent short-form content marketing piece for a Web marketing company or search engine optimization consulting firm.

Figure 9-6:
A guide to SEO as an infographic provides useful, shareworthy content.

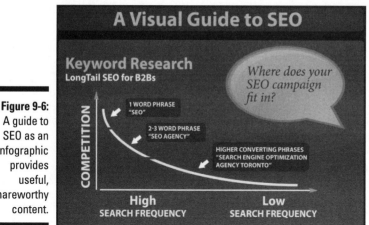

Infographics can be entertaining with few graphs and statistics or they can be highly detailed and researched. As long as they offer information that adds value, they have a chance of spreading virally across the Web as people talk about them and share them.

Companies like Infographic Labs are dedicated to creating infographics either using information you provide to them or conducting research related to a topic at your request. Prices vary depending on the amount of research the designer is required to do. Of course, if you gather all of the information for the infographic, you could use a traditional graphic designer to layout the information in a visual representation, too.

You can also use free online tools to create infographics, some of which are in the following list:

✔ **Paint.NET (`www.getpaint.net`):** Bring all the elements of your info-graphic together into one image document.

✔ **StatPlanet (`www.sacmeq.org/statplanet`):** Create interactive maps, graphs, and creative visualizations of world data.

✔ **Hohli (`http://charts.hohli.com`):** Create charts that look better than a simple Excel chart.

✔ **Creately (`http://creately.com`):** Quickly create great looking dia-grams and flow charts.

✔ **Many Eyes (`http://manyeyes.alphaworks.ibm.com/manyeyes`):** Upload your data and create excellent visual representations of that data.

✔ **Wordle (`www.wordle.net`):** Create images that look like tag clouds to show popularity or importance of specific words in a visually appealing manner.

✔ **Picnik (`www.picnik.com/app`):** Modify your images with this very easy-to-use image-editing tool.

Your infographic design will be limited by the functionality of the tool you use and your ability to create an aesthetically pleasing layout.

An infographic needs to convey interesting information and look great or it won't be shareworthy. Although it's tempting to cut corners and create your own infographic, don't risk losing shareworthiness in an effort to save money. Your time is valuable, too, and all the hours you spend creating an infographic will be for naught if it doesn't look good enough for people to take seriously or want to share with others.

Chapter 10

Writing in Short Form for the Web

Creating short-form content that effectively adds value to your audience's lives is challenging. For many people, it's difficult to write succinctly because it's common to add a lot of extraneous words and details to their thoughts. To be successful with short-form content marketing, you need to remove those filler words and communicate succinctly.

This chapter shows you how short-form content writing differs from the long-form content writing discussed in Chapter 6. You also find out how to find your voice and format your short-form content for maximum success. And of course, you discover how to say a lot in as few words as possible without breaking the unwritten rules of short-form content etiquette.

Comparing and Contrasting Short-Form to Long-Form Web Writing

The primary difference between short-form Web writing and long-form Web writing is the speed in which you must communicate your messages. In simplest terms, imagine that you have 30 seconds or less to communicate your message through short-form content versus three minutes or more with long-form content. Of course, these numbers aren't absolutes, but they give you an idea of how you need to modify your writing to communicate effectively using short-form content as opposed to long-form content.

You can communicate the same messages in short-form and long-form content, but by definition, long-form content allows you to include far more details and commentary than short-form content. That's why links are so important in short-form content marketing. You can include a link in your short-form content to your long-form content where your audience can get more details or you can include a link to someone else's additional content for more information. The links you include in your short-form content will change depending on the point you're trying to make. Figure 10-1 shows a great example of communicating a valuable point in short-form content and linking to more information.

Figure 10-1:
Publish
meaningful
short-form
content with
a link to find
out more.

It can also be more challenging to write short-form content in a manner that doesn't read like a marketing pitch because you can't give the details you can in long-form content. Choose your words carefully so the vast majority of your short-form content reads like original content rather than hyping your business or your long-form content. For example, when you're tweeting a link to your new blog post, don't just write, "Check out my new blog post," with a link to your post. Instead, tweet an important point you make in your blog post and include a link for people to get more details.

Much of your short-form content marketing success comes from the way you craft your content using carefully chosen words. If your Twitter stream reads like a list of links with no value visible without clicking one of those many links, people are less likely to pay attention to you.

Finding Your Voice

How do you create a personal voice and personality in just a few words? That's a common question that can't be ignored when you embark into the world of short-form content marketing. Not only do you need to provide useful content but you also need to let your personality shine through so your content seems more human and less institutional or corporate.

TIP

Use jargon and buzz words sparingly in short-form content only when they enhance your content or make it more meaningful to your audience. Otherwise, they simply use up valuable space and clutter your messages.

The easiest way to let your personality come through in your short-form content is to write the way you speak. However, you need to be certain that the way you speak matches your brand image and the expectations your target audience has for your brand. Just as you would modify the way you speak to your target audience in an in-person situation, you must modify the way you communicate in your short-form content.

As an example, imagine that you own a residential cleaning business. Your audience would probably respond best to your short-form content if it were written in a casual, personable voice. You might publish a Facebook update that says, "Listen to your grandma and use club soda on that stain. Seriously, it works." On the other hand, if you own a commercial cleaning business and your target audience is primarily large companies, your voice should be more professional.

The preceding Facebook update example would not offer the best voice to a highly corporate audience. Instead, you might publish an update that says, "Tested new marble cleaning process on atrium floors in downtown AT&T office. No smell, dried fast, and floor looks new. Watch the before and after video." This update is human and personable and offers useful information about a new service and a link to get more information in a separate video, which this business' target audience might be interested in viewing.

Take a look at Figures 10-2 and 10-3 to see how a different voice used in short-form content can affect a brand.

Figure 10-2:
For some businesses, a highly professional voice is appropriate.

Figure 10-3:
A casual voice might be the best choice for your target audience.

Before you begin publishing short-form content, take some time to analyze your brand's position in the marketplace, your best customers' expectations for your brand, and your goals for your brand. Then create short-form content using a voice that supports those elements and objectives. Make sure your voice is consistent, so you don't risk confusing your audience.

Formatting Tips

Short-form content marketing offers a great deal of flexibility when it comes to formatting, spelling, and grammar. Because you have fewer characters to work with and less time to get your message across to your audience, it's perfectly acceptable to use contractions, sentence fragments, abbreviations, and so on. In fact, depending on your voice and audience, it might even be okay for you to use slang and text messaging abbreviations and icons. For example, it's very common to see things like LOL (laughing out loud) or emoticons, such as the smiley :), in short-form content. Figure 10-4 shows how abbreviations or slang can be effective in short-form content.

Figure 10-4:
It's acceptable to break grammar rules in most short-form content.

Of course, the formatting you apply to your short-form content must be appropriate for your brand and target audience. A financial company with wealthy clients probably shouldn't use a slang term like *ya* instead of *you* in a tweet or *gotcha* instead of *understood*. When writing your short-form content, always use your best judgment based on your brand image and your audience's expectations for your brand.

It's also important to understand the limitations and capabilities of the tools you use to publish short-form content. As discussed in Chapter 9, you're limited to 140-character updates on Twitter. When people share your updates with their Twitter followers, your original tweet might get truncated to fit within the 140-character limit. Therefore, you should try to insert your vital links within your tweets rather than at the end of them. Alternatively, when you publish images on Flickr, you should take the time to write a keyword-friendly title and description to increase search traffic to your short-form content on that site.

Twitter apps and Twitter search tools enable people to search for tweets using keywords. Also, Google indexes tweets. Therefore, there can be great value in using keywords in your tweets, but don't overdo it!

Typically, short-form content is more difficult to craft with search engine optimization as a priority because you're limited in terms of space and time to convey your valuable content. Stuffing a tweet full of keywords will likely do more harm than good. However, some short-form publishing tools provide ways that you can make your content more search-friendly. For example, you can use hashtags to make it easier for people to find your tweets, as discussed in Chapter 9. You can tag people in images and updates that you publish on Facebook so they receive a notification about the publishing of those images and updates. Take some time to leverage the built-in capabilities of short-form content publishing tools to increase the organic exposure of your content. You can read more about short-form content and search engine optimization in Chapter 11.

Adding Value and Getting Shared with Fewer Words

It might seem impossible to create short-form content that actually adds value and is useful enough that people will share it with their own audiences. However, if you write succinctly, you can do it. In *Kick-ass Copywriting in 10 Easy Steps* (Entrepreneur Press), I introduced a tactic called the Red Pen Rule — a simple trick you can use to make your marketing communications more effective that you can apply to short-form content, too.

The Red Pen Rule instructs you to write your content, proofread it, edit it, and get it into the final version that you think is perfect. Then delete at least 30 percent of it. Chances are that 30 percent clutters your message, and your content would be better without it. Of course, 30 percent isn't a requirement, but it's a good target to help you trim your short-form content to be as clear and concise as possible.

An easy way to trim your short-form content is to delete filler words like *really* and *very*.

Another trick to make your short-form content more valuable and shareworthy is to stay focused and keep each message to one topic. Trying to communicate more than one message in a piece of short-form content reduces the strength of that content. Multiple messages make your content confusing and cluttered. Imagine that your audience is standing in front of you, and you have 30 seconds to communicate your content. It's more effective to pick a targeted topic that your audience is likely to be interested in and focus on that single topic than it is to try to talk as fast as you can and fit too much information into those 30 seconds.

For example, consider a florist who publishes photos on her Facebook Page. Creating focused albums for specific events that showcase the arrangement preparation and displays would be far more effective than showing random photos from picnics, weddings, and funeral gatherings all in the same album. The albums focused on an event type are likely to be more shareworthy because they appeal to specific audience segments that might be actively looking for the types of products and services the florist offers.

Most importantly, your short-form content should be original and convey a useful piece of information or it's unlikely that anyone will share it with his or her audience. The success of your content marketing efforts comes partly from how far your content spreads and the buzz it generates. If your short-form content is simply a list of links, random thoughts that aren't related to your business, or inappropriate for your brand, not only will no one share your content, but fewer people will follow you, engage with you, and trust you.

With that said, don't feel like every piece of short-form content you publish has to be amazing. However, make sure you offer more original and shareworthy short-form content than self-promotional or less meaningful content.

Following Short-Form Web Writing Etiquette

Because short-form Web writing is so short, there aren't as many etiquette guidelines to worry about as you encounter with long-form Web writing. Therefore, there is no reason why you shouldn't understand and follow them.

Most importantly, don't write offensive content. Not only could offensive content damage your brand image, but it can also cause people to stop following you or reading your short-form content. Your short-form content can't spread without the help of loyal brand advocate followers, so the last thing you want to do is offend your audience. If you wouldn't say something to your audience in a face-to-face situation, don't say it in your short-form content.

It's also very important that you are honest in your short-form content. Building trust with your audience is an essential step to content marketing success. Don't mislead your audience by publishing short-form content with a link that is unrelated to your short-form content. This type of bait and switch content is a surefire way to draw negative attention and lose followers.

You also need to take the time to determine how much short-form content is too much for your target audience. It's true that you need to stay active and publish short-form content frequently in order to stay in people's minds and increase the likelihood of having your content shared. However, if you publish too frequently, your audience could get annoyed. You don't want your content perceived as clutter or overkill. Unfortunately, there is no specific rule for how much short-form content you should publish each day or week.

Over publishing short-form content is similar to being stuck at a party with someone who won't stop talking. After a while, you stop fully listening to that person. Even if he eventually says something interesting or meaningful to you, you'll miss it because you've already stopped listening. Don't be that person who talks too much. It can be just as damaging to your conversational content marketing effort as publishing too little or too infrequently.

At the very least, try to publish new content at least two or three times throughout the day. The more the better, but if you find yourself publishing new content two or three times per hour, take a step back and evaluate that content for its shareworthiness as well as your audience's reaction to that content in terms of conversations and sharing. In time, you'll find the sweet spot for short-form content publishing frequency that delivers the highest return on investment for your business.

You should view your short-form content marketing efforts as reciprocal. In other words, if people share your content, communicate with you, and talk about you, you not only should acknowledge them so they understand that they're important to you, but also you should reciprocate when you can and share their content, communicate with them, and so on. Content marketing begins with publishing original, amazing content, but it doesn't stop there. As you find out in Part IV, conversational content marketing should be used to round out your content marketing plan.

Finally, as with all your content marketing efforts, your short-form content should not be solely self-promotional. Make sure at least 80 percent of the time you spend in your short-form content marketing effort is not spent on self-promotional activities and no more than 20 percent of your time is spent on self-promotional activities. This split offers a balance in your content that your audience is likely to accept without feeling that you're continually trying to sell your products or services through your short-form content. The majority of your time should be spent creating amazing content and participating in meaningful conversations without directly promoting your business, products or services.

Chapter 11

Discovering Ways to Improve Short-Form Content Marketing

In This Chapter

▶ Increasing the search engine rankings of your short-form content

▶ Abbreviating, truncating, and shortening content the right way

▶ Using tools and tricks to get more from short-form content marketing

*I*n Chapter 10, you discover ways to craft your short-form content so it's positioned for success. In this chapter, you find more specific tricks and tools that you can apply to your short-form content to make it even better. If you apply the suggestions included in this chapter to your short-form content, you will see an improvement in its performance.

Short-form content is a catalyst to action. In just a handful of words or a few seconds, short-form content can communicate an important piece of information, motivate people to action, or spark a conversation. Read this chapter to find out how to boost your short-form content return on investment by making sure the content is an effective catalyst to action rather than a message that's easy to bypass or ignore.

Increasing Your Search Engine Rankings

Even with just a handful of words or an image, you can drive traffic to your content from search engines. Short-form content can appear in search engine keyword search results and generate incoming links to your content and branded online destinations from other sites, which can help your content rank higher in those keyword searches.

In December 2010, both Google and Bing confirmed in interviews with Danny Sullivan of Search Engine Land that links shared on Twitter and Facebook have a direct impact on search engine rankings. The following search engine ranking factors related to Twitter and Facebook content were revealed during those interviews:

✔ Google and Bing both calculate and consider the social authority of Twitter users.

✔ Google and Bing both consider the number of times a piece of content is shared on Twitter as well as the social authority of Twitter users who shared that content when ranking search results.

✔ Google and Bing both calculate whether a link should carry more weight in terms of search rankings depending on who tweeted that link.

✔ Google and Bing both track links shared on Facebook Pages, and Google treats those links the same as tweeted links. However, both search engines only have access to public information published on Facebook.

You can read the complete published excerpts of Danny Sullivan's interviews at http://searchengineland.com/what-social-signals-do-google-bing-really-count-55389.

While search engine optimization experts have suspected that search engines have been including Twitter and Facebook links and activities in search engine rankings, the practice was not confirmed until December 2010. Because search engines typically guard the proprietary algorithms they use to rank search results, most search engine optimization tactics are guesses based on performance analysis. Some of those tips for Twitter and Facebook content follow:

✔ Try to write the first 42 characters of your tweets with keywords in mind. These characters are included in your tweet's title tag and can be great for search engine optimization.

✔ Try to include keywords throughout your tweets and Facebook updates to make it easier for search engines to identify the contextual relevance of your short-form content.

✔ Try to get authoritative Twitter users (and Facebook users) as well as a wide audience to share your content. The more retweets your content gets, the better.

✔ Try to keep your tweets under 120 characters so they aren't truncated when they're retweeted.

Don't fall into the tempting trap of writing short-form content solely for search traffic. Search engine optimization should be secondary to publishing amazing, shareworthy short-form content that generates organic retweets and conversations. People won't read your short-form content, follow you, or share that content with their audiences if it reads like a list of keywords with no real value. In other words, don't negate your short-form marketing efforts by prioritizing search engine optimization above quality.

Abbreviating, Truncating, and Shortening Content the Right Way

As you can read in Chapters 9 and 10, it's often necessary to use abbreviations, break grammar rules, and trim your content in creative ways in order to stay within the character limitations of some short-form content publishing tools.

When you create short-form content, make sure the most important details, such as links and keywords, are included at the beginning of your content. Because many short-form content publishing tools have character limitations, the end of your content could get cut off when it is shared. This is common on Twitter where retweets append the username of the person who originally published the content at the beginning of the retweet, which often causes the end of the original tweet to disappear. You never want your most important information to get lost when your short-form content spreads across the Web. Therefore, think strategically when you create your shareworthy original short-form content, so it's ready for sharing, retweeting, and so on.

The following sections describe common ways to keep your short-form content at the right length.

Using abbreviations, acronyms, and symbols

Using abbreviations and acronyms saves space in short-form content. For example, you can use an ampersand instead of spelling the word *and,* which saves two characters. If you're writing a tweet that must be 140 characters or fewer, those extra two characters could be very important to you! The same can be said of shortening *okay* to *OK*. It's not something you would do in business writing, but it's perfectly acceptable for short-form content marketing.

Short-form content uses common text messaging and instant messaging abbreviations. Online audiences who consume (or publish) short-form content have grown accustomed to the use of abbreviations for brevity and to save space. Even Fortune 500 companies use abbreviations like LOL in Twitter updates!

Following are some of the most common text messaging and instant messaging acronyms that you're likely to see and use in short-form content:

- ✔ **AFAIK:** As far as I know
- ✔ **B4:** Before

- **BBL:** Be back later
- **BFN or B4N:** Bye for now
- **BRB:** Be right back
- **BTW:** By the way
- **CNP:** Continued in next post
- **HTH:** Hope this helps
- **IANAL:** I am not a lawyer (but)
- **IAW:** I agree with
- **IMO:** In my opinion
- **IOW:** In other words
- **ITA:** I totally agree
- **JK:** Just kidding
- **JMO:** Just my opinion
- **KWIM?:** Know what I mean?
- **L8R:** Later
- **LOL:** Laughing out loud
- **MTF:** More to follow
- **NRN:** No response necessary
- **OTOH:** On the other hand
- **OTTOMH:** Off the top of my head
- **RL:** Real life
- **ROTFL:** Rolling on the floor laughing
- **TA:** Thanks again
- **TIA:** Thanks in advance
- **TPTB:** The powers that be
- **TTYL:** Talk to you later
- **TU or TY:** Thank you
- **UW or YW:** You're welcome
- **WFM:** Works for me
- **WTG:** Way to go

Short-form content often includes characters that represent symbols. For example, a smiley face might be typed as :) to communicate a happy emotion in a piece of content. You're likely to see and use these symbols on Twitter,

Facebook, and other short-form content publishing sites, and users expect to see them.

Following are some of the most commonly used text symbols that are used in short-form content:

- ✔ :) or :-) = smiling
- ✔ :(or :-(= sad
- ✔ :o or :-o = surprise or shock
- ✔ :'(or :'-(= crying
- ✔ :D or :-D = laughing
- ✔ ;) or ;-) = winking
- ✔ <3 = love heart
- ✔ @ = at

You can find more acronyms, abbreviations, and symbols for short-form content by searching for "text messaging abbreviations" or "text messaging symbols" on Google or your preferred search engine.

Make sure the symbols and abbreviations you use in your short-form content accurately represent your brand and business, and make sure you know what an acronym or abbreviation means before you use it in an original piece of content or a shared piece of content. For example, you don't want to retweet a piece of content that includes an acronym without realizing the acronym stands for a phrase with a profanity in it. If you're unsure of the meaning of a symbol or acronym, do a quick Google search to find out its meaning before you use it or share it.

Shortening URLs

Another way to trim your short-form content is to shorten lengthy URLs. Not only does using a URL shortener, such as the ones listed in Chapter 9, allow you to save valuable real estate for your useful content, but Twitter and social networking audiences expect them. In fact, finding a URL that hasn't been shortened in a tweet is surprising to most Twitter users.

Following are the standard link lengths of the URL shorteners introduced in Chapter 9:

- ✔ **bit.ly:** 14 characters
- ✔ **Ow.ly:** 17 characters

- ✔ **SnipURL:** 13 characters
- ✔ **TinyURL:** 25 characters

Some URL shorteners allow you to customize your shortened URL, which can affect the final length.

For example, following is a link to the introduction of the section of the U.S. Code of Federal Regulations that explains how testimonials and endorsements can be used in business, which can affect content marketers who publish them: `http://ecfr.gpoaccess.gov/cgi/t/text/text-idx?c=ecfr&sid=eb13e096b2e45337f1076b3b8fcb792c&rgn=div5&view=text&node=16:1.0.1.2.22&idno=16#16:1.0.1.2.22.0.5.1`. That's a useful link, but it's extremely long! The complete link is 155 characters and wouldn't fit in a 140-character tweet. It would also be quite an eyesore in a Facebook update. Not only does a URL shortener make the link short enough to tweet, but it also looks better and leaves room for you to include more useful, original content with the link.

Tools and Tricks to Get More from Short-Form Content Marketing

You can also improve the performance of your short-form content by applying some fairly easy tricks to it and using a variety of free tools to increase traffic to it. For example, as discussed in Chapter 9, using hashtags to identify your tweets as being related to a specific keyword topic can help people find your content while they search for content of interest to them. Similarly, making your Twitter, Facebook, LinkedIn, and other profiles public can increase the traffic to them significantly because more people can see your content and it might appear in search engine results. A private profile can't help your business when it comes to short-form content marketing.

It's important that you take the time to create complete profiles. Make sure your Twitter, Facebook, LinkedIn, and other online profiles are comprehensive and include keywords, links to your Web site and other branded online destinations, as well as any other information that can help people find you and take a closer look at what you have to say when they do find you.

You should also spend time connecting with other people and building relationships with them on your various profiles. As mentioned earlier in this chapter, Google and Bing count social authority in search engine rankings, so the more diverse followers you connect with, particularly people who already have authoritative reputations, and the more people that retweet and share your content, the better.

Search engines crawl the About box in your Facebook profile and Page (that's the box that appears in the upper left side of your profile beneath your profile image as shown in Figure 11-1), so be sure to write that text with keywords in mind. To boost internal Facebook search traffic, make sure you write keyword-rich content in your profile information page and work to increase your friends.

You can use a variety of tools to boost the chances that people will find your short-form content. For example, many Twitter apps allow you to find conversations to join and allow other people to find you based on interests and expertise. Because most Twitter apps are free to use, it's worth trying them!

Figure 11-1: Include keywords in the content of your Facebook Page's About box.

The About box

In addition to the Twitter apps introduced in Chapter 9, following are a number of easy-to-use Twitter apps that can help improve the exposure of your short-form content:

- ✔ **BackTweets:** Available at `http://backtweets.com`, BackTweets enables you to track and analyze your Twitter performance with information about your tweets, links, reach, influencer profiles, and more.

- ✔ **TweetReach:** At `http://tweetreach.com`, you can enter a URL, Twitter name, phrase, or hashtag and get reports about the reach and exposure for those tweets.

- ✔ **Twellow:** At `www.twellow.com`, you can create your own Twitter profile directory listing. Twellow is called the Yellow Pages of Twitter.

- ✔ **Twazzup:** At `www.twazzup.com`, you can enter keywords of your choice and track real time news related to those keywords as it's published.

- ✔ **Topsy:** Available at `http://topsy.com`, you can enter keywords to search the social Web for conversations people are having about a specific domain, page, term, or topic.

- ✔ **Retweetist:** At `http://retweetist.com`, you can find out what tweets Twitter users are retweeting at any given time.

- ✔ **Tweepz.com:** At `http://tweepz.com`, you can enter keywords of your choice to track conversations and offer content as appropriate. An advanced search feature enables you to search for more specific results.

- ✔ **TweetScan:** Available at `http://tweetscan.com`, TweetScan allows you to enter keywords of your choice and get real-time updates. You can see who is tweeting about topics of interest to you and what they're saying about those topics.

- ✔ **TweetBeep:** Available at `http://tweetbeep.com`, TweetBeep allows you to enter keywords and receive e-mails automatically when tweets are published with those keywords.

No Twitter app is perfect, so it's good to use a combination of tools as well as your common sense while you tweak your short-form content marketing tactics.

The most successful short-form content marketing efforts are fully integrated into a business' overall marketing plan, and cross-promotion is a crucial element of that success. In Chapter 15, you discover more about marketing integration and cross-promotion. For now, understand that publishing your content doesn't guarantee that anyone will see it. Without integration and promotion, your content can only get a limited amount of exposure. However, your first step is to create amazing, shareworthy content, or that content won't have a chance at success no matter how much you cross-promote it.

Part IV

Engaging in Online Conversations to Share Content

In this part . . .

An important part of content marketing is the conversations that happen that are based on that content. Part IV shows you how you can start and join online conversations to drive brand awareness, word-of-mouth marketing, and real business growth.

Chapter 13 introduces a variety of tools you can use for conversational content marketing, such as blog comments, forum posts, and more. Be sure to read Chapter 14 to find out how to get the most out of your online conversations for both direct and indirect marketing purposes. This chapter also includes a number of tools and applications that can make your life as a conversational content marketer easier.

Chapter 12

Defining Conversational Content Marketing

Conversational content marketing is a critical component of your content marketing plan. It's also the part that most closely aligns with social media marketing efforts, but at the heart of conversational content marketing is always some form of original content from which conversations emerge or evolve.

This chapter shows you what conversational content marketing is and how to start your own conversational content marketing initiatives. Most importantly, you read about the primary objective of conversational content marketing: building relationships.

Understanding What Conversational Content Marketing Is

Conversational content marketing is exactly what the name implies: conversations that happen between a business and target audience based on content. In other words, content can be the catalyst that either starts a conversation or moves a conversation in a specific direction.

Conversational content marketing can be called an emergence or evolution tool because the content can start or modify a conversation.

Unlike social media marketing (including all forms of conversation and two-way dialogue that happen on the social Web to directly or indirectly market a business), conversational content marketing is always rooted in some form of content that causes a conversation to emerge or evolve.

The purpose of conversational content marketing is to build relationships with your target audience through interaction based on your amazing, share-worthy, long-form and short-form content. First, you provide useful original content; then you lead people to that content and talk about it. Together, the three forms of content marketing (long-form content marketing described in Part II, short-form content marketing described in Part III, and conversational content marketing described in Part IV) are very powerful and can tell a comprehensive, interesting, and meaningful story.

In time, your audience will turn to you for more of the same useful content and conversations and trust that you know what you're talking about. They'll share your trusted content with their audiences and seek out your content rather than content from other sources. Ultimately, they'll become loyal brand advocates who spread your content through word-of-mouth marketing, which helps you build your brand and your business. You can't buy that kind of exposure and it's primarily free, aside from a time commitment.

Jumpstarting Dialogue

The key to conversational content marketing is to find the people who are likely to be interested in your content and then deliver that content to them in a way that invites them to talk about it. Often this requires that you reach out to people before you even begin creating and sharing content with them.

Take some time to find out where your target audience already spends time online and join the conversations happening on those sites and destinations. This is where social media marketing plays an important role in content marketing. As you get to know those people better and your name becomes associated with useful conversations, you can start bringing those people to your branded online destinations where they can experience your long-form and short-form content.

For example, when you've built a reputation on a forum, Facebook group, or another blog, you can begin referring those people to your content on your branded online destinations. Provide links for people to read more on your blog, in your Twitter profile, and so on. Use conversational content marketing efforts to describe in a few words or sentences what you have to say in your long-form or short-form content, so people understand the potential usefulness of it, and provide a link so they can access it quickly and easily. This is a great way to use conversational content marketing as a tool for emerging conversations.

Similarly, you can jump into conversations that are already happening online and offer a summary of your valuable short-form or long-form content that could be useful to the conversation participants along with a link to read more. As long as you present your content as helpful and meaningful information rather than a marketing pitch, there is a good chance that people will click your link to see what you have to say. If you've already spent time developing relationships with the conversation participants by establishing your reputation through social media marketing efforts, the chances that those people will click your links and read your content are even greater.

You can jump into conversations that you stumble upon online where your short-form or long-form content can be useful, but if you don't already have a relationship with the conversation participants, it's less likely that they'll engage with you. It's imperative that your tone and style is perceived as helpful rather than sales-oriented in these situations.

For example, if you use a Twitter app like monitter (discussed in Chapter 9) to keep track of keywords used in tweets, you can jump into conversations with people you don't know using the @reply feature introduced in Chapter 9 and offer a link to a piece of your content that you think will be of value to that person. However, if you simply tweet a link to a person you don't know, that person will probably ignore it. Instead, you need to try to communicate why you're contacting that person and how your content can help. This can be challenging on a site like Twitter where you're limited to 140 characters, but it's important to consider or your conversational content will fall on deaf ears and not have a chance to do its job of driving people to your other content or branded online destinations.

Being Personable and Engaging

Your conversational content should read the way you speak while accurately representing your brand image. The name says it all: Conversational content should be *conversational*. Don't speak *at* people in your conversational content. Instead, speak *with* people and invite them to respond to you, offer their opinions, and provide more information where they can.

Conversational content should not only be engaging and interactive, but it also has to sound human. Your personality should be evident in your content inasmuch as it reflects your brand. No one wants to converse with someone who sounds like they're expounding corporate rhetoric or quoting the company handbook. Be real and be honest and more people will want to communicate with you.

You also need to be consistent. The type of information you provide and conversations you participate in must appropriately promote your brand. If your conversations are inconsistent, your audience will get confused and won't know what to expect from you. Just as spending time with people whose conversations are erratic can be awkward and confusing, conversing with people online whose behavior and discussions are unpredictable can be undesirable, too. Consistency builds brands and builds loyal followers of your conversations and content.

As with all your content marketing efforts, your conversational content marketing must not be completely self-promotional. Stick with the 80-20 split suggested for your long-form and short-form content marketing efforts (where at least 80 percent of the time you spend on conversational content marketing efforts is not self-promotional and 20 percent or less of your time is self-promotional.) People don't want to converse with an ongoing sales pitch or advertisement. Your conversation has to be interesting, useful, and personable, or just as people hang up on sales calls or turn the television channel when a commercial comes on, they'll avoid your conversational content.

Conversing and Sharing Content the Right Way

As mentioned earlier in this chapter, a critical component to successful conversational content marketing is remembering that it's a two-way street. No businesses have found success with conversational content marketing that was all about them. Remember, your customers and audience are always the most important element of your business, and that applies to your conversational content as well.

That means your audience's opinions, conversations, and content are more important than your own. If you want them to talk to you and about you and share your content with their audiences, then you have to do the same for them. Following are some easy ways you can converse with your audience and share their content so they know you're efforts are not one-sided:

- Visit their Facebook profiles, friend them, and comment on their Wall updates and photo uploads. Like the content that they publish on their profiles.
- Follow them on Twitter and retweet their content.

✔ Share their content on social bookmarking sites like Digg or StumbleUpon, as discussed in Chapter 13.

✔ Write blog posts about the content published on their blogs, ebooks, YouTube channels, and so on. Publish comments on their blogs.

✔ Tweet their blog posts, Flickr images, videos, and so on to your followers even if they didn't tweet it first. An example is shown in Figure 12-1.

The goal is to let your audience know that you think what they say is important, even in their content and conversations that occur away from your profiles and branded destinations. If you want other people to visit your blog and talk about your content, then you might have to do the same for them, particularly when it comes to engaging with and building relationships with online influencers who already have large audiences of followers and are very busy.

Finally, make sure that you share content following accepted guidelines based on the Web site you're using. For example, write a retweet in a specific way so the original publisher is notified that you retweeted. Chapter 13 provides tips for sharing content using specific online sites and tools to ensure your efforts aren't missed.

Figure 12-1: Tweeting another person's content is a great way to start a conversation.

Building Relationships

Of all your content marketing efforts, conversational content marketing presents the biggest opportunity to build valuable relationships with online influencers and your target audience. When you develop relationships with people, they're more likely to look at your content, share your content, converse with you, and talk about you. This holds true in all aspects of life, not just in your content marketing efforts.

Therefore, you must take the time to reach out to people and engage with them rather than passively waiting for them to find you. When you make a connection, you can't disappear or there is no chance for you to develop a relationship with that person. That's why publishing fresh content that gives you a reason to talk to people is important. Your content can answer questions, clear up confusion, provide warnings, show people how to do things, and so much more.

Continually offer useful content that adds value to people's lives. Read and talk about other people's content, too, and your content marketing plan will achieve a higher return on investment than it would if you simply published some content once in a while and left it at that.

Connecting with influencers

Finding people who are likely to have the attention of your target audience and the ability to make your target audience listen and act is an important part of your content marketing plan. Be prepared to spend time searching for these people. It's not always easy to find niche online influencers through search engines, Twitter searches, Twitter directory apps, and so on. Sometimes you won't find the best online influencers for your business and target audience until you spend some time publishing content and participating in the online conversation.

Look for mentions of people as experts or knowledgeable in products and services like your own. Follow links published by other people that lead to useful content and see who published that original content. Look at the people your competitors are connected to on Twitter, Facebook, and LinkedIn to see whether they're connected to people who could be online influencers in your industry.

Use the tools and apps suggested in Chapters 8 and 9 to find online influencers on Twitter, Facebook, and LinkedIn.

When you find online influencers who you want to connect with, visit their blogs and leave useful comments on their posts. Connect with them on Twitter and start communicating with them via retweets and @replies. Friend them on Facebook and like their content. The more you appear on their radar screens, the more likely they are to take a closer look at you to see what you have to say.

If online influencers like what you have to say, and the content you publish, they'll begin to interact with you. That interaction is the start of an important relationship that you have to nurture on an ongoing basis. If you're committed to that relationship, the time might come when you can reach out to that online influencer and ask for help spreading a piece of content. In other words, the time you spend nurturing relationships with online influencers today could deliver big rewards in the future.

Whatever you do, don't send mass e-mails to online influencers or speak to them in a manner that can do more harm than good. For example, I receive e-mail messages all the time from bloggers who tell me I should exchange links with them because it can help my search engine rankings to get an incoming link from their blogs. This type of message tells me immediately that the sender spent no time learning about me before they sent a copy of a blanket e-mail to me. Suffice it to say, these messages are deleted instantly.

Bottom line, research online influencers before you communicate with them, so your conversations make it clear that you know who that influencer is and what that person does. Why should someone care about you are or take the time to learn about you if you don't do the same?

Developing a band of brand advocates

Conversational content marketing is extremely effective in helping you build your band of brand advocates who will help you spread your content across the Web. Branding theory says that *consumers* build brands, not companies. Brands are built based on consumer perceptions of them, which are created because of the brand image, message, and promise.

As consumers experience brands and develop expectations for them, the brand grows. If a brand meets customer expectations for it repeatedly, consumers begin to rely on that brand and trust it. That trust can lead to brand loyalty where a customer chooses that brand over all others and seeks that brand out even if they have to travel distances or spend more time to get it.

Loyal customers talk about the brands they love, and they defend those brands against naysayers. Word-of-mouth marketing is one of the most powerful forms of marketing, because research shows again and again that consumers trust the opinions of other consumers (even strangers) more than they trust advertising and marketing communications. That's why developing a band of brand advocates who talk about your brand, share your content, and defend your brand is so valuable. Brand advocates have the power to influence their audiences simply because they talk about the brands they love. They're not paid to talk about those brands. They actually want to do it.

When that brand advocacy occurs online, your business benefits not just from positive publicity, but also from increased search engine ranking, more incoming links to your content that bring more traffic, and a boost in exposure that costs little but can deliver big rewards. For example, individuals and businesses that have created bands of brand advocates can see their tweets retweeted hundreds of times, which brings significant exposure to that individual or business' content.

Developing a band of brand advocates comes from consistently and persistently publishing amazing, shareworthy content, engaging in useful conversations, being accessible, being human, and remembering that it's not all about you. You must always listen to your audience, find out what they want from you, and deliver that kind of content and conversations. Strive to meet their expectations for your content and brand, so they're motivated to keep talking about you and sharing your content.

Always acknowledge your audience and make sure they understand that each person is important to you. In time, your band of brand advocates will grow and your content will spread even further. That's how the power of conversational content marketing can take your business to new heights of success.

Chapter 13

Introducing the Tools of Conversational Web Writing

Chapter 12 defines conversational content marketing as the conversations that happen between businesses and target audiences based on content. In other words, content is the catalyst to conversations. In this chapter, you discover many of the tools you can use to effectively participate in online conversations that promote your business both directly and indirectly.

Just as you speak with people in face-to-face situations, you can speak with them online, from the comfort of your own home or office. With the widespread availability of smart phones, you can converse with people on the Web from anywhere and at any time. For your brand and business to grow through conversational content marketing, you just have to start talking virtually!

Commenting on Blogs

Blogs are an excellent tool for long-form content marketing. You can create your own blog and publish a wide variety of amazing, shareworthy content to drive awareness of your branded online destination, attract larger audiences to it, and jump-start conversations on and off the Web. However, there is more to blogging than publishing long-form content. Blogs also offer an amazing opportunity for conversational content marketing through a handy feature known in the world of blogging as *commenting*.

When you use blogs for social media marketing and content marketing, you want to provide a public commenting feature, which allows anyone who reads a post on those blogs to publish a comment about the post. Comments appear at the end of a blog post and typically appear in chronological order with the most recent comment published at the bottom of the list of comments (although some blogs do allow threaded comments, so individual comments and specific replies are published together making it easier to follow conversations). Figure 13-1 shows an example of blog comments published on a blog post.

Figure 13-1:
Comments appear at the end of a blog post.

Think of it this way — if your blog posts are the heart of your blog, then blog comments are the veins and arteries carrying blood to and from the heart so that it can live, breathe, and grow. Blogs that lack conversations offer limited growth potential because people innately want to talk about the topics that interest them and the ideas that they agree or disagree with. Blog comments allow them to do exactly that.

You can use blog comments in two distinct ways as part of your conversational content marketing efforts:

✔ You can write and publish comments on other people's blogs.

✔ You can allow people to write and publish comments on your blog and to respond to those comments.

It's true that blog comments can also be used as a tool to share links to other long-form and short-form content marketing. In short, consider blog comments an essential part of your content marketing plan, because quick comments can affect your brand or business success significantly.

Writing useful comments

As with all forms of content marketing, the success of conversational content marketing depends on the usefulness of the content you convey in those conversations. For example, a simple comment that says "Great post!" and nothing else isn't useful. In fact, the blog owner and other readers of the blog will ignore such a comment because it doesn't add value to the conversation happening around the content of the post. Even worse, the comment could be deleted entirely or flagged as spam, as discussed in the next section.

If you're not taking the time to write useful and meaningful comments, you're wasting your time. This doesn't mean, however, that you need to write a five paragraph comment. On the contrary, make your comments concise but with substance. Rather than simply writing "Great post!" add some details about why you think it's a great post and why you agree (or disagree, as the case may be).

You can also support your opinions by including a link to a useful piece of content you published elsewhere online. Adding a supporting link to a blog comment can add even more to the conversation and lead people to your branded online destinations where you can deepen conversations and relationships with them, as discussed later in this chapter. However, remember that the value of your comment comes from what you type in the blog comment, not from links to your site. The last thing you want is for people to view your comments as self-promotional or spam because they're filled with links to your own sites.

Try to include no more than one link in any blog comment you publish. Many blogging applications are configured to hold comments with more than one link in them for moderation or to automatically flag those comments as spam.

The same is true about the words you write in your comments. The 80-20 rule of content marketing, where at least 80 percent of the content (in this case, the conversations) you publish is *not* self-promotional and no more than 20 percent *is* self-promotional, applies to blog comments, too. Value and usefulness should always supersede self-promotion.

As you write blog comments, always consider the audience likely to be reading the blog where those comments will be published. Once a comment is published, you can't delete it. You need to tailor the content, the tone and voice, and the formatting of your comments to match the blog's audience as well as your brand promise. Blog posts can spread far across the Internet very quickly as people share links via Twitter and Facebook, write about those posts on their own blogs, and so on. In other words, you never know who might stumble upon your blog comments and judge you, your brand, and your business based on those comments. Think before you type!

If you write blog comments with the idea that you're joining a conversation (just as you would do in an in-person situation) and massage your comments to match the venue and audience (just as you would do in person), you should be able to confidently publish comments on blog posts that can help build awareness and recognition of your branded online destinations.

Avoiding spam tactics

Blog comment spam is growing quickly as Web site owners pursue link-building tactics to boost their own search engine rankings. In simplest terms, search engine optimization experts believe that Google and other search engines rank keyword search results in part based on how many incoming links come to a specific Web page. The assumption is that if a Web page is useless, no one will link to it. Therefore, pages with more incoming links, particularly pages with links from highly authoritative and popular sites, rank higher in keyword search results than similar pages with fewer incoming links.

In order to trick the search engine algorithms and get higher search engine rankings for specific keyword searches, some site owners pay companies or individuals to publish comments on many blogs to increase those incoming links. The comment writers either include the link with a specific keyword phrase within the comment form (in the Name and URL fields) or they include the link within the actual comment text. Either way, if the comment doesn't add value to the conversation happening on that blog post, it could be considered spam.

Following are several common types of blog comment spam that you want to avoid, either by writing on other blogs or by publishing on your own blog:

- ✓ **Gibberish comments:** Comments that are all or mostly written with symbols or text you can't understand are most likely spam.

- ✓ **Link-filled comments:** Comments filled with links either within the comment or at the end of the comment are usually spam.

- ✓ **Excessively complimentary comments:** Comments from random people that are overly complimentary, such as, "great info, keep up the amazing work that you do," are often spam.

- ✓ **Nice post comments:** Comments that say little more than "nice post" or similar acknowledgments are most likely spam.

- ✓ **Random character trio comments:** Comments that include three random characters at the end of the comment (such as *,~) are almost always spam.

The last thing you want is to spend a great deal of time writing comments on a variety of blogs only to have those comments flagged as spam and deleted. Similarly, you don't want your own blog to be filled with published spam comments, because they damage the user experience on your blog. Therefore, it's important that you take the time to write and publish useful comments that add value to the conversations happening across the blogosphere.

Leveraging comment form fields

Comment form fields like the one shown in Figure 13-2 provide at least three text boxes for you to complete when you submit a comment on a blog. These fields are where you can include your brand name and link as well as your valuable conversational content, so use them wisely.

Figure 13-2:
Always
complete
the
comment
form fields.

Comments

Got something to say?

Name (required)

Email Address (required)

Website

Speak your mind

Submit Comment

Some blogs might use special plug-ins and features that provide additional text boxes in the comment form field. For example, you might see a field to enter your Twitter ID. As part of your content marketing efforts, always provide as much information as possible when you're commenting on a blog. Comment forms typically have the following fields:

- ✔ **A Name field:** Keep in mind that you don't necessarily have to enter your personal name in this field. Instead, make sure that the name you enter in the name field is the best one for your search engine optimization efforts (to read more about search engine optimization, refer to Chapter 7). For example, your business name, a brand name, or your personal name might be the keyword term that you want to optimize for search across the Web. Always use the same name in the name field of all blog comment forms to maximize search traffic potential.

- ✔ **An Email Address field:** Enter your e-mail address. Only the blog administrator can see your e-mail address, so enter the e-mail address where you want the blog owner or person who moderates comments for the blog to reach you if they want to speak with you privately for any reason. Keep in mind, if you enter a fake e-mail address, the moderator could view your comment as spam, which means it won't be published.

- ✔ **A Website field:** This is the field where you can insert the specific URL you want people to arrive at after clicking your name in the published blog comments section of the post you're commenting on. As a rule, use the URL for your core branded online destination in this field. Because you're leaving a comment on a blog, it's best to provide your blog's URL in the URL field, but the URL really depends on your business and social Web presence. Your goal is to send people to the branded destination through this URL where they can continue the conversation with you, get more information from you, and build a deeper relationship with you. So, in this field, put the URL that will help you meet your goals.

- ✔ **A Comment text box:** Finally, the text box where you can enter your actual comment is included at the end of the comment form. Some comment forms allow you to use some HTML in the text box, which is usually noted beneath the text box. Depending on the special plug-ins or tools a blogger uses, you may have the opportunity to preview your comment before publishing it. Most importantly, use this text box to write interesting and useful content — with no more than one link to avoid automated spam filters, and try not to be self-promotional.

Very few blogs offer the ability to delete a comment once you submit it for publication. Therefore, always make sure you are absolutely satisfied with your comment before you click the Submit button.

Staying in the conversation

While it's good to submit a useful comment to a blog post, it's even better if you can stay in the conversation happening on that blog post as more comments are published by other people. Leaving comments on other blogs can be time-consuming, especially if you have to continually visit a specific blog post to see if someone responded to your comment or added a comment that you'd like to respond to.

Fortunately, some bloggers use plug-ins and tools that make it a bit easier to stay involved in conversations happening through comments. Look for a Subscribe to Comments check box or an option to subscribe to the blog's comments RSS feed. Both options automate the process to keep up with new comments that are published on the blogs. For example, the WordPress.org Subscribe to Comments plug-in (`http://wordpress.org/extend/plugins/subscribe-to-comments`) allows you to receive an e-mail message each time a new comment is published on a blog post that you subscribe to.

On the flip side, if your blogging application allows, provide ways for visitors to your blog to stay involved in comment conversations by offering an option to subscribe to comments. Furthermore, *you* need to stay involved in the conversations happening on your blog. If someone submits a comment to one of your blog posts, acknowledge that person by responding to his or her comment with a comment of your own.

As your blog grows in popularity, you won't be able to respond to every comment. However, as the community of people reading and commenting on your blog posts grows, they'll begin responding to each other and making your blog a truly interactive and conversational online destination. That's the ultimate objective of conversational content marketing on your blog.

Using an avatar

Avatars are self-identifying images that people upload using a tool like Gravatar (`www.gravatar.com`). When you upload your own image, your avatar appears next to your comments on all blogs that allow them, as shown in Figure 13-3.

Avatars are a great way to make your comments seem more human and further build relationships with people online. Instead of simply recognizing you from your name, people can also recognize you by your face or image. Your avatar is connected to the e-mail address you use when you create the avatar with Gravatar. Therefore, be sure to always use the same e-mail address in blog comment form e-mail fields to ensure your avatar displays with your comment.

Make sure that the avatar image you choose appropriately represents your brand and that you can use it in all your conversational content marketing activities. By using a single avatar, you can build a sense of brand consistency that helps your audience develop expectations for your brand. In other words, your avatar can become an important tangible representation of your brand.

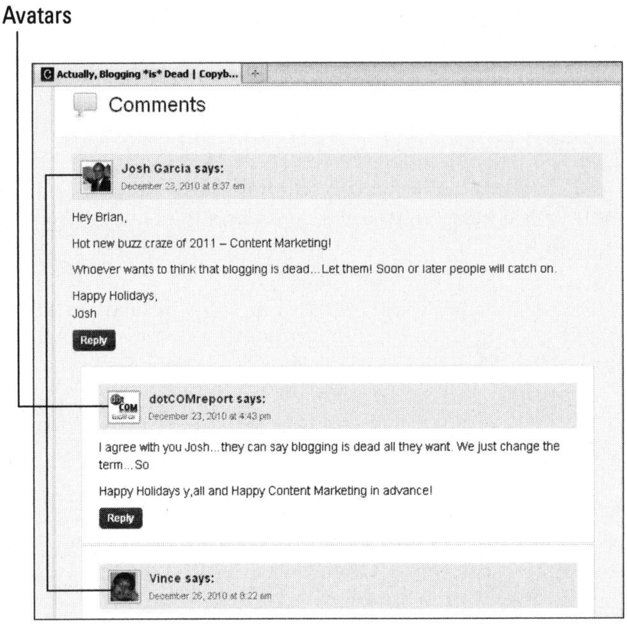

Avatars

Figure 13-3:
Avatars add
a face or
image to a
blog
comment.

Boosting comments on your blog

The vast majority of people who read your blog will be passive participants, meaning they won't leave comments. They might share your content, but they'll do so quietly. Getting your blog visitors to join the conversation by leaving comments on your blog posts can be difficult. Without comments on your blog, there's neither interaction nor a way to supplement your long-form content marketing efforts with conversational content marketing efforts.

You can use many tricks to increase comments on your blog posts. The options you choose to pursue should match your brand promise and your overall content marketing plan. Following are several suggestions to increase comments on your blog posts:

✔ **Ask for them:** At the end of your blog posts, ask readers to share their opinions by leaving a comment.

✔ **Get controversial:** Nothing gets people talking better than controversy. Play devil's advocate in your blog post, and readers might just come out of the woodwork and join the conversation.

✔ **Plant seeds:** You can seed your own blog discussions by publishing comments using a pseudonym or asking friends and family to publish comments. However, don't do this excessively because some visitors might view it as a deceptive practice.

✔ **Make it easy to subscribe:** Use a plug-in or tool (depending on your blogging application) that enables readers to subscribe to comments on your blog posts.

✔ **Respond:** Acknowledge people who publish comments on your blog and make them feel valued by responding to their comments with your own comments.

Publishing a comment policy

As your blog and the conversations happening on your blog grow, you may find people getting into heated debates that could turn ugly. You may also encounter *trolls* (people who leave comments for no other purpose but to incite your regular readers' ire). For these reasons, it's important to publish a comment policy on your blog.

Conversational content marketing should help your business, not promote inappropriate behavior. By publishing a comment policy, visitors to your blog can understand what is and isn't acceptable when commenting on your blog posts. Following is a sample blog comment policy, which you can tweak to fit your content marketing goals:

At their sole discretion, blog owners can edit or delete the following types of comments:

- Comments deemed to be spam or possible spam

- Comments including profanity

- Comments containing language or concepts that could be considered offensive or hateful

- Comments that attack an entity or person

- Comments that are irrelevant

Blog owners reserve the right to edit or delete any comments submitted to this blog without notice. This comment policy is subject to change at any time.

The preceding comment policy was not written by an attorney, so be sure to consult with your own legal advisor to develop the most appropriate policies and disclaimers for your blog and other branded online destinations.

Conversing on Twitter

Twitter is not only an excellent tool for short-form content marketing (refer to Chapter 9 for more on using Twitter for short-form marketing purposes), it's also perfect for conversational content marketing. Twitter offers a variety of features that enable users to converse directly either publicly or privately. There are even ways to speak with a group of people on Twitter.

The best part about conversational content marketing via Twitter is that it doesn't have to take a lot of time. You can find Twitter apps that make it extremely easy to join or start conversations at any time and from anywhere. This section shows you how to engage with other people conversationally on Twitter to grow your brand and business.

You cannot edit a tweet after you publish it. If you publish a tweet that you regret, your only recourse is to delete it. Even if you delete a tweet minutes after you publish it, that tweet could already be republished by content aggregators and syndicators. Depending on the timing, Google may have already indexed your tweet making it available through keyword searches for a short time. You never know where your online content could end up. Therefore, be careful what you tweet!

Using hashtags

Hashtags are keywords preceded by the # sign (refer to Chapter 9 for more on hashtags). They are used to informally group tweets that are related to a specific topic. Many Twitter users conduct hashtag searches to find tweets that interest them. Therefore, be sure to use hashtags in your tweets so that people can find them.

Similarly, you can use hashtags to connect conversations among Twitter users either formally in a tweet chat (discussed in the "Participating in Tweet Chats" section, later in this chapter) or as an informal conversation. You can even use hashtags to tie your own series of tweets together. For example, because tweets can be no more than 140 characters, you may need to publish a series of tweets to make a point. However, you might publish unrelated tweets in between that series of tweets. No problem! Just use the same hashtag in each tweet within the series.

Twitter applications like TwitLonger (www.twitlonger.com) enable you to tweet more than 140 characters, but sometimes you need to publish multiple related tweets at different times of the day. That's where hashtags are incredibly useful.

Retweeting other users' updates

The retweet feature in Twitter allows you to republish another Twitter user's update in your own Twitter stream with the click of the Retweet link, as shown in Figure 13-4. When you retweet a Twitter update, the update is republished on your Twitter stream preceded by RT @username, where @username is replaced by the Twitter ID belonging to the original publisher of the update you retweeted.

Retweeting another Twitter users' updates offers you two benefits:

✔ You can share useful information with your own Twitter followers.

✔ You can get on the original publisher's radar screen (who is likely to appreciate that you shared his content, because doing so gives him more exposure).

Because RT @username precedes your retweets, the original publishers will see your retweets within their Twitter profile lists of retweets, which they can access through their Twitter accounts. When you retweet other people's updates, you aren't giving them only pats on the back for publishing great content, but you're also taking a step toward build relationships with them. In time, they may start retweeting your content and putting it in front of a larger audience, too.

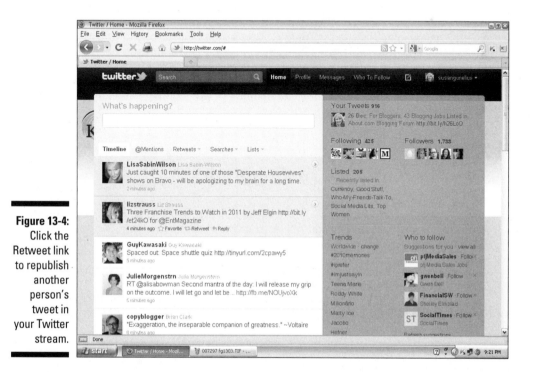

Figure 13-4:
Click the Retweet link to republish another person's tweet in your Twitter stream.

Think of retweets as an introduction to another Twitter user. Using retweets is a first step toward engaging that person in direct conversations through @replies and direct messages on Twitter.

Using @replies to build relationships

If retweets are virtual introductions, then @replies are the conversations that happen after those introductions. An @reply is either an indication that a tweet is meant to speak directly to another Twitter user (if it appears at the beginning of a tweet) or an indication that another Twitter user is mentioned in the tweet and is part of the conversation.

For example, if you wanted to tell me that you like this book publicly on Twitter, you could write a tweet that says, "@susangunelius I'm reading and learning a lot from Content Marketing For Dummies."

Because your tweet includes my username as an @reply, the tweet will appear in my list of @replies in my Twitter account. When I see your tweet, I'm likely to respond publicly to it. Not only do we share a conversation this way, but both of our audiences see who we are and what we're talking about. They might want to share our tweets with their own followers through the retweet feature or join the conversation through the @reply feature. We could continue the conversation back and forth through @replies.

Years ago, this type of conversation would have happened privately via instant messaging or e-mail only among people who knew each other's instant messaging handles or e-mail addresses, but today, it can happen publicly on Twitter, which gives all participants greater exposure to larger audiences and helps to build relationships between participants. In marketing terms, this level of broad reach is a gold mine that businesses would be crazy to ignore!

Responding to @replies

You need to frequently review your @replies through your Twitter account and respond to them. To do so, simply log into your Twitter account and make sure you're on your profile's home page. Then click the @Mentions link at the top of your Twitter timeline, as shown in Figure 13-5.

You can then scroll through the list of tweets mentioning your @username. From this page, you can easily reply to or retweet any of the tweets listed. It's important to go through your @replies at least once a day so that your responses are timely and make sense to other users. For example, if you wait a week to reply to an @reply, your response may not make much sense to the other person.

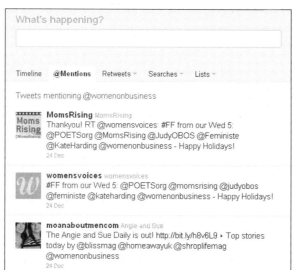

Figure 13-5:
Access your
@replies
from your
Twitter
account
home page.

Think of @replies as telephone messages or e-mail messages. The person who tweeted an update with your @username in it meant to say something to you or acknowledge you in some way. You wouldn't ignore a telephone call or e-mail for a week, and you shouldn't ignore an @reply for that long either.

That said, don't feel like you must respond to every single @reply. Use your best judgment as you review your list of mentions and be sure to respond to those that are appropriate for you to continue the conversation. For example, as you get more followers, you could get thousands of @replies each day. No one can respond to all of those. If someone simply retweets a link that you tweeted, you don't have to clog up their Twitter streams with thank you tweets. In other words, if your tweet response will add more clutter than value, then the intended recipient might not appreciate the intrusion at all. This is where your best social judgment is critical to your Twitter success. You don't want to be a nuisance to your followers.

Sending direct messages

You can also make your conversational content marketing efforts private on Twitter using the direct messaging feature. When you send direct messages to other Twitter users (you must be following another user in order to send a direct message to the user), they receive your message in a private inbox in their Twitter account. They can respond privately to your message if they choose to.

You can't send a direct message to people who don't follow you on Twitter. Likewise, another Twitter user can't send a direct message to you unless you are following that person.

The best content marketing plan is a fully integrated marketing plan, which means your online and offline content marketing efforts as well as all your other marketing initiatives need to work together for maximum success. Just because a direct message doesn't appear on the open Web doesn't mean it's not an important part of conversational content marketing. Your goal remains the same — to build relationships, build your brand, and build your business. Twitter direct messages can help you achieve those goals.

Not only do you work to make sure your direct message conversations are high in quality and help you grow your business, but also you want to lead participants to your branded online destinations whenever possible to deliver more of your content and to deepen relationships. Only so much can be said and done via a Twitter direct message. Providing people with various ways to find your content, so they can self-select how they engage with you is an essential part of your content marketing strategy.

Participating in tweet chats

Tweet chats are usually prearranged conversations that happen on Twitter among multiple users. You link tweets involved in the tweet chat using a specific hashtag; in this way, participants can keep up with the ongoing, real-time conversation.

A variety of tools can make arranging and participating in tweet chats easier. For example, you can use Eventbrite (www.eventbrite.com) or TicketLeap (www.ticketleap.com) to schedule tweet chats and manage RSVPs. When it comes time for your tweet chat, you can use a tool like TweetChat (www.tweetchat.com) to manage the entire process. Tools like Twazzup (www.twazzup.com) and TweetDeck (www.tweetdeck.com) make it a bit easier to follow tweets using specific hashtags. With Twazzup, you can follow and tweet about a specific hashtag in real time without being distracted from any unrelated tweets. Alternately, TweetDeck, a Twitter account management tool, allows you to follow and tweet from your desktop where you can follow and publish tweets related to a specific hashtag while doing other Twitter activities at the same time.

Some tweet chats happen spontaneously. Twitter users may stumble upon a tweet with a hashtag that interests them, or they could be conducting a keyword search using a tool like monitter (www.monitter.com) and find a related hashtag. Because tweet chats typically happen among public Twitter profiles (although private tweet chats can happen among groups of users with private profiles who follow each other), anyone can join the conversation at anytime.

That's another way Twitter can introduce people to each other through engaging dialogue, and it demonstrates how using Twitter for conversational content marketing can lead to indirect word-of-mouth marketing.

Facebook and LinkedIn also offer event-planning tools that you can use to schedule a tweet chat.

Using Social Networks for Conversations

Social networks like Facebook and LinkedIn offer some of the best options for conversational content marketing that can truly build relationships. Because social networks are typically more closed than blogs and microblogging, the conversations that happen on profiles, pages, and groups are often in-depth ones and can last for a long time.

Unlike a blog or Twitter feed that is updated frequently with new content and pushes older conversations deeper into archives, social networks allow individual users to converse on each other's profiles, thereby bringing old conversations front and center for participants. And because participants are typically automatically notified (depending on an individual's profile settings) when a conversation they're involved in is updated, it's easy to stay involved for a longer period of time.

Furthermore, social networks allow users to include links, videos, pictures, and more in conversations. Multiple people can easily participate in the same conversation, whereas others can ignore conversations that don't interest them.

Conversing on profiles and pages

When you publish a comment on another social network user's profile or a social network page (for brands, businesses, and celebrities on Facebook), that comment appears in the user's update stream. That person might even receive an e-mail notification when someone starts a new conversation or continues an existing conversation. Typically, anyone else who is connected with that user can view and join the conversation.

Facebook users can also start conversations by leaving comments on photos and videos that people upload. Facebook users can even participate in games that can spark more conversations.

Because social networks are more private than Twitter profiles, you might find it tempting to share too much information in conversations. However, you never know where your social network conversations will appear online, even if they happen on private profiles. Therefore, keep your conversations appropriate for your brand image at all times.

When other people publish comments on your social network profiles, be sure to continue the conversation by responding to them. Also, be sure that your social network tone is conversational, personable, and (as the name infers) social. Remember that you're not using a social network to sell, although selling is an excellent indirect effect of social networks and conversational content marketing. Instead, you're using social networks as a networking tool, just as you would if you were networking at a live event. Social network conversations need to be rooted in getting to know people, building coveted relationships, and indirectly marketing your brand and business.

Discussing in groups

One of the biggest conversational content marketing opportunities available through social networks is the ability to interact with people in groups. Both Facebook and LinkedIn allow users to create groups that people with similar interests can join. The purpose of a group is to give people a place to discuss, share, and learn about specific topics of interest.

For example, I belong to LinkedIn groups for writers and marketers. The conversations that happen between group members are highly targeted to my interests. You can start and join groups related to your business and that your target audience members are likely to be a part of, which gives you another line of access to them.

The best groups are highly interactive. You can start conversations, participate in ongoing conversations, ask questions, share information, and so much more in a social networking group. With time and dedication, a social networking group can lead to new relationships, learning, and opportunities.

Furthermore, when you join social networking groups on a site like LinkedIn, you often get additional access to other members. While you can't send private messages to LinkedIn users to whom you're not connected, you can send private messages to anyone who belongs to the groups you're in regardless of your personal connections. That means you can start conversations with any other group member outside the group setting, giving you one more way to reach out to people and indirectly market your business through conversational content.

The key to success is being active, persistent, and consistent. Don't just start conversations, join conversations, too. Vary your conversations from educational to entertaining, and present yourself as a multi-faceted, interesting person and as an expert in your field, rather than only a content marketer. Group members need to believe that you're there for more than self-promotion.

Finding creative ways to converse

Conversational content marketing through social networks includes more than simply publishing comments on profiles, pages, and groups. With a bit of effort and thinking, you can find some creative ways to jump-start a dialogue with other people on social networks. Poke around the social networks you belong to and learn about the various tools and features available to you. You'll probably find that a variety of creative opportunities wait for your use.

LinkedIn Answers

For example, if you use LinkedIn, you definitely want to leverage LinkedIn Answers. To find Answers, sign into your LinkedIn account and from the navigation bar at the top of the page, click More; then select Answers from the drop-down list that appears.

When you're not logged into your LinkedIn account, you can read, but not ask or answer questions, by clicking LinkedIn Answers in the links at the bottom of the LinkedIn home page.

You can ask and answer questions on LinkedIn Answers, as shown in Figure 13-6. Some questions get dozens of answers, allowing people to connect with one another in a different way than standard LinkedIn connections provide.

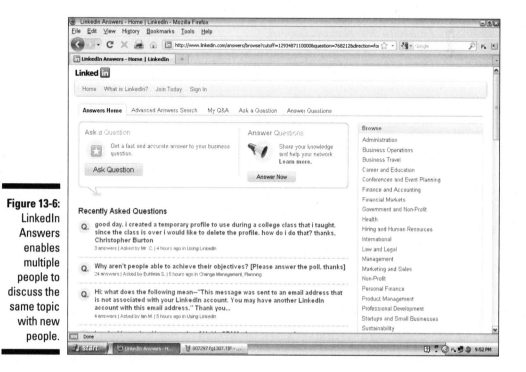

Figure 13-6: LinkedIn Answers enables multiple people to discuss the same topic with new people.

When multiple people answer the same question, a conversation can evolve. That conversation might continue through the Answers tool, or it could carry over to a LinkedIn profile, a group, private messages, or an external site. Because you don't have to be connected to other people to communicate with them through LinkedIn Answers, the tool is perfect for expanding your reach and networking with new people via LinkedIn.

Private messages

Don't forget that most social networks enable people who are connected to one another to communicate via private messages. These messages are similar to e-mail, but the communication is done through the messaging system within the social network. That means you can converse privately with anyone you're connected to on Facebook, LinkedIn, and other social networks, even if you don't know their e-mail address.

Because the most effective content marketing strategy is highly integrated, this type of private dialogue is very important. It can lead to deeper relationships and gives you the opportunity to steer people in the direction of your amazing content across your branded online destinations. Therefore, it's essential that you respond to the private messages you receive through your social networking profiles. They are just as important as traditional e-mail messages or in-person conversations. You never know where a conversation could lead, so treat each point of contact equally in terms of care and consideration.

LinkedIn Recommendations

At face value, writing recommendations about the people you're connected to on LinkedIn might seem very one-sided, but that's not the case at all. Typically, when you write a recommendation for someone, that person will reciprocate and write one about you. To write a recommendation, sign into your LinkedIn account and from the navigation bar at the top of the page, click Profile and select Recommendations from the drop-down list that appears. On the Recommendations page, shown in Figure 13-7, you can select a person and write your recommendation. It's that easy.

This type of indirect conversation is highly important to your conversational content marketing success. Talking *about* other people is just as important as talking *with* other people. That's because any type of content can lead to new conversations and introduce you to larger audiences. You need to be creative in thinking about new ways to jump-start conversations online, and writing recommendations on LinkedIn is a great way to do it.

Figure 13-7:
Writing
recommen-
dations is
a great way
to jump-
start a
conversation.

Adding tabs and features

Most social networks offer extra features that you can add to your social network profile, group, or page to open the doors to additional conversations.
These features may enable you to share your presentations or videos, or they
may allow you to spread the word about events and promotions. Any time
you can offer content that can lead to conversations, you want to do so.

Extra Facebook features are available through tabs and applications. Extra
LinkedIn features are available through applications.

If you use Facebook for content marketing purposes, then you should consider using the following applications to pique other users' interests and to
begin a dialogue:

- **SlideShare:** Share your presentations using the SlideShare tab.

- **Video:** Publish your videos on Facebook with the Video tab.

- **Events:** Spread the word about your online and offline events with the
  Events tab.

- **Promotions:** Announce your promotions with the Promotions tab.

For LinkedIn users, the following applications can help you begin conversations with your connections:

- ✔ **SlideShare:** Use the SlideShare application to publish your presentations.
- ✔ **Events:** Tell your connections about your upcoming events with the Events application.
- ✔ **Polls:** Gather market research with the Polls application.

Don't forget to automate processes that can start conversations. For example, feed your blog content and Twitter stream to your Facebook and LinkedIn profiles (refer to Chapter 8 for more on feeding blog and Twitter content to your Facebook and LinkedIn profiles).

As long as the content you're sharing on your social networking profiles, pages, and groups is useful to your target audience, it can be a catalyst to conversation. Just as your offline relationships grow from small talk, so do your online relationships. Give people something to talk to you about, and you're on the path to conversational content marketing success.

Communicating on Forums

You can find an online forum (also referred to as a bulletin board or a message board) on almost any subject. The purpose of a forum is to bring a group of people together to discuss a specific topic. Members have their own account that enables them to publish posts where they can ask questions or respond to other members' posts. Some forums are private (or partially private), allowing only members to see the posts and conversations, while other forums are completely open. The owner of the forum determines the level of openness of that forum.

Because the purpose of online forums is for people to communicate, it makes sense that forums should be a vital part of your conversational content marketing plan. When you find forums that your target audience is likely to spend time on, join those forums and get involved in the conversations happening there. Remember to publish useful content, be personable, and avoid self-promotion, and you'll find yourself building relationships with new people and increasing awareness of your brand and business.

Joining forums

When you find a forum you want to join, such as the forum shown in Figure 13-8, take some time to create a comprehensive profile. If people enjoy your content and conversations on the forum, they'll want to know who you are (particularly when you're a new member) so that they can evaluate the credibility and usefulness of your comments. To learn more about you, they may go to your Web site by clicking the links you include in your profile. As they communicate with you over time on the forum, they may return to your Web site via the links in your profile to deepen their relationships with you.

Make sure that your member profile is public and that the functions enabling you to receive e-mail from other members are activated. It's important that other members can contact you for more conversations via private message through the forum or via your e-mail account. Open the doors to conversations in as many places and in as many ways as possible.

When you join a forum, take some time to read through the conversations (referred to as *threads*) happening there. Analyze what gets people talking, what people like, and what they don't like. Click through to view profiles of the most active members and get to know who the moderators are. (*Moderators* are the designated leaders of a forum.) Also, look for forum rules and make sure you fully understand and follow them at all times.

When your primary research is completed and you have a good idea of how the forum operates, join the conversation. Respond to existing, current threads and offer meaningful, insightful information so other members understand that you have something useful to add. Don't be tempted to join arguments. Instead, ensure that your participation is always reflective of your brand promise.

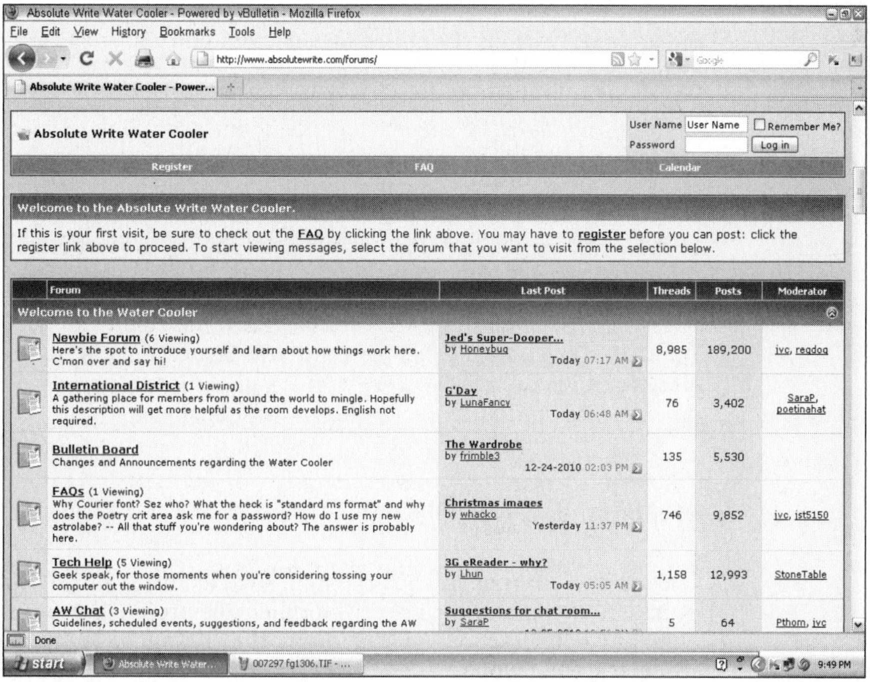

Figure 13-8:
Forums are made up of subtopic folders containing numerous discussion threads.

After you've spent some time participating in existing conversations, you can start your own by posting a new comment thread. Asking a question is a great way to start a conversation. Just be sure to search the forum before you do so to confirm the question you're asking hasn't already been asked and answered on the forum recently or repeatedly. Long-time members can get annoyed when a new member asks a question that has been rehashed time and again on the forum. Furthermore, make sure you post your new thread in the appropriate topic subfolder within the forum.

You can use handy forum tools to subscribe to threads that interest you so that you can easily reenter conversations that matter to you. When new comments are published on a thread you're subscribed to, you'll receive an e-mail notification message. You can also reach out to other members via private messages. Depending on the forum you belong to, features and functionalities can vary, so take the time to poke around and learn what tools and options are available to you to start and join conversations.

Creating your forum signature

A highly useful tactic to enhance your conversational content marketing success on forums is creating a great forum signature. A forum signature appears at the bottom of every comment you publish on the forum. Many people either don't use a forum signature at all or simply use their name as their signature. From a content marketing perspective, this is a huge lost opportunity. Your forum signature is the place where you can hype your brand and business for the entire forum community to see every time you publish a comment. Use it!

Your forum signature, at the least, needs to include a link to your core branded online destination. Don't simply use a link with anchor text that says, "My Web site." Instead, make the link seem useful to forum members. If you own an auto parts shop and you're a member of a Ford Mustang owners forum, use anchor text in your link that says something like, "Get ANY Mustang part with free shipping." You can see an example of a good forum signature in Figure 13-9.

While it can be tempting to fill your forum signature with links, it's better to stay focused and offer no more than three links. Too many links looks like spam. You don't want people to think that the only reason you participate in the forum is to get people to click through to your Web site and buy from you. Instead, in your forum signature, provide focused and targeted links for your business that match the forum members' wants and needs.

Of course, the links you provide might not lead to your Web site home page. They could lead people to a specific page or product listing on your Web site, or they could lead to your blog or your Twitter profile. The choice is yours and can change from one forum to another and from one time to another.

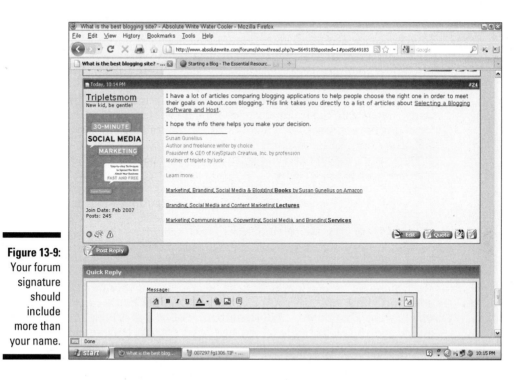

Figure 13-9:
Your forum
signature
should
include
more than
your name.

Most forum signatures allow you to use some HTML to provide links, images, and so on (images must be uploaded to a separate site before you can include them in your forum signature). The forum signature configuration page where you create your signature should explain the options available on that specific forum.

Uploading a forum avatar

As discussed earlier in this chapter, an *avatar* is an image that represents you online. Most forums allow you to upload an image to use as your forum avatar. This avatar displays with your forum member name on all the comments you publish. So, choose a forum avatar that consistently reflects your brand image.

If possible, use the same avatar across the Web so that the avatar you use on your blog matches the avatar you use on forums. Although there may be an instance in which a different avatar is more appropriate for a specific audience, brand consistency is usually best.

Some forums limit the types of files and sizes you can upload for your avatar. If that's the case in a forum you use, you can modify most images using a free image-editing tool such as Picnik (www.picnik.com).

At times, you may want to change your forum avatar. For example, it's not uncommon for a business to change an avatar when running a big promotion. When other members of the forum see the promotional avatar, they can click through to your member profile to find your Web site link where they can take advantage of the promotion.

Don't change your avatar until you've established your reputation on a forum. Again, you don't want members to think that you're there only for self-promotion. If you take the time to establish yourself as an integral member of the forum community, then your occasional promotional efforts will be better accepted.

Starting your own forum

If you can't find an existing forum dedicated to your topic of choice, start your own. A variety of free and inexpensive tools enable you to create a stand-alone forum or a forum that can be attached to your blog. Starting your own forum and growing the community on that forum can take a long time. You need to be very dedicated to promoting and driving traffic to your forum, and you also need to spend a lot of time moderating the forum to ensure that it works the way you want it to and that the community grows in the best way possible.

Creating your own forum is like creating another branded online destination for your business that's dedicated to conversational content and building relationships. Doing so offers an amazing opportunity, if you have the time and patience necessary to make it successful.

Don't try to start your own forum until you spend time on existing forums (even if those forums aren't directly related to your business) and gain an understanding of how forums work. Forums are a unique online destination, and you need to understand the dynamics of a forum community before you can successfully start one of your own.

When you're ready to start your own forum, check out the forum tools listed here and choose the tool that best meets your long-term goals:

- **phpBB:** phpBB (www.phpbb.com) is free and comes with a variety of deign choices so that you can brand your forum.

- **vBulletin:** If you're willing to spend some money on your forum, then vBulletin (www.vbulletin.com) is an excellent choice. It's feature-rich and customizable.

- **Simple:Press:** Simple:Press (http://simple-press.com) is a WordPress plug-in. It offers limited features, but the ease of integration and setup through WordPress makes it a popular forum choice.

> ✔ **bbPress:** bbPress (http://bbpress.org) was created by Automattic (the company behind WordPress), so it integrates easily with Word Press.org Web sites and blogs. bbPress doesn't offer the depth of features and customization that forum tools like vBulletin provide.

Your forum can be successful only if it's active, which means you must continually participate in conversations *and* promote the forum in order to boost membership. Forums can also be time-intensive because of spam. Many people use forums as a link-building tool, and sifting through spam comments and member accounts to ensure the user experience on the forum isn't damaged can take a lot of time and effort. Therefore, before you start your own forum, evaluate the amount of time you have to dedicate to it. Consider whom you might recruit to help you with moderation and participation. If you have the time and resources necessary to keep your forum active, then go for it!

Commenting on Other Forms of Social Media

Conversational content marketing can happen across the social Web. While blogs, Twitter, and social networks are likely the first places you think of when you consider two-way online conversations, many more options are available. Anywhere you can publish a comment along with other people is an opportunity for conversational content marketing.

Remember, a conversation doesn't have to be between two specific people. Group conversations are just as beneficial in terms of conversational content marketing as one-on-one conversations can be.

Videos

Online video is very popular. You can use a variety of sites to upload your own video content, respond to comments people post on your uploaded videos, or view and comment on other people's videos. As with all forms of conversational content marketing, the trick is to add value through your comments without directly self-promoting. A relationship lasts longer than a sales pitch, so view your conversational content marketing efforts as such to boost your long-term success.

You can search for videos by keywords related to your business on a multitude of video hosting and sharing sites, as well as on search engines like Google (http://video.google.com). Following are some of the online video sites you can browse:

- ✓ **YouTube:** www.youtube.com
- ✓ **TubeMogul.com:** www.tubemogul.com
- ✓ **blip.tv:** www.blip.tv
- ✓ **Dailymotion:** www.dailymotion.com
- ✓ **Viddler:** www.viddler.com
- ✓ **Vimeo:** www.vimeo.com

You have to create an account to post comments on most online video sites.

Also, take the time to subscribe to video channels related to your business and that your target audience will watch and connect with other users. Even the simple task of rating videos and marking videos in your list of favorites (on sites that allow ratings and favorites) can put you on other users' radar screens and open dialogues with them.

Social bookmark content

Conversational content marketing can also happen when short- or long-form content is shared via social bookmarking. Just as you bookmark your favorite Web pages using your browser so that they're easy to access later, you can bookmark Web pages using a social bookmarking site.

The benefits of social bookmarking are two-fold. First, you can access the Web pages you save via a social bookmarking site from any computer connected to the Internet because those pages are stored in your online account, not in your local desktop Web browser. Second, you can publicly bookmark Web pages using a social bookmarking site, which enables other users of that site to find your shared links and even to post comments on your shared links.

Different social bookmarking sites offer varied features, but most allow users to view other users' bookmarked (or shared) content, leave comments on that shared content, and add those bookmarks to their own lists of bookmarks. For example, Figure 13-10 shows a link to content that a user shared on Digg. As the image shows, other Digg users published comments on the shared link, and many users clicked the Digg icon that published with the submitted link to indicate they liked the shared video.

Popular social bookmarking sites include:

- ✓ **StumbleUpon:** www.stumbleupon.com
- ✓ **Digg:** www.digg.com
- ✓ **Delicious:** www.delicious.com

✔ **reddit:** www.reddit.com

✔ **Newsvine:** www.newsvine.com

✔ **Yahoo! Buzz:** http://buzz.yahoo.com

Many social bookmarking sites also allow you to connect with other users and become friends with them. This feature helps build a sense of community within a social bookmarking site. Friends can help draw attention to each other's bookmarks by commenting on and bookmarking one another's links. In other words, social bookmarking may seem like it's strictly a social media marketing tool, but the commenting feature makes social bookmarking a conversational content marketing opportunity, too.

Therefore, bookmark good content (not just your own) and comment on the content bookmarked by other people. Connect with other users who consistently share links that you and your target audience are interested in and comment on those links frequently. Review users' profiles and click through links that lead to their Web sites and other online destinations where you may be able to reach out further and provide more of your conversations and content. Even though social bookmarking starts with a shared link, the process can grow much bigger and go much further with a bit of additional effort.

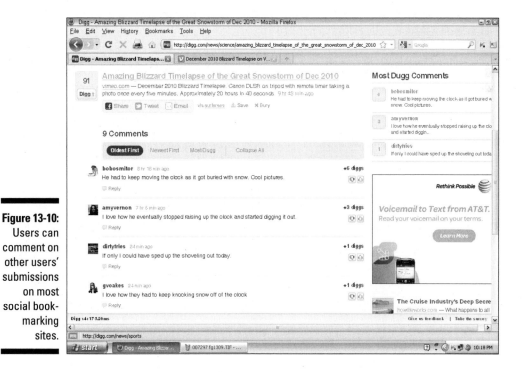

Figure 13-10:
Users can comment on other users' submissions on most social bookmarking sites.

Podcasts and audio content

Creating and publishing your own podcasts and audio content is an excellent short-form content marketing initiative (refer to Chapter 5 for more on using audio and podcasts). However, podcasts and audio content also offer an opportunity for you to engage in conversational content marketing — because many podcast, online radio, and online talk show sites allow people to publish comments on show pages and even to call into shows to participate via telephone.

BlogTalkRadio (www.blogtalkradio.com) is a great example of an online talk show site that allows listeners to publish comments on specific show pages and episode pages before, during, and after episodes, as well as call and participate in selected live shows. An example of a BlogTalkRadio show with conversational comments is shown in Figure 13-11.

You can use keywords to search for BlogTalkRadio shows related to your business and listen to episodes that pertain to you. Publish comments during the show to add value and begin a conversation with the host and other listeners.

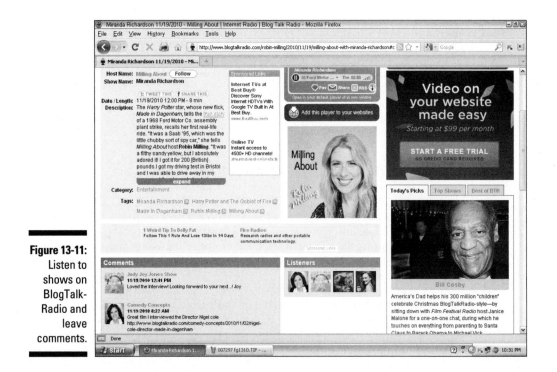

Figure 13-11:
Listen to shows on BlogTalk-Radio and leave comments.

Most podcast sites, including Podbean.com (`www.podbean.com`) and PodOmatic (`www.podomatic.com`) allow listeners to publish comments on shows and episodes (although you may not be able to comment in real-time during a podcast). Always look for ways to interact with the host and other listeners when you find a podcast or audio content of interest. It's a great way to strike up a conversation that can lead to better things!

Flickr and photo sharing sites

Uploading and sharing photos and images on sites like Flickr (`www.flickr.com`) and Picasa (`http://picasa.google.com`) is a popular form of short-form content marketing (refer to Chapter 9 for more on uploading photos and images); however, you can also use photo uploading and sharing sites for conversational content marketing. Any uploaded image that has the comment feature enabled on these sites offers a place for you to start and join conversations. Of course, you must have a registered account to post comments on images hosted on photo-sharing sites, but registration is typically free and easy to do.

Twitter provides applications that allow you to share pictures and comment on other users' shared pictures. Twitpic (`http://twitpic.com`) and yfrog (`http://yfrog.com`) are two such applications.

You can also upload your own images to image-sharing sites as part of your short-form content marketing efforts so people can publish comments on your pictures. Respond to those comments and keep the conversation going to extend those efforts into conversational content marketing opportunities. You'll be amazed at the relationships that can develop over shared images.

Chat tools and instant messaging

You can easily have real-time conversations with people around the world using various chat and instant messaging tools. Many of these tools are completely free to use and give you additional ways to pursue conversational content marketing initiatives. In fact, many social networks and online applications offer instant messaging and chat features within the applications, including Facebook.

Stand-alone chat and instant messaging tools used to center around the highly popular AOL instant messaging system (`www.aim.com`). That tool is still a viable option, as are Yahoo! Messenger (http://messenger.yahoo.com) and Windows Live Messenger (http://explore.live.com/windows-live-messenger?os=other). However, new, more feature-rich options are available that can take your conversational content marketing to new levels. For example, Google Talk (www.google.com/talk) integrates seamlessly with Gmail and other Google applications.

One of the best options is Skype (www.skype.com), which offers instant messaging, free online telephone calls (all you need is a microphone connected to your computer), and video calls (you just need a microphone and webcam connected to your computer). Skype is free, easy to set up, and very popular. You can use it for scheduled or spontaneous calls and chats, and you can even find software programs and add-ons to record calls on Skype if you need to access content from those discussions later. Skype does offer more advanced features for a fee, but the free version is more than enough to get you started with this part of your conversational content marketing plan.

As with all conversational content marketing efforts, you just have to get started, reach out to people, and be patient. Conversations will start to flow in time. Just as it can take time to break the ice in face-to-face conversations, the same holds true in virtual conversations — in fact, even more so virtually. Don't give up, and your efforts will be rewarded with great discussions, increased connections, and deeper relationships that help build your brand and your business.

Chapter 14

Getting the Most out of Online Conversations

Conversing with people can be fun, but it can also take a lot of time to do it well. Creating a conversational content marketing process that streamlines your efforts and ensures you're working efficiently is very important, or you'll find yourself spending far more time than you can afford in conversations that won't deliver the returns you want and need for your brand and business.

This chapter introduces you to tools and tricks that can help you save time and ensure that you focus on the conversational content marketing efforts that will drive results. While it's true that every conversation you join online can help your business and brand in some way, there simply aren't enough hours in the day to devote to all of them. This chapter helps you discover how to work smarter rather than harder.

Saving Time and Effort with Handy Tools

New tools launch frequently that can help you work more efficiently when it comes to conversational content marketing. You can automate many processes and pursue more targeted conversations simply by using a free or low-cost tool, add-on, plug-in, or application. Of course, just as new tools launch often, existing tools shut down frequently. With that knowledge in mind, make sure you don't become too dependent on any single tool, because you never know when the developers might stop supporting it.

Knowing that the lifespan of a free tool might be short doesn't mean you shouldn't test tools that might help you work more efficiently. On the contrary, I encourage you to experiment with the tools available in order to determine which ones will be most beneficial to you in reaching your content marketing goals. (Of course, what works for one person may not work for another, so some experimentation is necessary to find tools you like.) The vast majority of tools won't hurt your conversational content marketing efforts, as long as you don't become totally reliant on any particular tool.

URL shorteners

URL shorteners enable you to shorten links to approximately 20 characters, which is essential when using a tool like Twitter that limits the number of characters you can include in your short-form content. (Refer to Chapter 9 for more on using URL shorteners.) However, there is more to URL shorteners than the name implies. Many URL shortener tools allow you to track the number of clicks on your shortened links.

For example, if you tweet a link to one of your great blog posts and use a URL shortener such as bit.ly, you can also keep track of the number of people who click on that specific link within your tweet. If other Twitter users retweet your original Twitter update, they'll share your shortened URL link further, and clicks on those links (when the shortened URL is not changed) will also appear within the click statistics in your bit.ly account.

Tracking clicks on your published links is an excellent way to learn what type of content your audience wants from you. If a lot of people click on your link, it's safe to assume that link was interesting to them, and offering more content like it will interest them further and enable you to further engage with them, build relationships with them, and develop your brand and business.

Some URL shorteners are integrated into third-party applications such as HootSuite and TweetDeck for Twitter users, as discussed in the section "Third Party Apps," later in this chapter. Using integrated URL shorteners within these applications is a major time saver.

Plug-ins and add-ons

Depending on the content marketing tool you're using to publish your content, there might be add-ons and plug-ins available that enhance the features and functionality of that tool. For example, if you use the self-hosted WordPress application (available at www.wordpress.org) as your blog and Web site tool, you can choose from numerous free (and some for pay) plug-ins that enhance functionality and add features.

Some popular WordPress plug-ins that can help you streamline and boost your conversational content marketing efforts are in the following list:

- **Retweet.com Button:** (http://wordpress.org/extend/plugins/retweet) The Retweet Button makes it easy for visitors to your blog to retweet your posts with the click of the mouse.

- **ShareThis** (http://wordpress.org/extend/plugins/sharethis): The ShareThis plug-in adds link icons at the end of your blog posts so visitors can share them with their own audiences on a variety of social sites such as Facebook, Digg, and more with the click of the mouse.

- **Subscribe to Comments** (http://wordpress.org/extend/plugins/subscribe-to-comments): This plug-in allows people to subscribe to blog posts to which they submit a comment so that they receive an e-mail message when additional comments are published on that post, making it easy for them to stay in the conversation.

- **Most Commented Widget** (http://wordpress.org/extend/plugins/most-commented): This plug-in displays links to posts that have the most comments on your blog.

- **Top Commentators Widget** (http://wordpress.org/extend/plugins/top-commentators-widget): This plug-in displays the people who submitted the most comments on your blog.

- **Content Form 7** (http://wordpress.org/extend/plugins/contact-form-7): This plug-in makes it easy to create contact forms on your blog or Web site so that visitors can converse with you in additional ways.

You can also use a variety of add-ons to encourage conversations across your branded online destinations. For example, people love to give their opinions in polls. You can easily add free polls to your Web site, blog, and more using a tool like Polldaddy (www.polldaddy.com). Alternatively, you can answer questions using LinkedIn Answers (www.linkedin.com/answers?trk=hb_ft_answers) to participate in conversations related to your business.

You can also add the popular Facebook Like button to your blog (http://developers.facebook.com/docs/reference/plugins/like), Web site, and other branded online destinations so people can easily show their Facebook friends that they like your content. It's just one more way to jump-start a conversation.

The key is to keep your eyes and ears open for tools that can help you get people talking or streamline your efforts. You won't find value in every tool you try, and that's perfectly fine. Just don't be afraid to try them!

Third-party apps

A variety of applications created by third-party developers can help your conversational content marketing initiatives (third-party developers aren't affiliated with the sites and tools for which the applications are created). Some of these applications help you be more accessible to your audience. Some allow you to jump into relevant conversations in a timely manner, and some allow you to prioritize conversations so you know where to spend your time.

For example, most content publishing tools mentioned in this book offer mobile applications, so you can converse with people online at anytime. Whether you're waiting for a doctor's appointment or passing time during your lunch break, a mobile app can connect you to your Facebook Page, Twitter profile, blog, and more!

You can also find third-party applications that work directly with popular tools like Facebook and Twitter. Facebook Places is a fairly new application that enables you to see where your Facebook friends are and converse with them accordingly (`www.facebook.com/help/?page=18837`). Facebook Chat (`www.facebook.com/help/?page=713`) enables you to converse via online messaging with your Facebook friends, and the Facebook Birthdays app gives you a reason to reach out to your friends to wish them a happy birthday. Sometimes that's all it takes to get a conversation going and start building a relationship with another person.

Twitter applications that can help you join and start conversations are numerous. Some popular choices include the following:

- ✔ **TweetDeck:** (`www.tweetdeck.com`) Use TweetDeck to organize and prioritize your Twitter connections and conversations.

- ✔ **HootSuite:** (`www.hootsuite.com`) HootSuite makes it easy to automate tasks and prioritize and organize your Twitter activities.

- ✔ **monitter:** (`www.monitter.com`) Keep track of and join real-time conversations related to your business or local area.

- ✔ **yfrog:** (`www.yfrog.com`) Share photos and videos on Twitter with yfrog. It's a great way to start conversations.

- ✔ **Nearby Tweets:** (`www.nearbytweets.com`) Find tweets that reference a specific area and jump into conversations related to your business.

- ✔ **Twazzup:** (`www.twazzup.com`) Find real-time conversations to join through a keyword search.

- ✔ **SocialOomph:** (`www.socialoomph.com`) With SocialOomph, you can schedule tweets so that you appear active on Twitter even when you're not. You can also track keywords, extend your Twitter profile, automate processes, and more. You can get even more functionality with a paid account.

Most tools and applications are free, but you might stumble upon a tool that could help you with a price tag attached to it. Always look for a free trial before you commit to paying for a tool. If a free trial isn't available, do a Google search for reviews of that tool before you commit to paying for it to ensure it will do what you want it to do.

You can stop using a third-party application at any time, so you don't have to feel obligated to continue using a tool that doesn't seem to help you. Only you can truly know your audience and your goals, and that is the knowledge you have to turn to when you evaluate tools and applications.

Adjusting Your Conversations and Tone for Your Audience

As with all forms of content marketing, the tone that you write in can make or break you. Conversations are no different, and in fact, they could be more dependent on tone than long-form or short-form content marketing. A real person should be at the heart of your conversations. While an audience may accept an occasional corporate tone in long-form and short-form content marketing, it's unlikely they'll accept it in conversational content marketing. That's because no one wants to talk to a machine, and if your personality doesn't exude through your conversational content, you'll sound like a corporate robot.

The first step is finding out who your audience is and understanding that your audience is made up of various segments of similar people. One segment of your audience may want to discuss very different things with you than another segment does. When you understand which segments of your audience are represented on different online destinations, you can adjust your tone and voice to cater to them most effectively. For example, if you're conversing on a blog for corporate executive investors, your tone needs to be different than it would be if you were on a tweet chat with twenty-something customers.

Just as you adjust your tone in face-to-face conversations, you must also adjust your tone in online conversations. To do so, spend a significant amount of time listening to the conversations that happen on the various online destinations where you plan to participate. Listening should be a top priority for your content marketing plan. Therefore, listening and learning should be a continuous part of your daily content marketing activities. The online world changes quickly, and you need to be aware of how perceptions and actions are affected by those changes, or else your conversations will be stale before you click the Publish button.

On the other hand, you shouldn't alter your conversational tone to such a degree that it's inconsistent with your brand promise. Keep in mind that inconsistency sparks confusion in the minds of consumers. It's important that you consistently portray your brand across the Web so that you continually meet consumer expectations. So, while you need to modify your tone to match your audience, you always want to do so in accordance with your brand promise.

Using Keywords and Links in Conversations

Using search engine optimization tactics can enhance your conversational content by making it easier for other people to find that content, which gives them the opportunity to learn more from you. Chapter 7 provides more information about search engine optimization as it applies to long-form content marketing, and you can use many of those techniques in your conversational content, too. Most importantly, including keywords and links in your conversations in a manner that's not self-promotional can help you indirectly promote your business.

When it comes to using keywords in conversational content, you need to consider how people find online conversations. They might conduct a search using keywords on an online forum or by using a Twitter application or the search feature on Twitter. The point is that a person doesn't necessarily have to be following you or be connected to you online in order to stumble upon your online conversations. If they're actively looking for conversations with specific keywords, your conversations may appeal to them. Therefore, use the keyword research tips provided in Chapter 7 to decide which keywords will steer people to your conversational content.

Links are also important to your conversational content success, but in a different way. Of course, linking to your own short-form and long-form content in your conversational content can increase incoming links to that short- and long-form content, thereby boosting your search engine rankings for that content. Doing so can also help you get on other people's radar screens. For example, if you share links to other people's online content on Twitter or Facebook or in an online forum, the content owners could learn that you're linking to and sharing their content. They might reach out to you or share your content in return. It's just one more way to strike up conversations.

Bottom line, keywords and links not only help search engines find your conversational content, but also they can help people find you through third-party application searches and tools, and they can open doors to more conversations. Your goal is to publish useful information through your content, but always remember to incorporate any additional tricks (such as keywords and links) into your content so you can gain exposure in as many ways as possible.

Understanding Online Conversation Etiquette

All online publishing, including conversational content, is governed by written and unwritten rules of law and etiquette. When you participate in conversational content marketing, you need to be aware of the etiquette guidelines you're expected to follow. If you want to be a welcomed member of the online community and one with whom people want to interact, you need to play nice at all times. I suggest following this adage: "If you can't say something nice, don't say anything at all." And a simple rule of thumb to follow might be, "If you wouldn't say it to someone's face, don't say it at all." Both of these guiding principles will help keep you safe.

Your conversations should always complement your brand, not risk damaging it. Following conversational content etiquette is essential to building a business. While it might be tempting to respond to people who publish offensive comments, consider the source first. Often, people hide behind the veil of anonymity online and publish comments for no reason other than to incite anger. These people are referred to as *trolls*, and your best course of action is to ignore them (and delete the comments if they are submitted to your blog or site where you control the content).

Similarly, people fall into the trap of joining heated debates online, which can turn hateful and ugly. When a conversation escalates to these heights, they can be called *flame wars,* where participants try to damage each other's reputations. Again, consider the source and avoid these types of battles. They can do more harm to your brand than good, so don't feed the fire by participating.

If a heated online conversation warrants your participation, you can always choose to acknowledge the participants online with a note that you'd be happy to continue the discussion offline. Be sure to provide a link to your Web site contact page or another way for participants to contact you offline.

Evaluating Discussions and Tweaking Efforts

Your conversational content marketing success relies on your persistence in evaluating what works and what needs to be changed. Not only do you want to continually listen to the conversations happening among your target audience members, but you also need to use analytics tools to analyze the data behind those conversations. Chapter 16 offers a variety of Web analytics tools that you can use to gather information about your content marketing performance.

At the same time, you need to set up your branded online destinations so conversations flow freely and effectively. A blog filled with spam comments doesn't encourage visitors to join the conversation. You need to understand the types of conversations that happen on your branded destinations so you can ensure that the best conversations have the greatest chance to thrive.

Identifying key connections

Do you know who you're conversing with online? Think of it this way: You wouldn't want to respond to tweets by top search engine optimization experts by offering a simple SEO tip to help them get more traffic, would you? Doing so would be a surefire way to ensure that an SEO expert is insulted and annoyed and ignores all tweets from you in the future.

The lesson to take from this scenario is simple: Before you converse with people online, take a moment to find out who they are whenever possible. You need to tailor your conversations to match the person (or people) with whom you're interacting. This is particularly important when you converse with an online influencer or key person within your field or industry.

If you don't know who a person is and can't figure it out through a Google search, Twitter profile, Facebook Page, or other source, you can still interact with that person. Just stay tactful and polite. You never know where your online conversations could lead.

Handling conversations on your own blog

Your blog is one of the few branded online destinations that you can fully control. While you don't want to stop the conversations that happen on your blog through the comments feature, you should take some steps to ensure that conversations add value to user experience on your blog.

Using a feature called Comment Moderation, which is available in most blogging applications, you can configure your blog so that comments submitted to your blog posts don't publish live on your blog until you approve them. Although it takes a bit of time to moderate comments, you'll find doing so worth the time in terms of protecting the user experience on your blog. No one wants to read or comment on blog posts when the conversation is cluttered with spam.

As shown in Figure 14-1, you can configure comment moderation on a self-hosted WordPress blog in a variety of ways. I recommend the following settings:

✔ Select the Comment Author Must Provide Name and E-mail check box.

✔ Select the Comment Author Must Have a Previously Approved Comment check box.

✔ Enter **2** in the Hold a Comment in the Queue if It Contains *X* Or More Links text box.

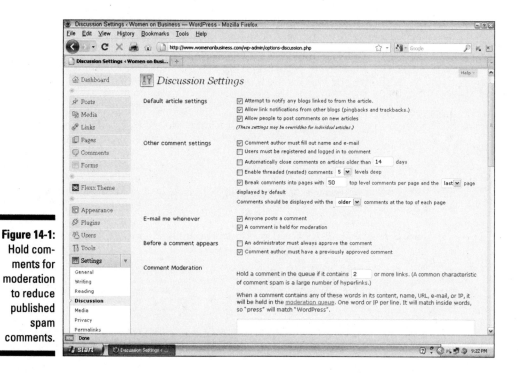

Figure 14-1: Hold comments for moderation to reduce published spam comments.

To set visitor expectations about the conversations that happen on your blog or branded online destination, I highly suggest publishing a comment policy like the sample comment policy in Chapter 13.

Recognizing and handling spam content and comments

Configuring your blog to require comment moderation is one step you can take to reduce spam clutter in your conversational content. However, you also need to be aware of the type of spam you're likely to come across on blogs, forums, social networks, and so on. Many people publish content or comments online for the sole purpose of boosting incoming links to a Web page or to promote products and services.

The difference between good content marketing and bad content marketing is a little something called *value.* If your content doesn't add value to the online conversation, then it's nothing more than a promotional pitch. If it's an over-the-top promotional pitch (such as a forum post filled with links) or a promotional pitch disguised as useful content, then it's spam. The last thing you want to have happen is for your content to be viewed as spam. If you're labeled as a spammer (whether you published spam intentionally or not), it can be difficult or impossible to remove that label.

Following are a variety of types of conversational content spam that you need to avoid writing and that you'll want to delete from your own branded online destinations whenever possible:

- ✔ Conversations filled with links.
- ✔ Conversations with a keyword link stuck at the end for no apparent reason.
- ✔ Conversations stuffed with keywords.
- ✔ Conversations that add no value but include a keyword link within the signature or other area.
- ✔ Conversations that have nothing to do with the content topic but include a keyword link.

Avoid encouraging this type of spam on your own sites or other sites, such as forums, by deleting spam comments when you can and ignoring them when you can't delete them.

Taking conversations beyond a single destination

Throughout this book, I mention that a goal of content marketing is to build relationships with people and slowly bring them back to your own branded online destinations where you can share more of your content with them and deepen your relationships with them. How do you do accomplish this goal? It's actually very simple. You offer more of your amazing, shareworthy content through your conversations.

For example, join an existing conversation related to your business where you can offer useful insight or helpful information. Answer questions and then offer a link to learn more on your blog. Alternatively, you could point them in the direction of one of your online videos or a discussion from your Facebook group that can help them further. The trick is to offer valuable, useful information that the person appreciates, and then offer them more on your branded online destination.

However, you can't just link them to any old page on your Web site and expect them to be happy that they clicked that link. If you want them to be happy that you offered that link with additional information, you need to make sure that you offer a link only if you truly have somewhere useful to direct them. If you have content published online that can be of additional value to them, then offer it. If not, then stop yourself. You don't want to annoy new connections by sending them to useless content. That's a guaranteed way to make them not want to converse with you in the future. Remember, content marketing is primarily an indirect marketing tool, so don't close conversations with a sales pitch. Offer more of your content only if the conversation warrants it.

Content marketing is a long-term strategy, so you need to be patient and persistent. If you push too hard, you'll destroy your chances of building your brand and business through content marketing. However, if you focus on building long-term relationships through organic growth, you'll achieve success.

Part V
Achieving Long-Term Success

The 5th Wave   By Rich Tennant

"I'm just not sure running a word processing program sideways without line breaks on butcher paper is the best way to start our long-form content marketing efforts."

In this part . . .

It's time to bring everything in Parts I–IV of this book together, so you can ensure your content marketing plan is set for long-term success. Content marketing is just one tool in your marketing toolbox, and Part V shows you how to make it a useful part that complements your other efforts rather than working against them.

In Chapter 15, you find out how to integrate your online and offline content marketing efforts — with each other and with other marketing initiatives. Chapter 16 shows you how to analyze your content marketing results so you can tweak your efforts and improve your results. Not only can you find tools you can use for your content marketing analysis efforts, but you also learn how to track results.

Finally, in Chapter 17, you discover how to build a content marketing team. Content marketing takes time, and you might need to recruit existing employees, hire new employees, or work with freelancers to ensure your content marketing efforts are the best they can be in order to deliver the results you want and need.

Chapter 15

Integrating Your Content Marketing Efforts

*A*s mentioned throughout this book, content marketing success can't reach full potential if your marketing efforts operate in silos. Instead, you need to integrate all of your online and offline content marketing efforts to achieve the highest results. Furthermore, you need to integrate your content marketing efforts with your other marketing efforts, such as advertising, research, direct response, and so on. To maximize your return on investments, develop an integrated marketing plan.

Integrating your content marketing efforts can be as simple as including a link to your Twitter profile in your e-mail signature or the address of your Facebook Page in a print ad. There are many ways to integrate your marketing efforts, and this chapter shows some of the most valuable integration tactics you can apply to your content marketing activities right away.

The Importance of Integrating Marketing Efforts

It's important to understand that content marketing can happen both online and offline. Whether you're writing a blog or sending an offline newsletter, you can use content to indirectly (and directly) promote your business and brand. However, those efforts can be more powerful and more far-reaching if they work together.

As you set your content marketing goals, try to surround consumers with branded experiences (using content) from which they can self-select how to interact with your brand. By integrating your online and offline content marketing initiatives, you can make it easy for consumers to find your branded experiences. Rather than receiving your printed newsletter and feeling annoyed by the mailbox clutter, consumers who are active Facebook users might notice the address of your Facebook Page on the front of the newsletter and add it to their list of likes.

In other words, just because consumers don't like your printed newsletter doesn't mean they don't want to consume your content, converse with you, and build a relationship with you. You need to give consumers options so they can make the best decisions as to whether they want to engage with you. Without all the information, they can't make an informed decision, and you may lose the opportunity to connect with them at all. Integrate your content marketing efforts to boost your chances of success.

The easiest and least expensive way to integrate your online and offline content marketing efforts is to indirectly promote them by adding references to other marketing tactics in *existing* activities. The preceding example that suggests adding the Web address of your Facebook Page in your printed newsletter is a great way to promote an online short-form content marketing effort in an offline long-form content marketing effort.

You can also directly promote your online and offline content marketing efforts in an effort to integrate your activities. For example, you can place an ad in your local paper inviting people to like your Facebook Page. The opportunities are limited only by your budget and creativity. However, you don't have to spend a penny if you don't want to. The choice is entirely up to you.

Interlinking Your Online Content

As you create and publish new content online, always consider how you can link to your existing online content or destinations. While you don't want to seem like you're always self-promoting with your links and references to other online content, you do want to offer useful content when it actually adds value to the conversation and audience that sees it. This type of cross-promotion can help you further engage people online and integrate your marketing efforts.

Keep in mind that you never want to *bait and switch* your audience, meaning you don't offer a link to your content that leads people to believe the content will deliver something specific and then not carry through by actually delivering. Don't try to promote your content or disguise it as something it is not. Doing so will accomplish nothing but annoy your audience and possibly flag you as a spammer. Instead, offer your links as additional, useful information and leave it up to the audience to decide whether to click those links.

When you offer links to cross-promote your content, follow what I refer to as the Catalyst to Click Theory:

> *Don't ask me to click something. Tell me something, and then I'll decide whether to click.*

Your goal in cross-promoting your content through links should be to tell your audience something meaningful that makes them feel that your link will help them even more. Give them the control they want, and let them decide whether your links are meaningful based on *what* you say to them, not on how nicely you wrap those links in promotional copy.

Feeding content from one branded destination to another

Chapters 4 and 8 cover how to automatically update your Twitter feed and Facebook Page with links to your new blog posts. You can feed content from one of your branded online destinations to another in many other ways. In order to save time and ensure that your online audience has the opportunity to consume your diverse forms of content, you can automate many publishing options.

When you automate content publishing processes, the important thing to remember is that you don't want any of your branded online destinations to include a long list of links to your other content but nothing original. For example, a Twitter stream that includes tweet after tweet with links to your blog content will be more useful and interesting if you intersperse those automated updates with short-form or conversational content marketing efforts. Although automated updates can offer your audience new ways to consume your content, don't consider them to be a replacement for publishing original content.

Following are a number of tools you can use to feed your content from one branded online destination to another:

- ✔ **Twitterfeed:** (`www.twitterfeed.com`) You can input an RSS feed URL (such as your blog's RSS feed) and feed it to your Twitter account. You can also enter your Twitter profile URL and configure Twitterfeed to automatically feed your Twitter updates to your Facebook profile.

- ✔ **RSS Graffiti:** (`http://apps.facebook.com/rssgraffiti`) RSS Graffiti is a Facebook app that makes it very easy to feed RSS or Atom feeds to Facebook profiles, Pages, groups, events, and more.

- ✔ **NetworkedBlogs:** (`www.facebook.com/networkedblogs`) Offers similar features to RSS Graffiti to make it simple to feed RSS or Atom feeds to Facebook profiles.

✔ **Facebook Pages Twitter app:** (`www.facebook.com/twitter`) Feed your Facebook Page updates to Twitter with this Facebook app.

✔ **Flickr to Facebook tool:** (`www.flickr.com/help/extending`) Configure your Flickr and Facebook account settings to allow your Flickr uploads to publish to your Facebook Page automatically.

✔ **Facebook SlideShare app:** (`http://apps.facebook.com/slideshare`) Automatically display your SlideShare presentations on your Facebook Page with this app.

✔ **LinkedIn Twitter app:** (`http://learn.linkedin.com/twitter`) You can feed your Twitter updates to your LinkedIn profile or your LinkedIn updates to your Twitter profile with this LinkedIn app.

✔ **LinkedIn Blog Link app:** (`http://learn.linkedin.com/apps/bloglink`) Feed your blog posts to your LinkedIn profile with this app.

✔ **LinkedIn SlideShare app:** (`http://learn.linkedin.com/apps/slideshare`) Publish your SlideShare presentations on your LinkedIn profile with this app.

✔ **LinkedIn Behance app:** (`http://learn.linkedin.com/apps/behance`) This app enables you to share your images on your LinkedIn profile as an online portfolio.

Depending on the blogging application you use, you may be able to add a variety of features (called *widgets* or *gadgets*) to your blog that display your various content feeds.

Of course, there are many ways to feed your online content from one destination to another, and new tools and applications pop up all the time. When you automate a process such as feed publishing, look to ensure that the content being published automatically reads the way you want it to and looks the way you want it to. It's not uncommon for a tool to have glitches, so ongoing review of the performance of tools you use to automate processes is essential to your long-term content marketing success.

Promoting content and online profiles on various branded destinations

Automating processes like the ones described in the previous section are just one step in integrating your content marketing efforts. You also need to make it easy for people to find your varied online content by promoting it in your online profiles and branded destinations. Truth be told, "promoting" can be a bit misleading in this instance, because you shouldn't try to sell your content. Instead, your goal should be to offer options. Just as a retail clothing store might offer the same shirt in multiple sizes and colors so customers can select the choices that are best for them, you also want to offer content choices to your online audience. Instead of hanging various shirts on a clothes rack, you can offer links, buttons, icons, and other ways to raise awareness of your varied content.

Options for cross-promoting your content online are offered throughout this book; the following subsections provide a more comprehensive list of options.

Social media icons on your blog and Web site

On your blog or Web site, you can display social media icons, which are images that link to each of your branded online destinations. For example, you can invite visitors to your blog to connect with you on Twitter, Facebook, or LinkedIn by displaying relevant social media icons that link directly to your profiles in your blog's sidebar, as shown in Figure 15-1.

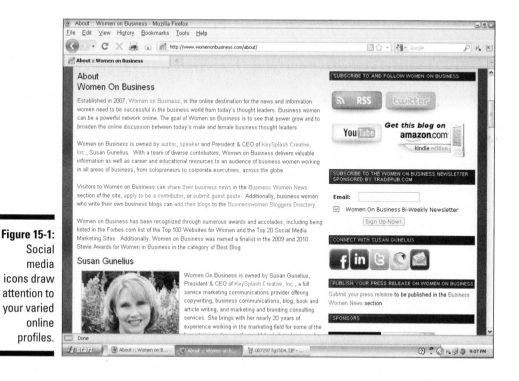

Figure 15-1:
Social media icons draw attention to your varied online profiles.

You can find social media icons to match any blog design. Following are several sites where you can download free social media icons for Twitter, Facebook, LinkedIn, YouTube, Flickr, RSS, Digg, StumbleUpon, and many more:

- ✔ **About.com Blogging:** http://weblogs.about.com/od/Social-Media-Icons/Social-Media-Icons.htm

- ✔ **WP Mods:** www.wpmods.com/ultimate-social-media-icon-list

- ✔ **Smashing Apps:** www.smashingapps.com/2010/03/08/the-ultimate-fresh-collection-of-high-quality-free-social-media-icon-sets.html

Facebook social plug-ins

You can add a variety of social plug-ins to your blog or Web site to connect your Facebook Page with your blog or Web site. You can add each plug-in to a blog or Web site simply by modifying some code, which is provided to you at http://developers.facebook.com/plugins.

The following Facebook social plug-ins are available:

- ✔ **Like button:** The Like button enables visitors to your Web site or blog to share pages from your site on their Facebook profiles with a single mouse click. You can see an example of a Facebook Like Button social plug-in in a blog footer in Figure 15-2.

- ✔ **Recommendations:** The Recommendations plug-in provides personalized suggestions for pages on your site that each visitor might like.

- ✔ **Login button:** If your blog or Web site includes a sign-up feature, the Login button shows a Facebook login button as well as Facebook profile pictures of each visitors' friends who have already signed up for your site.

- ✔ **Comments:** The Comments plug-in allows users to your blog or Web site to comment on any piece of content on your site.

- ✔ **Activity Feed:** The Activity Feed plug-in shows your blog or Web site visitors their Facebook friends' likes and comments on your site.

- ✔ **Like Box:** The Like Box lets people view your Facebook Page stream and to like your Page directly within your Web site or blog.

- ✔ **Facepile:** The Facepile plug-in shows Facebook profile pictures of everyone who has liked your Page or signed up for your site.

- ✔ **Live Stream:** The Live Stream plug-in allows visitors to share their activities and comments during a live event in real-time.

Each of the Facebook social plug-ins can add value to your blog or Web site where you publish them, but don't overdo it. Limit the number of Facebook social plug-ins you use on a single site or page so as not to clutter your valuable original content on those pages.

Facebook badges

Facebook badges (www.facebook.com/badges/?ref=pf) enable you to show off information from your Facebook Page or profile on your other branded online destinations, such as your Web site or blog. You can add each of these badges to one of your online destinations simply by copying and pasting some code.

Here are the Facebook badges that are available:

- ✔ **Profile Badge:** The Profile Badge allows you to share your Facebook profile information on your blog or Web site.

- ✔ **Like Badge:** The Like Badge enables you to show your favorite Facebook Pages on your Web site or blog.

- ✔ **Photo Badge:** The Photo Badge lets you share photos that you've uploaded to Facebook on your blog or Web site.

- ✔ **Page Badge:** The Page Badge allows you to publish your Facebook Page information on your blog or Web site.

Facebook badges aren't very intrusive and can give your audience an idea of your activities on Facebook and the popularity of those activities. Sometimes a visitor just needs to see other people interacting with you or your activities in order to feel motivated to join the conversation.

Twitter resources

Twitter offers a variety of free tools that you can use to promote your Twitter profile across your branded online destinations at http://business.twitter.com/optimize/resources. Twitter separates these free resources into three categories:

- ✔ **Follow buttons:** You can add a Twitter follow button to any other site where you can paste HTML code.

- ✔ **Tweet button:** The Tweet button can be added to most Web sites, making it easy for people to share your content in a Twitter update with the click of a mouse.

- ✔ **Widgets:** Twitter widgets work with many other applications, including Facebook, MySpace, Blogger and more. Simply paste some HTML code, and either your Twitter profile updates or a live stream of updates from a live tweet session is published on your blog, other profile, or Web site. As shown in Figure 15-3, you can create a widget to show off your profile, tweets based on a specific keyword search, favorite tweets, or lists of favorite Twitter users.

Figure 15-3: Twitter widgets allow you to promote your profile, specific tweets, or Twitter users.

Online profiles

When you create profiles on Web sites, always look for opportunities to include links to your other branded online destinations. Most social sites allow users to provide at least one URL in their profiles, but that doesn't mean you can't include additional URLs. For example, include the URL to your primary branded online destination in the area of your profile designated for your Web site URL, and then include additional URLs in the longer description section of your profile.

The key is to work around profile limitations so that you can share the most important information with your audience. Sometimes, the design of your profile might provide additional space to include links to your other branded online destinations. Chapter 9 covers tools you can use to customize your Twitter profile background, which is a creative way to include additional URLs on your Twitter landing page.

TIP

Even if you can't include active hyperlinks within an online profile, include the URL for interested visitors to copy and paste into their Web browser search bars.

REMEMBER

Every online profile offers a chance for you to cross-promote at least some of your other branded online destinations. Make sure you set up your online accounts so that you can leverage that promotion. For example, don't just create a YouTube profile. Instead, create a YouTube channel where you can publish links, a biography or description of your business, and more. Integrating your content marketing efforts shouldn't be an afterthought. Instead, it should be a core component of your strategies and tactics.

Hyping content through offline activities

Promoting your content marketing efforts and creating a fully integrated marketing plan means you need to leverage offline activities to hype your online content, too. Research shows that even when people hear about businesses, products, and services offline, they're highly likely to go online in search of additional information, reviews, comparisons, and more. If they're going to go online anyway, you should nudge them in the right direction by including URLs to your branded online destinations in your offline marketing materials.

Even your non-promotional materials could offer opportunities for you to hype your online content. For example, you can include the URL for your blog on your business cards, or hype your Twitter profile on customer receipts. You could even include a note inviting people to like your Facebook Page so they don't miss upcoming sales and discounts on your shopping bags or in-store signage. The options are limited only by your creativity.

Ways to integrate content marketing efforts

Following are easy ways that you can integrate your content marketing efforts in order to surround consumers with branded experiences:

1. Include social media icons in your blog's sidebar.

2. Include your branded online destination links in your e-mail signature.

3. Include your branded online destination links in your forum signatures.

4. Include links to your content in blog comment forms.

5. Include links to your content in your ads.

6. Include links to your content on your business cards.

7. Include links to your content in your e-mail newsletter.

8. Include links to your content on your receipts.

9. Include Facebook social icons on your blog or Web site.

10. Include Twitter widgets on your blog or Web site.

11. Publish your YouTube videos on your Facebook Page and profile.

12. Feed your blog content to your Twitter, Facebook, and LinkedIn profiles and your Facebook page.

13. Feed your blog content to LinkedIn groups that allow the News feature.

14. Use the SlideShare app to share your presentations on Facebook and LinkedIn.

15. Include links to your blog in your online profiles on Facebook, Twitter, LinkedIn, and so on.

16. Include links to your content in the biography you include in guest posts that you write for other people's blogs.

17. Include Facebook buttons on your blog and Web site.

18. Include the URLs to links to your content in your brochures and other marketing materials.

19. Include the URLs to links to your content in your store or event signage.

20. Feed your Twitter, LinkedIn, and Facebook updates to your blog.

Making It Easy for Others to Share and Talk about Your Content

Promoting your own content across your branded online destinations is just one part of your marketing integration efforts. You also need to make sure that your audience helps you integrate your efforts by spreading your content across varied online destinations and tools. In order to achieve this type of integration, you must make it easy for your audience to share your content with their own audiences. Fortunately, a variety of free tools can help you do so.

Chapters 8 and 9 cover how to write short-form content that is more likely to be shared via Twitter, social networking, and social bookmarking tools. However, writing shareworthy content is only the first step. You also need to make it easy for people to share your content, because if it takes longer than a couple of seconds for them to do so, they might not share it at all. Online audiences move very quickly, and pausing more than a couple of seconds might feel like an eternity to them.

Instead of requiring your online audience to take multiple steps in order to share your content with their own connections, try to make it possible for them to share your content with just one or two clicks of the mouse. Adding the Facebook social plug-ins listed earlier in this chapter can help visitors to your Web site and blog share and like your long-form content with a single mouse click. So take the time to set up those plug-ins and integrate them into your branded online destinations that allow them.

Following are additional tools that can help your audience quickly share your online content:

- **AddThis:** (www.addthis.com) With AddThis, you can customize how you want your sharing icons to look on your Web site or blog, as shown in Figure 15-4. AddThis works with WordPress, Blogger, TypePad, Tumblr, MySpace, Web sites, e-mail newsletters, and flash video. You can include links to share your content on Twitter, Facebook, e-mail, Digg, Delicious, StumbleUpon, and over 300 more social sites and services. You can choose to track analytics about the clicks on your AddThis links, too.

- **ShareThis:** (http://secure.sharethis.com/publishers/get-sharing-button) ShareThis works with Web sites, WordPress, Blogger, and TypePad and enables you to easily add links to share your content on Twitter, Facebook, LinkedIn, Delicious, Digg, StumbleUpon, and over 50 more social sites and services. You can customize the look of your ShareThis links, as shown in Figure 15-5, and include analytics for tracking purposes.

- **Retweet button:** (http://tweetmeme.com/about/retweet_button) You can add the popular retweet button from TweetMeme to your Web site, blog, e-mails, or RSS feed. If you use the self-hosted WordPress application available at WordPress.org, you can add the retweet button to your blog posts using the TweetMeme Button plug-in, which is available at http://wordpress.org/extend/plugins/tweetmeme.

Figure 15-4:
You can choose the size of your AddThis sharing icons as well as whether or not you want to display share-counts.

Figure 15-5:
You can customize the display of icons using ShareThis.

Finding Content Marketing Opportunities

Content marketing can happen on and off your own branded online destinations. Whether you're publishing a blog post on your own blog for long-form content marketing purposes or participating in a forum that you don't own for conversational content marketing purposes, both activities can help you build relationships, your brand, and your business.

With that in mind, actively seek opportunities to publish your appealing, shareworthy content on a variety of online destinations. Finding relevant online destinations that cater to your target audience can take time, but when you do find those sites, reach out to the site owners and offer your original content in the form of a guest blog post, guest article, free video, or in another form appropriate for each site.

You can actively offer your content or search for open opportunities to provide your content for publishing on sites that you don't own in many ways. As long as you offer original content that is relevant to the site's audience and not self-promotional (although a link to your core branded online destination in your accompanying bio is acceptable), many site owners will be happy to publish it. All you can do is ask, and the worst that can happen is that the site owner rejects your offer. You'll never know unless you try.

Help a Reporter Out

Help a Reporter Out (HARO) can be found at www.helpareporter.com. The purpose of HARO is to connect journalists and writers with credible sources for stories, quotes, interviews, and more. You can register for a free HARO membership as either a journalist or a source. As a journalist, you can complete the query form shown in Figure 15-6 and request sources when you need them. Sources receive e-mail messages from HARO three times per day with new opportunities from journalists included in them. If a source matches your query, he or she will e-mail you directly (per the instructions you provide in your query form) to discuss the opportunity with you.

On the flip side, you can register for HARO as a source so that you receive e-mails with opportunities listed in them each day. You can respond to queries that match your knowledge, skills, and expertise in an effort to share your story, indirectly promote your brand and business, or spread your original content. For example, an online magazine editor might submit a query looking for writers for an upcoming issue. If the magazine is related to your business and one that attracts your target audience, then that's a query you might want to respond to.

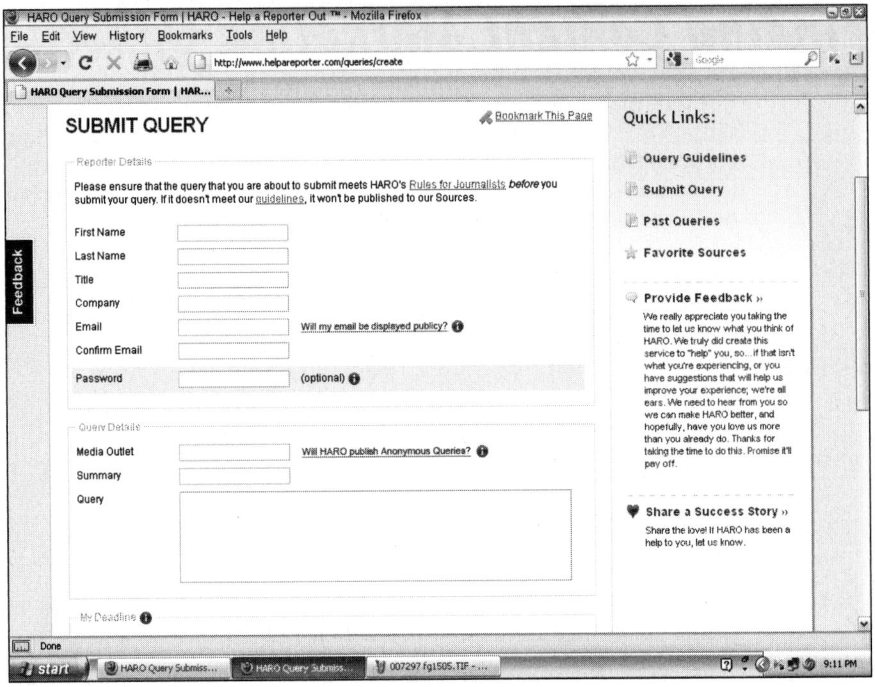

Figure 15-6:
Complete
the query
form to
solicit
sources for
your own
needs.

Always read queries carefully and respond as instructed, or your query might be deleted before it's reviewed.

HARO requests can vary from content requests, interview requests, quote requests, and more. Registration is free, so there's no downside to joining and keeping your eyes open for opportunities that can benefit your content marketing plan and your business.

ProfNet Connect

At www.profnetconnect.com, ProfNet Connect is owned by PR Newswire and connects journalists, bloggers, and writers with experts on a wide variety of subjects. It's free to join ProfNet as an expert source, and submitting your requests for sources is easy using the ProfNet Opportunity (Query) Submission Form at www.prnewswire.com/contact-us/ProfNet-Query.html, shown in Figure 15-7.

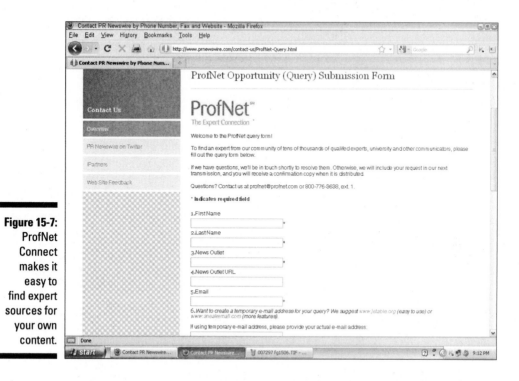

Figure 15-7:
ProfNet
Connect
makes it
easy to
find expert
sources for
your own
content.

ProfNet Connect categorizes experts into the following primary institutional categories: activists, analysts, authors, bloggers, corporate social responsibility officers, colleges and universities, corporations, government agencies and laboratories, hospitals and medical centers, legislative offices, nonprofits, public relations agencies, and small businesses. You can send your expert queries to all or some of those institutional categories as well as to specific geographical regions. Similarly, you can create your own expert profile with all of your industry and geographical details to ensure that you receive and can respond to the most relevant opportunity requests.

Guest blogging

Writing guest blog posts for blogs you don't own (refer to Chapter 4 for more on being a guest blogger) is a great way to integrate your content marketing efforts. The critical element of guest blogging is ensuring that you can include a short biography (usually a few sentences) with your post that includes a link to your core branded online destination. It's even better when you can include a few links — such as your Twitter, Facebook, and other social profile links — so readers can connect with you and get more of your content online.

Guest blogging opportunities are typically voluntary (that is, you aren't paid for them).

Finding guest blogging opportunities can be as easy as sending an e-mail or tweet to a blogger and asking if you can submit a guest post. Most popular bloggers are very busy and welcome quality guest posts that aren't completely self-promotional. Some Web sites also connect writers with blogs that accept guest posts, including these:

- **My Blog Guest:** www.myblogguest.com

- **About.com Directory of Sites that Accept and Publish Guest Blog Posts:** http://weblogs.about.com/od/Sites-to-Guest-Blog/Sites-That-Accept-And-Publish-Guest-Blog-Posts.htm

- **About.com Blogging Forum:** http://forums.about.com/n/pfx/forum.aspx?folderId=16&listMode=13&nav=messages&webtag=ab-weblogs

Searching for opportunities

You can find other creative ways to cross-promote your content through your online activities by conducting simple searches. The trick is taking the time to notice people who are creating content that is relevant to your brand and attracting your target audience. When you find that type of content, reach out to the publisher. Comment on the blog. Follow the publisher on Twitter and retweet his content. Friend the publisher on Facebook and comment on his Facebook Page. These efforts help you to get on his radar screen, so when you finally reach out to offer your content, your request is more likely to be noticed and responded to.

Following are a variety of tools you can use to conduct searches for people publishing content relevant to your brand and business:

- **Google blog search:** http://blogsearch.google.com/?hl=en&tab=wb

- **Twitter advanced search:** http://search.twitter.com/advanced

- **Twellow:** www.twellow.com

✔ **YouTube channel browse:** www.youtube.com/members?hl=en_US

✔ **BlogTalkRadio talk show search:** www.blogtalkradio.com/search/search-blogtalkradio.com/

✔ **SlideShare search:** www.slideshare.net/search

The more time you spend publishing long-form and short-form content and participating in discussions through conversational content, the more you'll get to know the people you interact with online. In time, you might even find people contacting you directly and asking if you'd be interested in sharing your content with their audiences.

Your content lives online for a very long time, and you never know how or when someone might find it. What you publish today could open doors to new promotional opportunities tomorrow or even two years from now. As long as you strive to continually publish interesting, shareworthy content, you'll increase your chances of content marketing success in the long-term, and it's that long-term growth that can deliver significant results to your brand, business, and bottom line.

Chapter 16

Analyzing Results and Fine-Tuning Your Strategy

Key components of successful content marketing are ongoing analysis of results and strategy revision. The Internet changes quickly, and the online audience moves even faster. What works today may not work tomorrow, and the best way to accomplish a specific task one day may not be the best way to do the same task the next day.

This chapter shows you how to analyze the performance of your content marketing initiatives so that you can appropriately modify your strategy to effectively meet your goals. Fortunately, many free and inexpensive tools can help you along the way, and this chapter points you in the right direction to start gathering useful and actionable data without spending a fortune.

Monitoring Your Online Reputation

One of the biggest opportunities that content marketing offers is the ability to listen to conversations happening about your brand based on the content you publish. You can also see who is sharing your content and where they're sharing it. This type of information is very valuable in helping you identify which content marketing efforts are working and which need to be changed or abandoned completely.

Monitoring your online reputation starts with finding the conversations happening about your content. Whether people are sharing and discussing your content on Twitter or writing about it on their blogs, you need to find those sources of sharing and discussing so that you can determine when to let conversations and content flow and when to jump in to nudge conversations in the right direction.

In order to find online content related to your business and brand in a timely manner, you need to determine which keywords to track.

Following are ten suggestions to help you put together your own list of keywords for online reputation management tracking:

1. Your business name

2. Your brand name

3. Your product names

4. Your competitors' business names

5. Your competitors' brand names

6. Your competitors' product names

7. Your personal name

8. Your Web site or blog domain name or title (if they're different from your brand or business name)

9. Names of employees who spend time online on behalf of your company

10. Nicknames, acronyms, or other keywords used to refer to your business, brand, or products

You need to do online reputation monitoring every day. By automating some processes, you can streamline your reputation monitoring efforts and free up more time for content creation.

As you monitor your online reputation, read through the content and conversations you find to determine how to proceed in order to maintain a positive online reputation. Of course, you can join any online conversation to boost your conversational content marketing efforts when you find appropriate opportunities to do so, but specific options are described in the section, "Responding to Criticisms and Inaccuracies," later in this chapter. These options can help you evaluate content and conversations before you respond.

Google Alerts

Google offers an excellent tool for monitoring specific keyword mentions across the online space. To set up Google Alerts for your chosen keywords, visit www.google.com/alerts and complete the form shown in Figure 16-1.

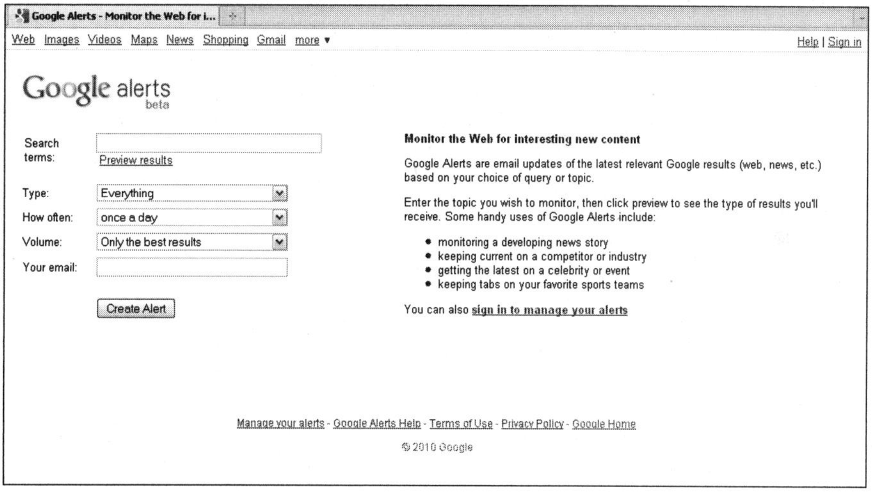

Figure 16-1:
Set up
Google
Alerts for
your busi-
ness name,
brand name,
and other
keywords
related
to your
business.

Simply enter your chosen keywords into the Search Terms text box, select the type of content you want to be included in your alerts from the Type drop-down list (I recommend selecting Everything to see all results), the frequency you want to receive alerts from the How Often drop-down list (I recommend selecting daily so you're not overwhelmed with updates nor do you miss seeing something important for days), and the volume of results you want to receive from the Volume drop-down list (I recommend starting with Everything so you don't miss anything). Enter the e-mail address where you want to receive your Google Alerts in the Your Email text box, and click the Create Alert button. You'll automatically receive e-mail messages at the frequency you selected containing links to content related to your chosen search term (see the Google Alerts message shown in Figure 16-2).

When you receive a Google Alert message, click the links in the message and read through the content and conversations published to determine how to respond or whether you should respond at all.

Keep in mind that Google Alerts catches a lot of content, but not everything. In fact, no tool can catch all keyword mentions across the Web. So, be sure to supplement Google Alerts' reputation monitoring efforts with other tactics like the ones described in this chapter.

Figure 16-2:
Google
Alerts
messages
include links
to content
relevant to
your search
term.

Google Advanced Search

Daily Web searches are an important part of your online reputation monitoring efforts. Visit www.google.com/advanced_search to access the Google Advanced Search form, shown in Figure 16-3, where you can conduct specific daily searches to find content published about your business or brand.

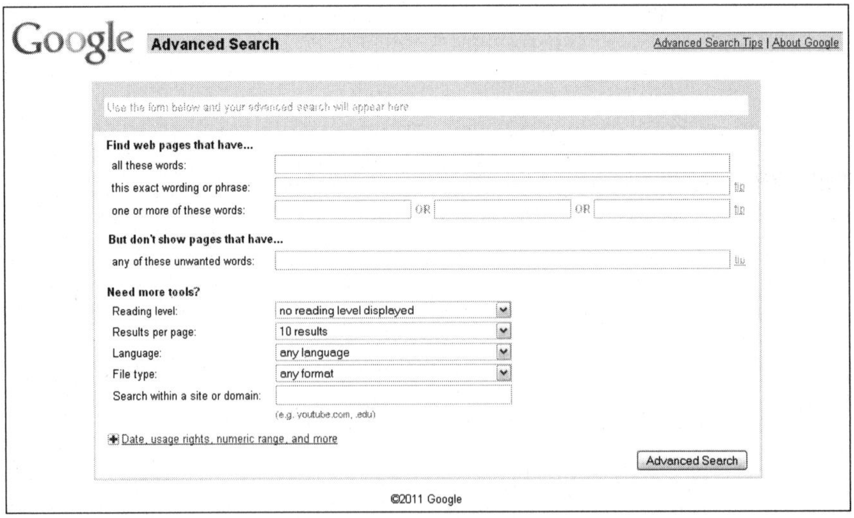

Figure 16-3:
Use the
Google
Advanced
Search form
to do daily,
specific
searches for
mentions of
your brand
and
business.

A daily Google Advanced Search can pick up additional mentions of your brand or business name that Google Alerts or other online monitoring tools might miss. Follow these steps to conduct a specific daily reputation monitoring search:

1. **Visit www.google.com/advanced_search and enter your search phrase in the This Exact Wording or Phrase text box.**

   Here, enter your brand name, business name, or other keywords to search for mentions across the Web.

2. **Click the Date, Usage Rights, Numeric Range, and More link at the bottom of the page.**

   This step expands the search form to reveal additional fields, as shown in Figure 16-4.

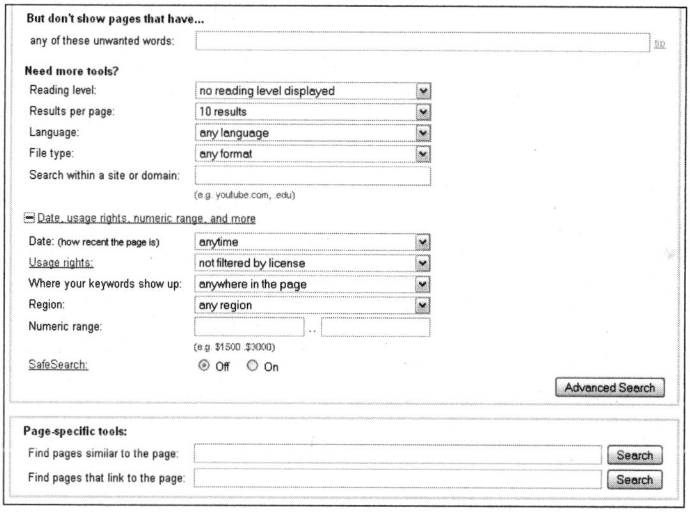

Figure 16-4: Expand the Google Advanced Search form to narrow search results.

3. **From the Date drop-down list, select Past 24 Hours.**

   This narrows your search to content indexed by Google within the past 24 hours.

4. **Click the Advanced Search button.**

   Matching results are returned to you.

Advanced Google Search results aren't perfect, and you're likely to find duplicate results, old results, and even spam results mixed in with useful results. If the results you get from your daily searches are too numerous to review, you can narrow your search using additional fields in the Advanced Google Search form. For example, you can limit your search results to content that was published from specific geographic areas using the Region drop-down box, or you could use the Language drop-down box to limit your results to content published in specific languages. This is useful for businesses that operate in specific parts of the world.

Keep a look out for sites where your content is shared and discussed frequently. These are likely to be sites where you'll want join the conversation and build relationships with the site owners and audience.

monitter

A variety of applications can help you monitor your brand reputation on Twitter. One of the most popular options is monitter (www.monitter.com), shown in Figure 16-5, which allows you to enter keywords of your choice and receive a list of real-time Twitter updates and conversations using those keywords. It's an excellent tool for finding and jumping into conversations.

Figure 16-5: Use monitter to keep track of real-time conversations on Twitter related to your brand or business.

Follow these instructions to conduct searches using monitter:

1. **Visit www.monitter.com and enter up to three search terms in the search boxes (refer to Figure 16-5).**

   You can enter Twitter hashtags or keyword phrases into the search boxes.

2. **Press Enter on your keyboard to reveal real-time tweets using your chosen keywords.**

3. **(Optional) Limit your results to a specific location by entering a city and state or zip code into the text box in the top-left navigation bar and choosing a distance using the drop-down lists.**

TECHNICAL STUFF To get a more comprehensive understanding of tweets mentioning your brand name or other keywords of choice, supplement your efforts with monitter with additional applications such as Twazzup (www.twazzup.com) and TweetDeck (www.tweetdeck.com) to capture more results.

Advanced Twitter Search

As with the Internet as a whole, there is no single way to capture all keyword mentions on Twitter because no tool is perfect. However, you can get more comprehensive results by using both advanced Twitter searches and Twitter applications for monitoring brand reputation.

Follow these steps to conduct an advanced Twitter search:

1. **Visit http://search.twitter.com/advanced and type your chosen keyword or keyword phrase in the This Exact Phrase text box, as shown in Figure 16-6.**

   Alternatively, you can search for hashtags by entering your chosen hashtag into the This Hashtag text box.

2. **Scroll down to the Places section of the form, as shown in Figure 16-7, and enter a location, city, or zip code to narrow your results.**

   You can also limit results to a surrounding area using the Within This Distance drop-down list.

3. **Scroll to the Dates section of the form and enter the timeframe within which you want to search in the Since This Date and/or Until This Date text boxes.**

   You can click the calendar icons to select dates from a calendar image.

4. **Click the Search button to get your results.**

   Of course, you can add any other search criteria into the form to narrow your results further.

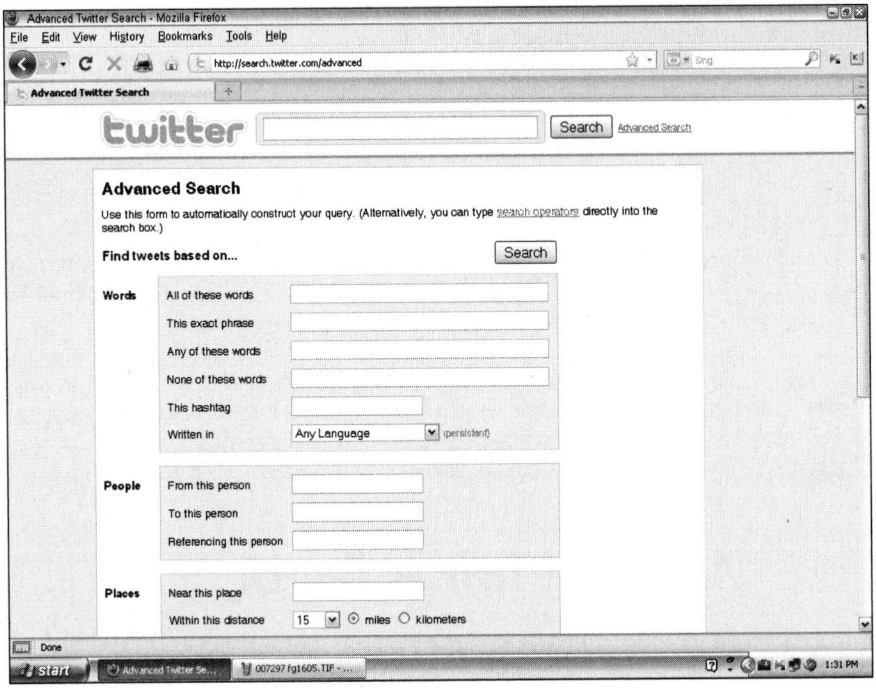

Figure 16-6:
Use the
Advanced
Twitter
Search form
to search
for specific
keyword
phrases or
hashtags
related
to your
business.

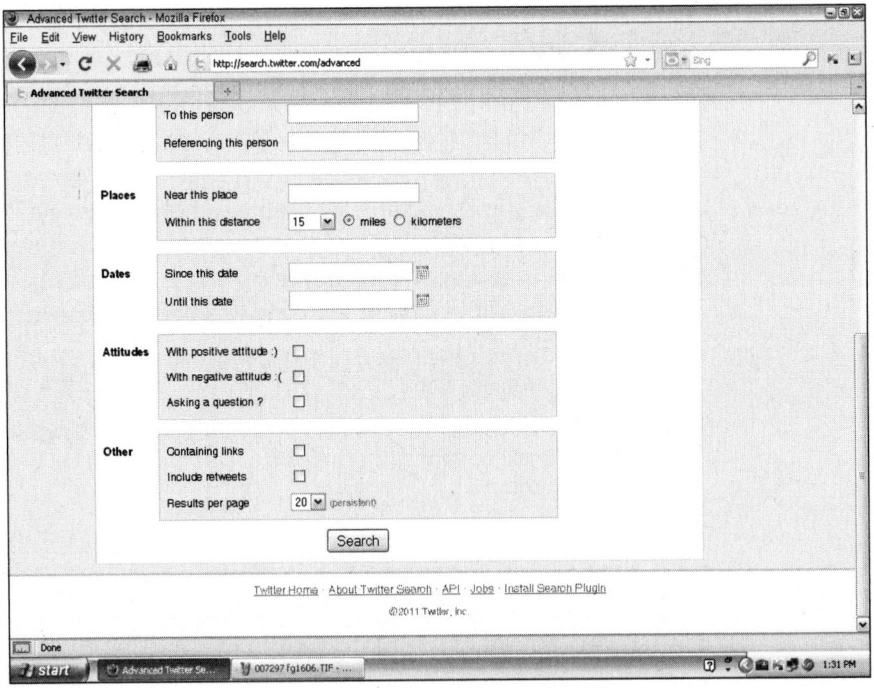

Figure 16-7:
Enter a
location
to narrow
your search
results.

Try to conduct an advanced Twitter search every day to pick up Twitter mentions of your brand, business, or yourself that don't appear in other tools or within your own account list of retweets and @mentions. You won't find every mention, but you'll undoubtedly find some that other tools missed.

Responding to Criticisms and Inaccuracies

As you monitor your online reputation, you're apt to come across negative content and conversations. It's inevitable. No one, including businesses, can please everyone all the time. While you might be tempted to jump in and defend yourself when you find negative commentary about your business online, joining the conversation may not always be the best option. Sometimes responding simply ignites the flames, allowing the negative content to spread further, while ignoring the fire might have allowed it to simply die out on its own.

A variety of well-known quotations attributed to famous people such as P.T. Barnum, Oscar Wilde, and Brendan Behan tell us there is no such thing as bad publicity. However, the social Web provides the opportunity to nudge conversations in the direction you want them to go and correct inaccuracies before they spread too far.

That's why it's essential that you analyze each negative criticism or inaccuracy that is published about your business in the online space. Take a deep breath, avoid simply reacting, and choose the best response to negativity, which might be no response at all.

The 3 Fs of Online Reputation Management

Determining how to respond to negative criticisms and inaccuracies online differs with each circumstance, but three basic tactics can guide your responses. I call these responses the 3 Fs of Online Reputation Management, which you can see visually in Figure 16-8.

Flight

The first basic response tactic in the 3 Fs of Online Reputation Management is *flight,* which directs you to not respond at all. In other words, simply ignore the negative criticism or inaccuracy when you find it.

Figure 16-8:
Follow the 3
Fs of online
reputation
management
to respond
to content
and con-
versations
about your
business.

The flight response is appropriate in specific circumstances. For example, if the source of the negative content or conversation has a very small audience so the negativity or inaccuracy is unlikely to spread, then ignoring it is probably the best course of action. Another possible time to consider ignoring a negative comment is when it comes from someone with an established reputation as a complainer or squeaky wheel. In other words, if people expect little more than negativity and complaints from a particular source, they're unlikely to be greatly affected by that source. Sometimes ignoring negative conversations or content allows it to die a quick death.

When deciding how to respond to negative criticisms or inaccuracies online, always consider the source first.

Fight

The second basic option to respond to inaccuracies or criticisms about your business or brand online is to *fight* by responding to it. However, it's important that you don't come across as overly defensive in your response. Instead, work to massage perceptions and gently nudge conversations in the direction you want them to go. Offer your own useful and meaningful content to support your response, and demonstrate your willingness to go the extra mile to ensure that people are satisfied with your business.

The biggest mistake you can make when utilizing the fight response to negativity online is to enter heated debates or arguments. Again, consider the source and ensure that your responses always stay true to your brand image and promise. Some people enjoy inciting others and starting arguments for no reason, and there's no value to falling into their traps.

Flood

The third basic response to negativity about your business online is to bury those negative conversations and content by *flooding* the online space with your own amazing, shareworthy content. The goal in employing this response is to bury negative content about your business in relevant keyword searches on search engines like Google.

Because most people find content using keyword searches on Google, you don't want negative content about your business to appear in the first several pages for Google searches on your business name or in other highly relevant keyword phrases. That's another reason why it's important to conduct Google searches on your business name frequently, so you know what potential customers see when they perform similar searches. By flooding the online space with shareworthy content that is shared by your connections and discussed across the social Web, you can push negative results further down in the search engine results pages.

Be sure to use search engine optimization tricks like the ones discussed in Chapter 7 to boost your content in search engine results pages for your targeted keywords.

Knowing What to Track

While keeping track of what is being said about your business across the Web is the first step to online reputation management, it's only the beginning of the analysis of your content marketing performance. Actually, a lot of your content marketing success comes from building brand value, which is an intangible business asset. That doesn't make your brand any less important than other assets, but it's far more challenging to quantify using hard numbers.

When it comes to tracking content marketing performance, you need to be prepared to invest for the long-term, because success doesn't happen overnight (although it is possible to get lucky). The value that comes from the relationships you build, the reputation you develop for your brand, and the band of brand advocates you acquire can last for many years and deliver immeasurable benefits to the bottom line.

Identifying hard and soft metrics for analysis

Tracking content marketing performance requires a focus on both hard and soft metrics. In the simplest terms, hard metrics include quantitative data that can be collected objectively, whereas soft metrics include qualitative data that is collected subjectively. Both forms of metrics offer important insight into your overall content marketing performance.

Specifically, hard metrics offer hard numbers such as the following:

- ✔ Number of page views on your Web site and blog
- ✔ Number of retweets of your Twitter updates
- ✔ Number of @replies and @mentions you receive on Twitter
- ✔ Number of views of your online videos
- ✔ Number of times your shortened links in Twitter, Facebook, and so on are clicked
- ✔ Number of comments published on your blog
- ✔ Number of responses to your comments published on other blogs, forums, and so on
- ✔ Number of subscribers to your newsletter or RSS feeds
- ✔ Number of incoming links to your blog or Web site
- ✔ Number of Twitter followers, Facebook friends, LinkedIn connections, Facebook Page fans, and so on
- ✔ Number of times your content is shared on social bookmarking sites, Facebook, LinkedIn, and more

Any metric that offers insight into how many people consume, share, or discuss your content is a hard metric that you need to track to quantify your content marketing results. As long as you see a continued increase in those metrics, you're on the right track to growing your online presence.

Soft metrics are far more subjective. They focus on the perceptions and sentiments the online audience has about your brand and business, based on the content and conversations the audience publishes online. In fact, it's many of these unquantifiable performance results that actually drive hard metrics. For example, as brand awareness and positive brand sentiment about your business grow among your target audience, an increase in hard metrics such as Web site page views and Twitter followers will likely follow.

By allowing the online audience to take control of the online conversation and to experience your brand in the ways they choose, your online presence will grow. This type of growth isn't always measurable, but this fact doesn't make it any less valuable.

Understanding the new ROI: Return on Impression

Tracking content marketing performance begins by understanding the new ROI that applies to social media and content marketing. No longer does the term ROI stand only for Return on Investment. Today, ROI also stands for Return on Impression, which encompasses two primary values, one of which is a hard metric and the other a soft metric.

Eyeballs

Impressions can be a quantifiable, hard metric related to how often the online audience views your content and conversations. In this case, the term *impressions* is used similarly to how it's used in impression-based online advertising. However, impression-based online advertising is limited to the site where the advertiser paid for ad placement, whereas content marketing impressions can happen across the Web as people share and discuss that content.

For example, a piece of content that is originally published on your blog can be shared on Twitter, Facebook, LinkedIn, Digg, StumbleUpon, in other blog posts, in online forums, and so on. Your valuable, shareworthy content can spread and boost impressions. When measuring content marketing results, you can calculate this form of return on impression by counting the actual number of people who view, share, and discuss your content.

Not all eyeball impressions are the same. For example, eyeball impressions can range from a person who simply views your content all the way to a person who passionately discusses and engages with your content. This is where the *perceptions* aspect of return on impression comes into play.

Perceptions

Impressions can be an immeasurable, soft metric that represents added value related to how your content and conversations are received by the online audience and how that content affects their perceptions of your brand and business. In other words, *how* your content makes people feel about your brand and the emotional involvement that develops with your brand and business have a direct effect on your content marketing success.

Unfortunately, you can't directly measure those feelings, but by listening to conversations and monitoring your online reputation, you can get a clearer understanding of how your audience perceives your brand and business. Positive brand perceptions and emotional involvement in a brand lead to brand loyalty and advocacy, which typically lead to increased business.

Evaluating Return on Opportunity, Return on Objectives, and Return on Engagement

Content marketing can also be measured using methods frequently referred to as Return on Opportunity, Return on Objectives, and Return on Engagement. The purpose of each method of tracking performance is to focus more heavily on soft metrics and long-term strategies than on hard data and short-term tactics.

Measuring Return on Opportunity is as simple as evaluating the opportunity that specific content marketing efforts present versus the time and monetary commitment they require. The purpose of Return on Opportunity analysis is to allow room to account for indirect marketing success. For example, a content tactic that offers a big opportunity might not add to the business's bottom line immediately, but the indirect marketing opportunities that it could lead to are worth the effort. It's this type of analysis and balancing that is necessary to create a successful content marketing plan.

Similarly, Return on Objectives may not be measurable with hard data but rather with an analysis of whether content marketing efforts are moving the business in the right direction to meet its long-term objectives. It's this area of performance analysis that reminds you content marketing is a long-term strategy. As long as your efforts are moving you toward your objectives, you're on the right track.

Finally, Return on Engagement may not be quantifiable, but that doesn't make it any less important to your content marketing performance analysis. It might require a subjective analysis to review how people engage with your content and interact with you and your business through content and conversations, and that's absolutely fine. The important thing is that you keep track of *how* people engage with you and your content, not just that they do or do not engage with you.

Return on Opportunity, Return on Objectives, and Return on Engagement each rely on three core pieces of information — traffic (which is a form of eyeball impressions), sentiment (which is a form of perception impressions), and sharing (which is a combination of eyeball and perception impressions). You need to consider all three forms of data in order to fully analyze your content marketing performance.

Finding Tools to Analyze Marketing Metrics

A variety of free and paid tools are available to help you track hard metrics related to your content marketing efforts. When it comes time to track metrics on your own Web site or blog, you can choose among several free tools. Each offers similar information, which you can use to tweak your content marketing efforts to boost results on your own sites.

When you start using a Web analytics tool, you may be overwhelmed by the amount of data that's available to you. To make it easier, following are some of the key statistics you can track to gauge which content is helping you the most:

- ✔ **Visitors:** So that you can make sure your audience grows over time and determine whether that audience is becoming loyal to you, it's important to discover how many unique and repeat visitors are coming to your Web site each day.

- ✔ **Traffic sources:** Review the data in your analytics tool to find out where the people who visit your site come from. Traffic sources are typically broad categories grouped by people who come from search engines, other Web sites, and direct traffic (people who typed your Web site address directly into their browser's search bar). This data can help you find out about other sites that are sharing your content and sending traffic to you.

- ✔ **Referrers:** Referrers is a more specific metric that breaks down traffic sources into the exact Web addresses where people clicked on links to get to your site. Visit the top referrers of traffic to your site to see how and why they're sending traffic your way and what they're saying about you and your content. These referrers are likely to be sites and people you'll want to connect with and begin building relationships.

- ✔ **Keywords:** It's important to track the specific keywords and keyword phrases that people typed into search engines that led them to your site. With this knowledge, you can rewrite your Web content to leverage those keywords further and use them to boost your search engine rankings and increase eyeball impressions on your content.

- ✔ **Top content:** The top content data refers to the pages on your Web site that are getting the most visits. By analyzing your top content, you can create more content like it and boost your traffic even higher. You can also find which pages on your site are underperforming so that you can make that content more meaningful and shareworthy.

When you know what to track, you need to choose a Web analytics tool to automate the process of gathering data. The following sections describe several popular Web analytics tools you can use to track your Web site and blog content performance.

No analytics tool (free or paid) is 100 percent accurate.

Google Analytics

I recommend Google Analytics (www.google.com/analytics) because it offers a huge amount of data for free, is easy to use, and integrates with other Google products such as Google Webmaster Central (www.google.com/webmasters), which can help you improve your Web site, blog, and content even more with Google Webmaster Tools that provide useful information about how Google crawls your site, who is linking to your site, how people are finding your site through keyword searches, and more.

As you can see in Figure 16-9, Google Analytics offers information about visitors, traffic, content, and much more. Each section can be expanded, enabling you to access a wealth of additional data.

To use Google Analytics, you just need to create a free Google account, enter your site's URL into the provided form, and paste the provided tracking code into your Web site or blog as directed. (Note that it may take a day or two for data to appear in your Google Analytics account.)

Site Meter

Site Meter (www.sitemeter.com) offers basic site data free. Site Meter can be a good option to help you become familiar with Web analytics without feeling overwhelmed with data. However, Site Meter counts up to only 100 visitors at a time and then resets and starts counting again, so this is not the option you want to use if you're ready for deep analysis. You can also use a paid version of Site Meter that provides more detailed information, so it's up to you if you want to pay for Site Meter when Google Analytics is free.

Figure 16-9:
Google Analytics offers a huge amount of data free.

StatCounter

The free version of StatCounter (www.statcounter.com) is a bit more detailed than Site Meter, but for enhanced details, you'll need to use the paid version. StatCounter works the same way as Site Meter in that only the first 500 visitors are counted in displayed results unless you upgrade to the paid version. Again, it's up to you to determine whether you want to pay for StatCounter when Google Analytics is free.

Adobe Online Marketing Suite

The Adobe Online Marketing Suite of products (powered by Omniture), including Adobe SiteCatalyst, Discover, Digital Pulse, and more are available for purchase at www.omniture.com/en/products/online_marketing_suite. These products are some of the higher priced Web analytics tools, which are used by many large companies, and pricing is not available unless you speak directly with a sales representative about your individual needs for a custom solution. Expect the price tag to be significantly higher than the paid versions of Site Meter or StatCounter.

Radian6

To monitor hard metrics related to your social media mentions and engagement efforts, Radian6 (www.radian6.com) offers products that are popular for larger companies. Pricing starts at $600 per month, so it's a big investment. However, if you really need hard metrics related to how your content performs on the social Web, Radian6 offers viable options.

Conducting Ongoing Research

Conducting trend analysis and reviewing Web analytics data are essential to track your content marketing performance, but you also need to conduct your own market research to get a full picture. That research can be both quantitative and qualitative, but remember, unless your research is conducted with truly random audience samples, data collected should be considered exploratory only. In other words, don't bet the farm on insights you gather through your own online market research. This type of data can help guide you in a certain direction but should not be used as the foundation of your marketing strategy development.

You can conduct your own informal market research online in a variety of ways in order to develop your content marketing plan for the future. The following sections provide just a few examples of free or low-cost methods you can use to gather qualitative and quantitative data from your online audience.

Pricing varies depending on the size of your research project and the audience.

E-mail and online surveys

A number of companies offer free or low-cost e-mail survey tools, which you can use to create and send marketing surveys or invitations to participate in your survey online. Typically, your surveys can include closed-ended and open-ended questions, and pricing depends on the length of your survey, the number of people you're sending it to, and the number of responses you receive. Survey tabulation is usually included, but be sure to confirm that before you commit to paying for a specific tool or service (unless you're willing to tabulate the results yourself).

Popular options for creating e-mail or online surveys (including e-mailing invitations) include the following:

- **SurveyMonkey:** www.surveymonkey.com
- **SurveyGizmo:** www.surveygizmo.com
- **VerticalResponse:** www.verticalresponse.com
- **Constant Contact:** www.constantcontact.com
- **Emma:** www.myemma.com

Online polls

Publishing polls online is not only a great way to gather market research data about your existing audiences but also a great way to motivate people to actively participate on your site or blog. Anything you can do to move people to action and get them to start engaging with you and interacting with your content is a good thing. Sometimes all it takes is that first interaction to get people to engage on a regular basis.

You can find a number of free tools to publish online polls and even embed them into your own Web site or blog. These are usually simple one-question polls with a number of possible answers a respondent can choose from. Sometimes, an Other response is included where respondents can enter their own answer if it's not in the list provided. You can see an example of an online poll in Figure 16-10.

So what do you think? Is the new Kululua Airlines rebranding initiative a good long term strategy or a short term tactic that will fizzle out sooner rather than later? Take the poll below and share your opinion. If you can't see the poll, follow this link to take it.

> What do you think of the Kululua Airlines rebranding effort?
>
> ○ I love it!
>
> ○ I hate it!
>
> View Results
> PollDaddy.com
>
> vote

Figure 16-10: Online polls can be informational or just for fun.

Following are popular tools for creating online polls:

- ✔ **Polldaddy:** www.polldaddy.com
- ✔ **Poll Authority:** www.pollauthority.com
- ✔ **Zoomerang:** www.zoomerang.com

Online poll tools typically offer free and paid accounts, so be sure to compare current features and pricing before you select a tool or pay for anything (typically, a free account is fine to start with).

Some online poll tools enable you to create polls to publish on sites like Twitter and Facebook in addition to on your Web site and blog!

Listening to and joining conversations

One of the best ways to monitor your content performance is simply by paying attention to what people are saying about you, your content, and topics related to your business. At the same time, you need to understand which content and conversations get the greatest response from your target audience. For example, take note of which of your Twitter updates receive the most clicks, responses, and retweets and then publish more of the same type of content. Analyze which types of posts on your blog get the most comments or incoming links and publish more of the same kind of posts.

Listening and joining conversations is only the first part of improving your content marketing efforts. By looking for consistent threads, trends, and similarities, you can identify the types of content and conversations that strike a chord with your target audience and better predict the type of content and conversations that will get them emotionally involved in the future.

Emotionally involved audience members are likely to become loyal to your brand, and there's no better form of word-of-mouth marketing than loyal and vocal brand advocates.

In other words, by listening to and joining conversations that happen online, your content marketing efforts can come full circle. Few other marketing opportunities allow you to get broad feedback on an ongoing basis. Leverage that information to improve your efforts in the future and boost your Return on Investment, Return on Impression, Return on Objectives, Return on Opportunity, and Return on Engagement.

Retooling a Content Marketing Strategy

It's important to understand that there's no written recipe for content marketing success — because content marketing is still in its infancy, and companies of all sizes and in all industries are in the very early stages of experimentation. In other words, if you pursue a specific content marketing tactic and it doesn't work, don't be overly disappointed. Instead, remember that you're not the only one who is continually testing and tweaking. Look at each tactic and the subsequent result of implementing that tactic as a learning experience, knowing that you can develop more effective content marketing initiatives in the future.

Because of the newness of content marketing, you need to view your content marketing strategy as ever-changing. Not only should you review the performance of each content marketing tactic you use, but you also need to listen and monitor your online reputation on a constant basis to ensure that you're always heading in the right direction.

Understanding the ever-changing online world

The Internet changes faster and more frequently than any other medium, and the online audience *expects* that constant change. The Web-savvy audience is always looking for the next great thing and something better than what they currently have. Rather than fearing change, the online audience embraces it with the hope that change will make their Web experiences and their lives easier or better.

As part of your content marketing strategy, you need to keep your ears and eyes open so you find out about new tools that can enhance your content marketing efforts. You can't be afraid to experiment with new tools, and you certainly can't ignore them. Your audience is apt to expect that you'll use new tools that gain a significant buzz online. Again, listen to your audience so you're sure you're always delivering what they want, need, and expect from your business and brand.

To get started with your efforts to discover new content marketing tools that can help you, take some time to follow content marketers and social media marketers online. These people are likely to hear about new tools, discuss them, and offer their opinions, which can help you determine which tools to try. For example, you can follow me at `www.twitter.com/susangunelius`, and search for more experts using keyword searches on Twitter or with Twitter apps such as WeFollow (`www.wefollow.com`).

Evaluating results against goals

Earlier in this chapter, I discuss analyzing Return on Objectives to evaluate the performance of your content marketing efforts. This is an important concept that bears repeating. Remember, content marketing is a long-term brand building and marketing strategy. Don't sweat the numbers, or you might set yourself up for disappointment.

When it comes to content marketing success, quality always trumps quantity. By publishing amazing, shareworthy content, you'll have a better chance at developing followers who are loyal brand advocates and relationships with key individuals across the Web. It's better to have 100 quality connections share and discuss your content than 1,000 connections that can't help your business at all.

Therefore, spend your time creating quality content and building quality relationships. Your efforts will result in a steady movement toward meeting your goals, and that's where true content marketing success comes from.

Revising goals

As you evaluate your content marketing results in terms of your goals, you may realize that the goals you originally established aren't the right goals. That's to be expected, so don't view the need to revise your content marketing goals as a failure. Instead, view the need to revise your goals as a positive, because it shows that you've effectively monitored your performance, your audience, and the changing online landscape and that you're flexible enough to change with the people and environment around you.

As you begin implementing your content marketing plan, schedule a monthly review of that plan to determine where goal revisions are warranted. When a new tool is launched that can significantly affect your content marketing efforts and the results of those efforts, take some time to compare your goals to those opportunities and make the necessary changes.

Again, your content marketing plan is a moving document that grows and changes. A static content marketing plan is doomed to failure, but a flexible content marketing plan is positioned for success.

Introducing new content efforts

As new tools are launched and you gather more information about your audience, the online space, and the performance of your content marketing efforts, you'll undoubtedly find new content efforts that you want to add to your content marketing plan. Don't hesitate to do so, but always proceed with the understanding that a new content effort shouldn't take so much time away from your existing content efforts that those original efforts will suffer.

Quality trumps quantity, and while it's essential that you diversify your content marketing efforts, increase your branded online destinations, and offer new ways for audiences to consume and engage with your content, it's even more important that each of your content marketing efforts is of high quality and representative of your brand promise. The last thing you want to do is confuse consumers who have established expectations for your brand by creating content that is sub-standard and counterproductive to your brand building efforts.

As you create content for new sites that you don't own or develop new branded online destinations to publish your content, be sure to interlink and integrate your varied efforts. Announce your new content's presence on your existing online destinations so that your audience knows there's a new way to consume your content and engage with you. If you build it, they won't necessarily come. Instead, you need to tell people about your new destinations and content, but avoid spreading the word in a self-promotional manner.

While announcing a new branded online destination or content marketing initiative is fine, don't repeatedly promote it. Instead, indirectly market that content by integrating your content marketing efforts (refer to Chapter 15 for more on this topic). In time, your new destinations will grow just as your original destinations grew. However, if you spend all your time self-promoting, no one will want to visit your new destinations, and they might even leave your existing destinations and conversations.

Always make sure that you give new content efforts a fair chance at success. Each effort is different from the next, so monitoring performance and listening to conversations is just as important for new content efforts as it is for existing efforts. It's unlikely your original content marketing initiative was a success overnight, and your new efforts aren't likely to be overnight sensations either. Patience and persistence are required for every content marketing effort to have a chance at long-term success.

Chapter 17

Building a Content Marketing Team

Content marketing can be time-intensive. While monetary investments don't have to be big, you do need to commit a portion of your time each day to content marketing. Whether you're strategizing future efforts, writing and publishing content, listening to online conversations, monitoring your online reputation, or analyzing results, every part of executing your content marketing plan requires a time investment.

You might even need to find help creating content and managing your content marketing efforts. With proper planning, you can put together a content marketing team, recruit employees to help, or hire freelancers to give you a hand when you need it. This chapter shows you how.

Identifying Resource Needs

The first step to building a content marketing team is identifying the resources that you need in terms of manpower. Content marketing is about more than just writing content. While you need at least one person on your team who can write quality content for varied online destinations, you also need someone who can share and discuss content effectively, and provide the behind-the-scenes site maintenance and support necessary to implement an effective content marketing plan.

Depending on the size of your content marketing efforts, you could perform all of these duties yourself, or you may need to divide responsibilities among a number of people. Only you can make the determination about whether you need to spread responsibilities across additional people in order to meet your content goals. In fact, most content marketing efforts start as a one-person show and grow to include more team members as necessary.

Content creation needs

First, you must determine the type of content that needs to be written, created, and published on a daily basis. You may also need a team member who can write or create excellent audio or video content if your content marketing plan includes those kinds of long-form content marketing.

Not only do you need the tools to create and publish these types of content, but you also need the expertise to accomplish these tasks. Writing a single blog post each day may not seem overly time-intensive; however, when you add in the time it takes to carry out all your other content marketing activities, you may find that you don't have time to write one quality blog post.

To make sure you can realistically handle all the content creation requirements you need to fulfill, put together a monthly editorial calendar that outlines the content you'll need on a daily basis. For example, how many blog posts, tweets, Facebook updates, videos, and so on do you plan to publish each day or week? Identify your content needs before you do anything else.

Sharing needs

When your content is published, you need to indirectly promote it by integrating your varied content marketing efforts, sharing links to your own content, and sharing links from your audience, too. Remember, successful content marketing is not one-sided. You have to give as much as you receive, so you need to spend a significant amount of time sharing content that you did not create but that your audience is likely to find valuable.

It takes time to share your own content and integrate it with your other online efforts, and it takes even more time to read through the content published by others and then share the meaningful content you find with your audience. In addition, to establish new relationships that can benefit your business in the future, be sure to share content from people and sites that you're not already connected to, if that content will benefit your target audience. None of these activities are difficult, but they do take time.

Discussion needs

If your content marketing efforts are working, your content will create discussions. Be prepared to join discussions about your own content as well as join in online discussions across the Web where you can demonstrate your expertise, build relationships, and ultimately share more of your long-form and short-form content.

Discussions in support of your overall content marketing plan can take up a significant amount of your time each day. You can't ignore your online connections if they engage with you through your content, so you must be available to respond to these online conversations. This form of content marketing is essential to your overall content marketing success.

Offline and behind-the-scenes support needs

On a daily basis, a wide variety of behind-the-scenes activities happen in support of your content marketing efforts. For example, answering e-mails; paying bills; maintaining your blog, applications, and hosting accounts; researching trends and new tools; listening to conversations; evaluating results; and much more. Someone needs to be available to keep up with these activities, or your content marketing efforts will suffer.

These offline and behind-the-scenes support responsibilities may not get the recognition they deserve, but that doesn't make them any less important. The different parts of your content marketing team must be seen as equally important, or your entire plan will not reach its full potential. Don't try to cut corners or skip responsibilities, because the result will be reduced performance.

Asking Employees to Help

If you have a staff of employees, then you might be in luck. You may already have people working for you who understand the social Web and content creation. In fact, you may be able to tap into your existing staff's skills without having to pay additional salary.

For example, if you have an employee who has been hiding her writing talents, have her take 30 minutes each day to write a blog post. If you have a person on staff who uses Twitter avidly, ask him to take on the tweeting duties for your company profile. He could spend just 10 minutes in the morning, 10 minutes midday, and 10 minutes in the late afternoon tweeting. Every effort helps boost your content marketing results and alleviates some of the time you have to devote to content marketing each day.

It's very possible that some of your existing employees have the skills you need to take some of the content marketing responsibilities off your plate. Even if you don't need help today, you may need it in the future as your content marketing efforts become more successful. Prepare in advance by gathering information about your employees' skills related to content marketing. Ask your employees what their writing experiences are, if they have a blog, use Twitter, use Facebook, know how to create and post YouTube videos, and so on. Each of these skills could be very helpful to you in executing your content marketing plan.

Considering the Budget

If you don't have the content marketing skills that you need in-house, you may have to hire new staff or contract with freelancers to get the skills and help you need. However, hiring additional staff or paying freelancers to help you costs money. You need to weigh the cost of hiring additional help against the potential returns that acquiring additional content marketing assistance can deliver to ensure that the investment is worth it.

You get what you pay for. Highly skilled and experienced writers are likely to charge a significant amount for their services. It's up to you to determine if you're willing to pay the writer's fees for quality content.

Fortunately, content marketing help doesn't have to cost a fortune. By outsourcing very specific skills, you can get the help you need without breaking the budget. For example, you can hire a freelance writer to supplement your blog content or hire a person to start conversations about your content on Twitter, online forums, and so on. In other words, you can choose tasks to assign to others in order to free up your schedule for more advanced projects.

When you search for freelancers or new employees to handle content marketing tasks for your business, make sure that you familiarize yourself with the going rates for the type of work you need done. If you don't know what the going rate is, then ask applicants to provide their expected salaries or payments. It's very possible that you may be able to negotiate rates for content marketing tasks that can help a writer or marketer build his own online presence and reputation.

For example, if your business blog is very popular, you may be able to find a freelance writer to write content for your blog at a discounted fee if she can include her byline and a link to her own Web site or blog with her articles. This type of exposure can be very useful to writers who are trying to build up their portfolios, so be prepared to mention these types of opportunities to potential hires.

Establishing Expectations and Requirements

For employees or freelancers to be successful in providing content marketing services to you, you need to provide them with detailed requirements that fully describe your expectations of them. The more specific you can be, the better they can deliver the type of content and conversations you want and need.

Consequently, you need to provide written style requirements, audience descriptions, and specific content requirements, including length, voice, formatting, and more. If you're not writing content yourself, you need to let the people writing it for you know what you want the content to look and sound like, as well as what you want the content to do and to whom you want to speak.

Identifying specific content requirements

You need to offer specific requirements for each type of content an employee or freelancer is expected to create. For example, blog post requirements might include the following details:

- Word count
- If images are required
- If keywords are to be included
- Link formatting requirements
- If posts must be categorized
- If keyword tags are to be included with posts
- If plug-ins or add-ons used on the blog require extra steps to be performed when a new post is written

✔ If posts must be promoted

✔ If comment moderation is required

✔ If comment responses are required

Each of these tasks not only enhances a blog post, but it also adds to the amount of time a person must devote to that post. If you don't specifically tell a writer that he must perform all of these tasks when creating blog posts for your business, he might skip tasks or not perform them in the way you want them to be completed.

Explaining style expectations

Style expectations are a bit more difficult to explain because they can be somewhat objective. For example, do you want your content to be highly professional or highly personal? The style of your content must match your brand promise, so the first step in communicating style expectations is to make sure your content marketing staff fully understands your brand's promise, message, and position.

Provide your content marketing staff with links to your existing content so they can read it and get a feel for your preferred style. If you don't have existing content published yet, point them in the direction of other sites that provide content in the style you want to use for your own content. Also, provide them with content from your competitors and describe how you'd like your content to be different or the ways in which your content can be similar. Finally, lead them to sites where your target audience already spends time so they gain an understanding of how your style will fit into the conversations happening there.

You can also use offline content to demonstrate your style expectations. If you have marketing materials, correspondence, or other content that uses the same style that you want your online content marketing to use, allow your content marketing staff to read that offline content. You can even write some sample content to more clearly demonstrate the style you want them to use when they create new content for you.

Writing policies and guidelines

As more people begin creating content and conversations for you in support of your content marketing efforts, you need to create policies that will help them understand what they are and aren't allowed to do on behalf of your company.

In addition to being representatives of your business, your employees and the people who create content for you are also some of your most valuable brand advocates. You have to give them the freedom to create content related to your business, but you also have to give them some guidelines to follow as representatives of your brand.

Your content marketing guidelines might be as simple as list, such as the following:

✔ Be professional.

✔ Follow copyright, plagiarism, and libel laws.

✔ Don't reveal private company information.

✔ Don't talk about specific clients or customers without permission.

✔ Link to sources.

✔ Avoid participating in conversations that attack individuals or entities or paint the brand in a negative light.

✔ Don't participate in or publish content or conversations that could be deemed offensive, hateful, or obscene.

✔ Use common sense, exercise good judgment, and when in doubt, ask.

Of course, you can create more specific guidelines, but don't scare employees away from creating content and conversations with heavy-handed content marketing policies and guidelines. If they're afraid to participate in the online conversation, they won't be much help to you or your business.

Finding Help with Content Creation, Sharing, and Promotion

When you're ready to look for help in creating, sharing, and promoting your content, you need to identify the skills you require before you hire anyone to help you. By writing specific job postings that clearly communicate your expectations, you'll be better prepared to select the most qualified people from the responses you receive.

Be prepared to receive a wide variety of responses to your requests for content help. Only you can determine the exact skills you want, so make sure you're patient and hire the best person for the job.

Knowing what skills you need

It can be challenging to define and write the specific skills required of the people you hire to help you with your content marketing efforts. Try to envision the tasks you expect the person you hire to perform on a day-to-day basis and make sure every one of the skills required to perform those duties are included in your job posting.

Following are a variety of high-level areas to consider when you put together your job posting:

- ✔ **Experience:** The person you hire should not only have experience using the tools required to perform the job's duties, but should also have experience writing and conversing on the social Web. Potential hires need to understand the online environment and how people interact online. Similarly, if your business requires hiring someone with industry-related experience (for example, a person trained in the medical field if you own a medical business), then you need to make those requirements clear.

- ✔ **Grammar and proofreading skills:** The person you hire should be capable of writing well without the need for you or another person to edit his or her work for clarity, grammar, and spelling.

- ✔ **Specialized knowledge:** If you're hiring a writer, that person should have knowledge of writing with search engine optimization in mind, and how to write content that attracts traffic and sparks conversations. In other words, the duties that your content marketing workers perform may require specific knowledge, which you need to mention in your job posting.

Before you sit down to create a job posting, define the skills the person you hire will need to do the job effectively and meet your expectations. You don't want to set up yourself, your business, or the person you hire for failure by not being clear and specific from Day One.

Writing a job posting

When you're ready to write a job posting to find a person (or people) to help with your content marketing initiatives, you need to include various pieces of information. Not only do you need to describe what the person will be doing on a daily basis, but you also need to include the skills and experience you expect that person to bring to the table and how that person's performance will be measured. You need to include information about the pay rate and how the person will be paid. Finally, you need to provide information about your business that demonstrates the legitimacy of your company and job posting and your company's reputation for demanding quality content.

Use the job requirements and skills listed earlier in this chapter to help you create your own content marketing job posting, and be sure to request that applicants provide you with links to or copies of samples of their work. Make sure you take the time to read applicants' clips and samples when you receive them. These samples can reveal a lot about a person's actual skills, experience, and abilities.

Finding qualified help on Web sites

Many Web sites enable you to publish content marketing job postings and get qualified responses. Remember, those qualified responses are likely to be mixed in with many unqualified responses, so be patient. If you don't find the right person the first time you publish a job posting, you can always publish it again or publish it on a different site.

Following are a number of Web sites where freelance writers and content marketers search for opportunities where you can publish your job postings (be sure to check for potential fees that a site might charge you):

- ✔ **Craigslist.org:** You can publish job postings on your local craigslist.org site.

- ✔ **About.com Blogging:** You can publish blogging jobs free in the About. com Blogging forum at `http://forums.about.com/n/pfx/forum. aspx?folderId=13&listMode=13&nav=messages&webtag= ab-weblogs`.

- ✔ **ProBlogger Job Board:** You can pay a fee and post jobs on this popular site at `http://jobs.problogger.net`.

- ✔ **Freelance Writing Jobs:** You can post jobs on this popular blog for writers for a fee at `www.freelancewritinggigs.com/freelance- writing-job-ads`.

- ✔ **AbsoluteWrite.com:** This forum for writers allows you to post jobs free at `www.absolutewrite.com/forums/forumdisplay.php?s= 0d0d7c2123cc2d8bbe9fd40334410cb9&f=24`.

- ✔ **Mashable Jobs:** This site's job board (`http://jobs.mashable. com/a/jbb/find-jobs`) is powered by SimplyHired.com, but because it appears on one of the most popular blogs online, your posting is likely to get many responses. As you might expect, the posting fee is high.

- ✔ **Freelancer.com:** This is a popular site for freelancers to find work.

- ✔ **Elance.com:** This is another popular site for freelancers to find work.

- ✔ **Guru.com:** This is one more site that freelancers use to find work.

You can publish content marketing job postings on many other sites. In fact, you should always make sure that you publish them on your own Web site, blog, Twitter profile, Facebook Page, and so on. Your own network of connections may already include the right person for the job, or your connections might share your job posting with their own audiences where the right person could be waiting!

Monitoring Performance

Be sure to read the content your employees and writers create for you, and review their online activities in support of your content, brand, and business to ensure that it's appropriate and that it accurately reflects the reputation you want to develop online. If your staff is veering off course or not meeting your expectations, let them know immediately, and give them specific directions to correct any problems. This kind of supervision is particularly important when working with freelancers who aren't physically located in your office.

Content marketers and writers often work remotely, which means lower costs for you. However, managing virtual workers requires a different communication style. Make sure those lines of communication are always open and workers feel like they can ask questions at any time. Weekly or bi-weekly phone calls are a great way to stay on track, and using a free tool like Skype, you can conduct these calls without incurring long distance telephone charges.

Use your Web analytics tools and trend analysis to determine which content your writers create and which conversations they participate in are driving positive results for your branded destinations and online reputation — and make sure they're aware of your findings. This information will enable them to plan better content and pay closer attention to people and sites that are generating useful conversations. The more information you can give them to do their jobs effectively, the better.

Just as it's important to create a sense of community among online connections and networks, so is it important to create a sense of community among your content marketing staff. Their efforts shouldn't operate in silos anymore than their outputs should. Instead, an integrated content marketing plan and an integrated content marketing team will yield the best results for your business in the long-term.

Part VI
The Part of Tens

The 5th Wave   By Rich Tennant

"Jim and I do a lot of business together on Facebook. By the way, Jim, did you get the sales spreadsheet and little blue pony I sent you?"

In this part . . .

The Part of Tens offers quick information about tools and information you're likely to need as you foray into content marketing. In fact, you're probably going to visit the Part of Tens frequently for quick access to extremely useful information.

Review the Part of Tens to get information about free tools you can use to get started with content marketing, sites where you can publish your content free, and resources where you can get content marketing help.

Chapter 18

Ten Free Tools to Get Started with Content Marketing

• •

*T*he first step to beginning your journey into the world of content marketing is registering for accounts with the tools you need to use to create that content online. Fortunately, you can use a wide variety of free tools to get started immediately. This chapter points you in the direction of ten free tools that I can't live without.

If you're looking for Web sites where you can actually publish your content, check out Chapter 19. This chapter provides tools that you can use to create, enhance, and manage your content. From analytics tools to image-editing tools, you'll find ten free ways to make your content look great and perform well.

WordPress.org

www.wordpress.org

WordPress.org is the free version of the popular WordPress blogging application that you can only use if you pay for your own Web hosting through a provider, such as Bluehost.com or GoDaddy.com. WordPress.org offers far more customization, flexibility, and features than the WordPress-hosted version available at www.wordpress.com. If you're serious about developing a professional Web presence and brand identity, then WordPress.org is the way to go.

Learning how to use WordPress.org can take a bit longer than WordPress. com, not because the application is more challenging, but because you need to know how to work with a Web host and how to use the many additional features available to you. Check out *WordPress For Dummies,* by Lisa Sabin-Wilson, to find out more about WordPress. Additionally, the WordPress.org Codex (a Wiki-type site that WordPress developers contribute to) offers a huge amount of documentation to help you use WordPress.org (http:// codex.wordpress.org/Main_Page).

stock.xchng

www.sxc.hu

A great way to enhance your content is to add images to it. However, you can't add just any image to your content. You need to make sure that the images you choose carry copyright licenses that allow you to use them, or you need to obtain permission to do so first. Chapter 3 discusses copyrights in detail.

To find a good selection of images that you can use in your online content, search the free images available on stock.xchng. Simply conduct a keyword search, and click the free image you want to use (note that images in the premium section are offered for a fee). The image page opens, as shown in Figure 18-1. Check the usage options in the right sidebar next to the image. If it says "royalty free," then click the Usage Options link to see whether you must follow any specific requirements to use the image (for example, you might have to send the image owner an e-mail with a link showing where the image was used). If you can meet the usage requirements, you are free to use the image in your content.

Figure 18-1: Check the usage options before you use an image in your content.

Paint.NET

www.getpaint.net

Paint.NET is an excellent, free image-editing tool available to Windows users. Don't be misled by the rudimentary Web site where the Paint.NET download links are found, as shown in Figure 18-2. This great free tool rivals the expensive Adobe PhotoShop software that graphic designers use.

Be sure to download the Paint.NET application by clicking the Get It Now link in the upper right of the Getpaint.NET home page, and then click the Download button (sometimes more than one is available) from the table in the Download section, as shown in Figure 18-3.

There are other free image editing options if Paint.NET isn't right for you. GIMP (www.gimp.org) is even more robust than Paint.NET and is available for free download for both Windows and Mac OS X users. However, GIMP can be difficult for beginners to learn because it is more technical. For a Web-based tool, Picnik (www.picnik.com) is not as feature-rich as Paint.NET or GIMP, but it does offer many great options.

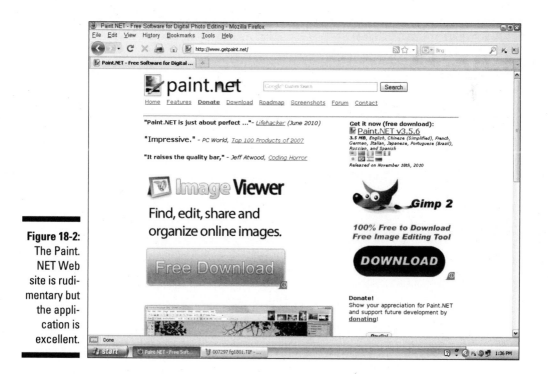

Figure 18-2:
The Paint. NET Web site is rudimentary but the application is excellent.

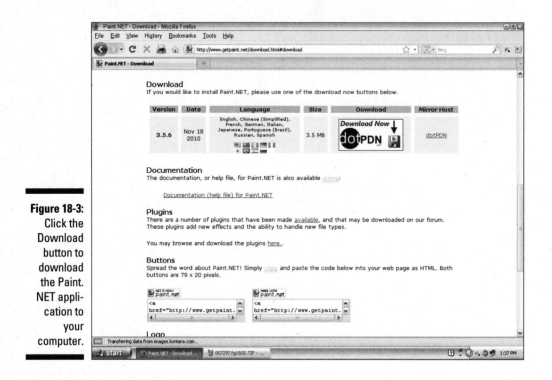

Figure 18-3:
Click the Download button to download the Paint. NET application to your computer.

Polldaddy

www.polldaddy.com

Many tools enable you to create free online polls, but Polldaddy is one of the easiest to use and offers a great selection of free features. You can register for a free Polldaddy account and create a variety of types of polls, modify the design and size, and embed them into your online content. A simple visual step-by-step poll creation tool makes it easy for even beginners to use Polldaddy.

Adding polls to your content is a great way to boost interactivity. It's also a great way to conduct market research, so you can learn about your audience and provide better content to them. Polls can also be a lot of fun!

Core FTP

www.coreftp.com

You can use a number of free FTP tools, and Core FTP is a popular option. A premium version of Core FTP is available, but the free version, Core FTP LE, should suit your needs. You can use Core FTP to transfer files between computers or to upload large documents to your Web site, blog, and so on.

You can download and use the Core FTP application on the Windows platform only. If you need help using Core FTP, check out the active Core FTP forum at http://coreftp.com/forums.

 Another popular FTP tool for Windows users is SmartFTP (www.smartftp.com), and both Windows and Mac users can use FileZilla (www.filezilla-project.org).

CoffeeCup

www.coffeecup.com/free-editor

The more time you spend creating online content, the more likely it will be that you'll need to edit some HTML code. You can learn just a bit of HTML and use a free HTML editor tool like the one offered by CoffeeCup to make the changes you need to your content. CoffeeCup offers a free HTML editor for Windows users that provides enough functionality for most beginners.

Fortunately, most content publishing tools are easy enough to use that you might never need an HTML editor. However, if you do find yourself in need of an easy way to view and edit HTML code, a free tool like CoffeeCup is a great option.

 If you use a Mac or want a different free HTML editor for your Windows environment, the free version of Komodo Edit (www.activestate.com/komodo-edit) is a popular choice.

Google Analytics

www.google.com/analytics

Google Analytics is the best and most comprehensive free Web analytics tool. You can create a free Google account, set up Google Analytics to run on your Web site or blog within minutes, and then analyze your site's performance in a wide variety of ways to ensure it's as successful as possible. Chapter 16 discusses Google Analytics in detail.

Google Analytics also integrates seamlessly with other Google tools and applications, such as FeedBurner, which you can use to manage your blog RSS feed and subscriptions. You can read more about feeds and subscriptions in Chapter 4.

Google Alerts

www.google.com/alerts

Google Alerts is one of the best tools you can use to monitor your brand, business, competitors, and more online. Simply complete the Google Alerts form indicating the keywords you want Google to track, and you'll receive automatic e-mail notifications when new content matches are found across the Web.

Google Alerts can also be used to give you ideas for content topics and to help you find conversations to join. Chapter 16 offers additional tools that you can use to monitor your online reputation and more.

bit.ly

http://bit.ly

Shortening URLs in links used in your online content can help you in a variety of ways. For example, you can fit more characters into a tweet with a shortened URL. You can also track the number of clicks on a shortened URL to determine which content you share via a link is most popular. This helps you plan your content marketing initiatives.

A popular free URL shortener is bit.ly, which enables you to shorten URLs, customize your shortened URLs, and track the number of clicks on your shortened URLs. You can find more on URL shorteners in Chapters 9, 11, and 14.

Google Bookmarks

www.google.com/bookmarks

Google Bookmarks is a great tool to save the links to content you want to write about or reference. The best part is that it's free!

Simply create a free account with Google (or use your existing account), sign in to Google Bookmarks, select the Add Bookmarks link in the right sidebar, and drag the Google Bookmarklet button that appears on the right side of your screen to your Web browser's toolbar. Select View from your Web browser's top navigation bar, click Toolbar, and then click Bookmarks Toolbar. This will make the Google Bookmarks toolbar visible in the top navigation area of your We browser, so you can start bookmarking Web pages in your Google Bookmarks account with a single click. Your links are saved as private, so only you can see them when you're logged into your account.

When you save a bookmark using Google Bookmarks, you can tag it with keywords that will help you remember why you saved it, and access it from any computer at any time. Content marketing organization just got easier!

Chapter 19

Ten Sites to Publish Your Content for Free

· ·

*N*ot only do you need tools to create and enhance your content (you can find ten free tools to do so in Chapter 18), but you also need tools to actually publish the content you create online. Similar to having many free tools that you can use to create your content, you can use a wide variety of free tools to publish that content.

This chapter introduces you to ten popular tools that you can use to publish your content online without paying a penny. These tools and many others are discussed throughout this book, but these are some of the most popular options to get you started.

Blogger

www.blogger.com

In Chapter 18, I discuss that WordPress.org is the best blogging application choice because it offers the most functionality and flexibility. However, to use WordPress.org, you have to pay a small monthly fee to a Web host to store and serve your content online. If you're not interested in paying that fee, Blogger is the best free option. You can't do everything with Blogger that you can with WordPress.org, but for no out of pocket expenses, it's fairly feature-rich.

You can create a free account at Blogger and get your blog up and running within minutes. Be sure to read *Google Blogger For Dummies,* by Susan Gunelius, to discover everything you need to know about using Blogger.

Twitter

`www.twitter.com`

Twitter is the most popular microblogging application, and it's likely to become a core component of your short-form and conversational content marketing efforts. It's completely free to use, and the learning curve is very short.

The wide variety of free Twitter applications that are available to Twitter users makes it easy to take your Twitter content to the next level in terms of indirectly marketing your business, analyzing your audience, connecting with people, and joining conversations. You can read more about using Twitter for short-form and conversational content marketing in Chapters 9 and 13, respectively.

Facebook

`www.facebook.com`

Over 500 million people use Facebook, and the opportunities to market your brand and business (or yourself) through content via Facebook are numerous. You can start a personal Facebook profile and a business or brand Facebook Page, and you can even start and join Facebook groups where smaller audiences of users participate in niche conversations.

In Chapter 8, you find out about using Facebook for short-form content marketing, and Chapter 13 offers information about using Facebook for conversational content marketing. Facebook is the most popular social networking site, so, undoubtedly, many people you want to talk to are there.

LinkedIn

`www.linkedin.com`

LinkedIn is the most popular social network for business people and career-minded individuals. You can create a personal LinkedIn profile or a company LinkedIn page to promote yourself, your brand, or your business to the 90 million LinkedIn users.

LinkedIn is a more private social networking site than Facebook, so be sure to read Chapters 8 and 13 to get all the details about using LinkedIn for content marketing purposes.

YouTube

www.youtube.com

Google owns YouTube, which is the most popular online video publishing tool. You can upload your video content to your YouTube account or create a branded YouTube channel and upload all of your brand-related content to that channel. It's a great way to create a branded online destination where you can share your content and discuss it with visitors.

You can also embed your YouTube videos into your Web site and blog, and you can share them on your Facebook and LinkedIn accounts. Those are just a few of the tactics you can pursue to market your company through video content. Chapter 5 discusses YouTube and video long-form content marketing in detail.

SlideShare

www.slideshare.net

SlideShare is an excellent tool for publishing and sharing your presentations. You can upload a presentation and allow people to comment on it, share it, embed it on their own sites, print it, and download it. Your presentations are likely to be great representations of your expertise, so promote yourself by letting the world see and share them!

A free SlideShare account is typically enough for beginner users, but there is a Pro option available for a fee if you ever want to upgrade. You can find more about SlideShare and long-form content marketing in Chapter 4.

Flickr

www.flickr.com

Flickr is the most popular photo uploading and sharing site. You can create a free account and begin uploading your photos or images immediately. Flickr allows you to tag images that you upload with keywords and even create image sets to keep specific groups of images together. Visitors can comment on images you upload, and sharing uploaded images across the social Web is easy.

Chapter 8 offers more information about Flickr and using images for short-form content marketing. Remember, when you upload images to Flickr, you have an option to set the copyright license on each individual image. Figure 19-1 shows how the copyright license appears with an image on Flickr. Although it isn't guaranteed that people will respect that copyright and not use your images in other places, the copyright does offer you some form of recourse.

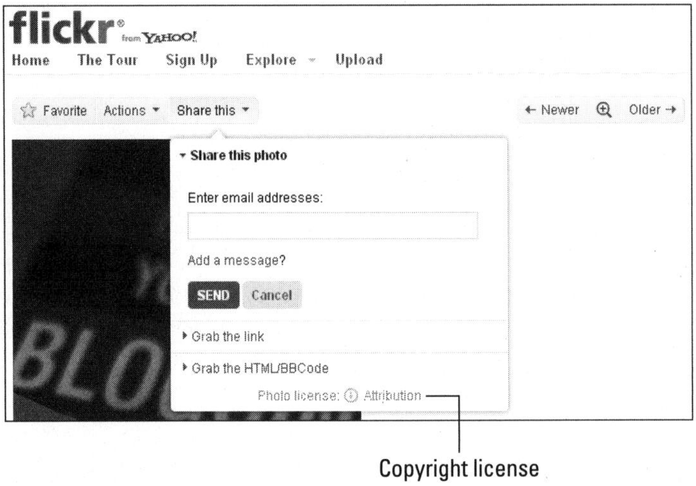

Figure 19-1:
Apply a
copyright
notice to
every image
you upload
to Flickr.

flickr® from YAHOO!

Home   The Tour   Sign Up   Explore ▾   Upload

☆ Favorite   Actions ▾   Share this ▾   ← Newer   ⊕   Older →

▾ Share this photo

Enter email addresses:

Add a message?

SEND   Cancel

▸ Grab the link

▸ Grab the HTML/BBCode

Photo license: ⓘ Attribution

Copyright license

Don't upload images to Flickr and set them as public (for the world to see) unless you are okay with those images spreading across the Web and being seen by more than just Flickr users. You never know where content published online might turn up despite the copyright restrictions you put on that content. You can find more on copyrights in Chapter 3.

BlogTalkRadio

www.blogtalkradio.com

You can create a free account on BlogTalkRadio and become the host of your own online talk show! BlogTalkRadio lets you create your own branded show page, invite guests, allow listeners to call in with questions and comments, and enable people to publish written comments on your show. It's a great way to add interactive audio to your long-form content marketing plan.

You can find more on using audio for long-form content marketing and BlogTalkRadio in Chapter 5. A benefit of using BlogTalkRadio is that you can upload your show to iTunes, so people can listen to it on their iPods and other MP3 players.

Podbean.com

www.podbean.com

Although BlogTalkRadio enables you to be the host of your own online talk show, Podbean.com allows you to publish more traditional podcast content. When Podbean.com hosts your audio content, that content is automatically available on iTunes, too.

With Podbean.com, you can easily integrate your audio content into your other branded online destinations, such as your blog or Facebook Page, so it's exposed to wider audiences. Chapter 5 discusses audio long-form content marketing and Podbean.com in detail.

EzineArticles.com

www.ezinearticles.com

A popular form of long-form content marketing is article publishing. Using a site, such as EzineArticles.com, you can publish your original content or content that you own which you've already published on your blog or other branded online destination in an effort to expose it to a broader audience.

The important thing to remember about article publishing sites like EzineArticles.com is that submitting your content may be giving permission for your content to be republished by other people both online and offline. Be sure to read all the details to ensure they match your goals before you publish your content on an article publishing site. You can find more on long-form content marketing with articles in Chapter 4.

Chapter 20

Ten Resources for Content Marketing Help

. . . .

*I*f you're ready to dive deeply into specific content marketing tools and tactics, then the resources offered in this chapter can help you. Whether you want to find out how to blog, how to write content for better search engine optimization, or how to use Facebook, this chapter sends you in the right direction to take the next step.

Content Marketing For Dummies introduces you to the tools and concepts you need to understand in order to develop a content marketing strategy and plan for executing that strategy, but to learn the ins and outs of those various tools, you might want to use one of the resources offered in this chapter along the way.

Blogging All-in-One For Dummies

Blogging All-in-One For Dummies, by Susan Gunelius, is over 700 pages and teaches all aspects of blogging that a beginner needs to know to successfully enter the world of blogging. As a content marketer, you need to understand how to set up your blog and publish posts effectively to get the most from your time investment. This book can help you.

Topics include choosing a blogging application, writing content, promoting content, and even making money from a blog. The book is written in modular format, so you can choose the chapters or parts that you want to read at any given time.

About.com Blogging

http://weblogs.about.com

About.com is a New York Times company, which employs experts to publish useful content to help beginners learn about specific subjects. About.com Blogging is dedicated to delivering information about blogging and micro-blogging (particularly with Twitter).

The site is divided into topic categories, such as starting a blog, blogging tools, marketing a blog, and more. A weekly newsletter, a forum, and a blog offer real-time content to supplement the evergreen article content found within the site.

WordPress Codex

http://codex.wordpress.org/Main_Page

For people who use the self-hosted version of WordPress available at WordPress.org to create their Web sites and blogs, the WordPress Codex is a valuable resource. The documents in the WordPress Codex are written by contributors and teach just about every aspect of using WordPress.org that you can think of.

The Getting Started with WordPress section of the WordPress Codex (http://codex.wordpress.org/Getting_Started_with_WordPress) is particularly useful as you build your Web site and blog to begin your content marketing initiatives.

Google Blogger For Dummies

If you choose to use Blogger as your blogging application, then *Google Blogger For Dummies,* by Susan Gunelius, is one of the most comprehensive guides available. It covers all aspects of using Blogger, such as account creation, blog set-up, blog design, content publishing, and adding additional features.

Blogger is updated continuously, and *Google Blogger For Dummies* is updated and re-released from time to time with necessary revisions incorporated. Be sure to purchase the most current edition.

Facebook Help

www.facebook.com/help/?ref=pf

The Help section of the Facebook Web site includes documentation where you can discover just about every aspect of how to use Facebook. Sections are dedicated to Facebook profiles, Facebook Pages, Facebook groups, Facebook applications, and more.

If you have questions about Facebook while you're using it, the Help section is likely to have the answers you need. It's the first place you should go to search for information.

LinkedIn Learning Center

http://learn.linkedin.com

The LinkedIn Learning Center (shown in Figure 20-1) is different from the LinkedIn Help page (http://help.linkedin.com), which offers a keyword search tool to find answers to common LinkedIn user questions. The LinkedIn Learning Center offers more comprehensive guides to using LinkedIn.

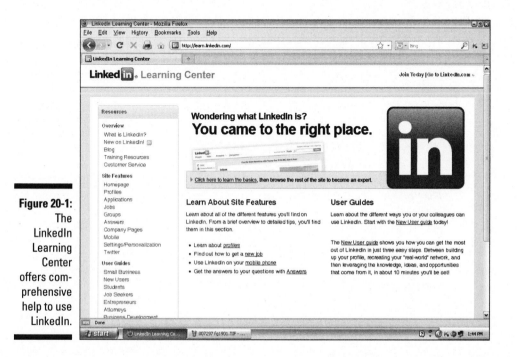

Figure 20-1: The LinkedIn Learning Center offers comprehensive help to use LinkedIn.

The LinkedIn Learning Center offers video and text instruction related to getting started with LinkedIn and using the site features, including profiles, applications, jobs, answers, groups, company pages, mobile, personalization, Twitter, and more. Links to a variety of guides targeted to specific users are also available. For example, there are user guides for businesses, students, job seekers, entrepreneurs, non-profits, journalists, consultants, and more.

Twitter For Dummies

Twitter For Dummies, by Laura Fitton, Michael Gruen, and Leslie Poston, is one of the best books to read if you want to learn how to use Twitter. Chapters include information about setting up your Twitter profile, finding people to follow, and using applications. There is also a great deal of information about using Twitter for business and networking.

Twitter might seem simple enough to use, but you can get a lot more out of it if you understand how it can be used and what applications and features are available to you to boost your chances for success. This book introduces you to many of those concepts and tools.

SEOmoz

www.seomoz.org

SEOmoz is one of the best Web sites to learn about search engine optimization, so you can write content and setup your branded online destinations to boost the traffic that comes to them from keyword searches on such popular search engines as Google, Yahoo!, and Bing. The site offers both free and paid content, but the free content is more than suitable for anyone who is not trying to become an SEO expert.

SEOmoz offers a useful blog (www.seomoz.org/blog) and guides to learn SEO (www.seomoz.org/learn-seo). Paying pro members can also access webinars and training seminars.

W3Schools

www.w3schools.com

W3Schools offers a variety of free online training. If you want to learn HTML or CSS, then this is the site to check out. The free HTML training (www.w3schools.com/HTML/default.asp) is split into chapters that offer beginner and advanced instruction. Examples, references, and quizzes are also included.

The free CSS course from W3Schools (www.w3schools.com/css/default.asp) is divided into chapters with basic, styling, box model, and advanced instruction. Like the HTML course, the CSS course also includes examples, references and quizzes.

30-Minute Social Media Marketing

30-Minute Social Media Marketing (by Susan Gunelius, McGraw-Hill) offers strategic and tactical instruction to small and mid-size business owners and individuals who want to build their brands, businesses, and online reputations on the Web through social media. It's written in an easy-to-read manner that explains complex and overwhelming topics in simple and succinct ways.

Social media marketing and content marketing go hand-in-hand, and *30-Minute Social Media Marketing* teaches readers how to implement a social media marketing plan effectively by spending just 30 minutes each day on social Web activities. This book offers sample 30-minutes per day plans, links to hundreds of resources, and tips to make the time you spend online drive real results.

Part VII
Appendixes

The 5th Wave   By Rich Tennant

"Look—you can't just list an extraterrestrial embryo on eBay without using some catchy phrases or power words to make it seem interesting and unique."

In this part . . .

Appendix A offers several sample plans that you can use to create your own content marketing plan. These samples can help you think creatively and come up with ways to jumpstart your business with content and conversations.

This book concludes with a glossary of terms that you might see while you're diving into the world of content marketing. If you come across a term that's unfamiliar to you — in this book or while implementing your content marketing plan — peek at Appendix B for an easy-to-understand definition.

Appendix A

Sample Content Marketing Quick Start Plans

• •

*U*se the sample content marketing quick start plans offered in this appendix to start your journey into the world of content marketing and building your brand and business. Keep in mind that these sample content marketing quick start plans are not requirements. They're provided to help you start thinking about simple ways to add content marketing tactics to your existing marketing plan. If you're having trouble deciding where to begin and what to do first, follow one of the plans provided in this appendix, modify one of these plans, or combine different elements from different plans to create your own.

The more time you spend creating content and listening to your online audience, the more your content marketing will evolve. A static content marketing plan is unlikely to succeed because the world of content marketing continually changes. Therefore, remember that the sample content marketing quick start plans included in this appendix should be used as guides not rules.

Each sample content marketing plan includes a series of five specific steps and tactics you can pursue to jumpstart your content marketing efforts. Of course, you can do many more things to enhance your content marketing plan, which you read about throughout this book. However, these sample content marketing plans are intended to help you quickly implement a content marketing plan, which you can build upon over time. You can't enjoy the benefits of content marketing until you get started, and these sample content marketing plans enable you to do exactly that — get started today!

A Blog-Focused Content Marketing Quick Start Plan

This sample content marketing quick start plan focuses on using a blog as your core branded online destination and building your content marketing tactics around that central hub.

Long-form content marketing tactics:

1. Create a blog for your business using a blogging application, such as the self-hosted version of WordPress (www.wordpress.org).

2. Design your blog to accurately communicate your brand promise and ensure your blog is linked to your business Web site.

3. Write and publish amazing, shareworthy content on your business blog to build up your content archives and get indexed by search engines to build up entry points.

4. Syndicate your blog's RSS feed with a Web feed management service provider, such as FeedBurner (www.feedburner.com), and make it easy for visitors to subscribe to your blog via feed reader or e-mail.

5. Make sure your blog posts are open to comments.

Short-form content marketing tactics:

1. Create a Twitter profile for your business and use Twitterfeed (www.twitterfeed.com) to publish your blog posts automatically to your Twitter feed.

2. Publish interesting, useful tweets to build up your archive of meaningful short-form content on Twitter.

3. Search for people to follow on Twitter who would be interested in your content using the Advanced Twitter Search tool and such Twitter apps as Twellow (www.twellow.com) and WeFollow (www.wefollow.com).

4. Add a Twitter "follow me" icon on your blog, inviting people to follow you on Twitter.

5. If you already have profiles on social networking sites, such as Facebook or LinkedIn, use the tools and applications available through those sites to publish your Twitter updates and blog post links automatically to those profiles.

Conversational content marketing tactics:

1. Search for blogs related to your business where your target audience spends time and begin leaving useful comments on posts where you can add value. Make sure the name and URL you input into the comment form are representative of your brand and useful for search engine optimization.

2. Search for forums related to your business where your target audience spends time and create a profile for yourself. Join conversations, answer questions, and be personable. Make sure that the forum signature that appears at the bottom of your posts is representative of your brand and includes your Web site, blog, Twitter, and other important URLs.

3. Respond to comments submitted on your own blog posts by visitors to your blog. Make sure you respond in a timely manner.

4. Follow the links in the useful comments submitted to your blog to learn about the authors. If the links take you to the authors' blogs or social profiles, comment on those blogs or profiles in return to deepen the relationships and show that you value those people.

5. Spend time conversing with people on Twitter using @replies and direct messages.

A Facebook Page Content Marketing Quick Start Plan

This sample content marketing quick start plan focuses on using a Facebook profile and Page as your core branded online destination for content marketing purposes.

Short-form content marketing tactics:

1. Create a Facebook profile for yourself and take some time to write a great bio that leads with your business information.

2. Take some time to build up some postings and content by adding applications and feeding your blog and other online content feeds (such as Twitter) to your profile.

3. Search for people to become friends with and send them friend requests.

4. Search for groups related to your business where your target audience is likely to spend time and begin publishing content to those groups.

5. Create a Facebook Page for your business, begin publishing content to it, and invite your Facebook friends to like your Page.

Long-form content marketing tactics:

1. If you create YouTube videos for a branded channel or publish presentations on SlideShare, be sure to add those applications to your Facebook Page and profile and publish that long-form content to your Facebook profile and Page, too.

2. Feed your blog content to your Facebook profile and Page.

3. Use the Facebook social tools, such as the Like button, to cross-promote your long-form content. For example, add the Like button to your blog and all of your blog posts, and add Facebook Page widgets to your blog and Web site.

4. Use the Facebook Events application to promote your long-form online or offline events, invite guests, and accept RSVPs.

5. Promote your Facebook Page and profile through your long-form content, such as your blog, Web site, and so on, by adding social media icons to other branded online destinations, in your e-mail signature, and so on.

Conversational content marketing tactics:

1. Respond to comments that people publish to your Facebook profile and Page.

2. Visit your Facebook friends' profiles and Pages and join conversations.

3. Join conversations happening in Facebook groups that you belong to that are related to your business.

4. When you publish content, images, or conversations on Facebook that reference another user, use the tagging feature to tag that person in the content, image, or conversation. By tagging that person, he or she is notified that you referenced him or her, which could strike up a conversation.

5. Don't forget to use the Facebook private message feature to reach out to people outside their public Walls and Pages, too. Just as it's important to communicate with people via email, telephone, and in-person when you can, using the Facebook private message feature gives you another way to interact with people in your online network.

A YouTube Channel Content Marketing Quick Start Plan

This sample content marketing quick start plan focuses on using a YouTube channel as the core branded online destination for a business.

Long-form content marketing tactics:

1. Create a branded YouTube channel and be sure to allow comments and subscribers when you create your account and channel.

2. Create several videos that your target audience would find useful.

3. Upload your video content to your YouTube channel. Be sure to write useful descriptions and include keywords that people are likely to use when searching for video content like yours. Also, to increase exposure, make sure your uploaded videos can be shared and embedded into blogs and Web sites by other people.

4. Create playlists made up of similar video content or a video series to boost search traffic and make it easy for people to watch videos that should be played in a specific order.

5. When you publish a new video, be sure to write a blog post about that video and embed the video into your blog post.

Short-form content marketing tactics:

1. Use a social media icon to promote your YouTube channel and invite followers on your blog and Web site.

2. Add the YouTube application to your Facebook profile and Page and publish your videos there, too.

3. Share relevant video content in comments you publish on forums where it's useful to do so.

4. Take screenshots of useful parts of your online video content that can stand alone as images and publish those on your Flickr profile or Twitpic (www.twitpic.com) to create another way for people to consume and share your content.

5. Share your video content links on your Twitter feed.

Conversational content marketing tactics:

1. Respond to comments that people post on your video content.

2. Find video content and channels related to your business that your target audience produces or is likely to view. Subscribe to those channels and publish comments on interesting videos.

3. Bookmark and share your video content and others' interesting video content using StumbleUpon or your preferred social bookmarking tool.

4. Hold a tweet chat to discuss one of your videos or to get feedback about how to improve your video content or come up with ideas for new video content.

5. Take the time to delete spam comments on your YouTube videos. YouTube videos get a lot of spam comments and offensive comments that can damage the user experience people have when viewing your video content. Don't let that happen.

Appendix B

Glossary

● ●

@mention: A Twitter update that includes @username within the tweet. See also *@reply*.

@reply: Pronounced *at reply*. A Twitter update that begins with @username, which identifies a tweet as being directed at a specific Twitter user. See also *@mention*.

archive: The location on a blog where posts that are not current are stored for easy access by visitors.

Atom: A type of syndication format used to deliver feeds. See also *feed, feed reader,* and *RSS*.

attribution: Citing the source of a story, quote, or image used within online content.

avatar: An online identity's visual representation, such as a picture of a person or logo of a company.

bandwidth: The amount of data that can be transmitted through a network, modem, or online connection, typically measured in bits per second (bps).

blog: A fusion of the words *Web* and *log*. Originally dubbed *Weblogs, blog* quickly grew to be the preferred nomenclature. Blogs began as online diaries with entries listed in reverse chronological order. As blogging grew in popularity, individuals, groups, and businesses joined the blogosphere. Blogs are unique in that they provide a two-way conversation between the author and visitors through the comment feature. Blogs are considered one of the first methods of bringing user-generated content to the mainstream.

blogger: A person who writes content for a blog.

blogging: The act of writing and publishing blog posts or entries.

blogging application: The program used by bloggers to create and maintain blogs, such as Blogger, WordPress, TypePad, Movable Type, and LiveJournal.

blogosphere: The online blogging community made up of bloggers from around the world creating user-generated content as part of the social Web.

blogroll: A list of links created by a blogger and published on his or her blog. Typically, links in a blogroll relate to the blog topic or other sites the blogger enjoys or recommends.

blog comment: An opinion or reaction by a blog reader to a specific post. Comments can be submitted at the end of blog posts when the blogger has chosen to allow them. Comments make a blog interactive.

blog comment moderation: The process of holding comments for review prior to publishing them on a blog. Comment moderation typically ensures spam and offensive comments aren't published on a blog.

blog comment policy: A set of rules and restrictions published on a blog to set visitor expectations related to the types of comments allowed on the blog and what types of comments are likely to be deleted.

blog posts: Individual entries written by a blogger and published on a blog.

blog statistics: The data used to track the performance of a blog.

bounce rate: The percentage of people who leave a Web site immediately after finding it.

brand: The image, message, and promise perceived by consumers when they encounter a tangible representation of a business, product, or service, such as a logo, store, or ad.

browser: A program used to surf the Internet including Internet Explorer, Firefox, Opera, Google Chrome, Safari, and more. Also called *Web browser*.

buzz: The online conversation related to specific topics, words, or other content that draws widespread attention.

CAPTCHA: The acronym for Completely Automated Public Turing test to tell Computers and Humans Apart. It presents a challenge or question that a user must complete before submitting data through a Web site, such as a blog comment.

category: Used in some blogging applications, such as WordPress, to separate similar blog posts so it's easier for readers to find them.

content management system (CMS): A tool for creating and maintaining online content that separates design, content, and interactivity and allows multiple users to easily manage the Web site.

content marketing: The practice of developing awareness, recall, purchases, and loyalty through the use of content published online or offline.

conversational content marketing: Any form of conversation related to a form of content that is created, published, distributed, and consumed for promoting a business or brand.

copyright: Legal ownership of intellectual property giving the owner exclusive right to reproduce and share that property.

Creative Commons license: Created to give copyright holders more flexibility in allowing reproduction and sharing of their property.

CSS: The acronym for Cascading Style Sheets, which is used by Web designers to create blog layouts and Web pages. In other words, CSS works behind the scenes to configure the look and feel of a blog.

dashboard: The primary account management page of an online software program, such as Blogger or WordPress, where users can access the tools and functionality to modify settings, create content, and more.

domain name: The part of a URL that represents a specific Web site. Typically, domain names are preceded by *www.* and end with an extension such as *.com* or *.net.*

ebook: A short electronic book that typically focuses on a single topic. (Ebooks for content marketing purposes are usually around 20 pages long.)

fair use: An exception to copyright laws that allows limited use of certain copyrighted materials such as images, video or text for commentary, criticism, or educational purposes.

feed: The syndicated content of a blog or Web site. See also *RSS* and *feed reader.*

feed reader: A tool used to read RSS feeds. Feed readers receive feeds from blogs and Web sites and deliver them to subscribers in aggregated format for quick and easy viewing in one place.

flash: Streaming animation that appears on Web pages.

footer: The area spanning the bottom of a blog or Web page, which typically includes copyright information and may include other elements, such as a contact link or ads.

forum: An online message board where participants post messages within predetermined categories. Other participants respond, creating an online conversation between a potentially large group of people.

freemium: A fusion of the words *free* and *premium*. Web sites may offer a freemium content model wherein some content on the site is available free and other premium content is available for a fee.

FTP: The acronym for File Transfer Protocol, which is the process used to transfer files from one computer to another across the Internet.

Google: A company based in California that produces software, programs, tools, and utilities to help people leverage the Internet to accomplish tasks. Popular Google programs include Google search, Google AdSense, Google AdWords, Google Docs, Google Groups, and more.

guest blogging: The process of writing free posts to appear on another person's blog or accepting free posts from another blogger to publish on your blog with the purpose of networking and driving blog traffic or indirectly marketing a brand or business.

hashtag: An informal categorization system for Twitter that helps users identify tweets related to topics of interest. Hashtags include the # symbol followed by a keyword, such as #olympics.

header: The area spanning the top of a blog or Web page where the site title, graphics, and possibly navigational links or ads appear.

hit: A Web statistic counted each time a request is made to a Web server to display files on a Web page. Each page in a blog or Web site typically contains multiple files such as numerous images, text, video, flash elements, and so on. Therefore, when a page loads in a Web browser, multiple hits are counted equal to the number of files on that page.

home page: The first page a visitor sees when he or she enters a root domain name without an extension, such as www.keysplashcreative.com.

host: A company that provides space on its servers to store and maintain blogs. Also called *Web host* or *blog host*.

HTML: The acronym for Hypertext Markup Language, which is a programming language made up of tags used to create Web sites and blogs.

integrated marketing: A marketing strategy focused on linking all business marketing tactics to each other either directly or indirectly.

keyword: A word or phrase used to help index a Web page, allowing it to be found by search engines.

link: A connection between two Web sites. When selected, a link takes the user to another Web page. Also called *hyperlink*.

linkbait: A piece of content written for the primary purpose of attracting traffic and links. Linkbait content typically relates to buzz topics.

long-form content marketing: Any form of detailed content that takes more than a few minutes to create, publish, distribute, and consume for the purpose of promoting a business or brand.

long tail search engine optimization: The process of optimizing Web pages for highly focused searches based on specific keywords and keyword phrases.

message board: See *forum*.

microblogging: Short snippets (typically 140 characters or less) published through a site, such as Twitter.

niche: A specific and highly targeted segment of an audience or market. A niche blog is written about a focused topic and appeals to a very specific group of people.

page rank: A ranking used to determine a Web page's popularity, typically based on traffic and incoming links.

page view: A statistic that tracks each time a Web page is viewed independent of who is viewing that page.

permalink: A fusion of the words *permanent* and *link*. A link to a specific page on a Web site that remains unchanged over time.

ping: A signal sent from one Web site to another to ensure that the other site exists. Pings are used to notify sites that receive updates from ping servers of updates to a blog or Web site.

podcast: An episodic series of audio files that are recorded digitally for playback online or on mobile devices and uses a mobile RSS feed for syndication purposes.

press release: A news article created by a company to promote company news and distributed to journalists and audiences in an effort to generate publicity.

professional blogger: A person who writes blogs as a career.

profile: A blogger, Facebook user, Twitter user, LinkedIn user, or other social site user's About Me page that describes who the person is.

referrer: A Web site or search engine that leads visitors to a Web page.

retweet: A Twitter term used to identify updates that are copied from another user's Twitter stream and republished. Retweets are preceded by *RT*.

RSS: The acronym for Really Simple Syndication. The technology that creates Web content syndication, which allows users to subscribe to Web sites and blogs and receive new content from those Web sites and blogs in aggregated format within a feed reader. See also *feed* and *feed reader*.

search engine: A Web site used to find Web pages related to specific keywords or keyword phrases. Search engines use proprietary algorithms to spider the Internet and return results, which are typically presented in a ranked order. Google, Yahoo!, and Bing are popular search engines.

SEO: The acronym for search engine optimization. The process of writing Web content, designing Web pages, and promoting online content to boost rankings within search engine keyword searches.

SERM: The acronym for search engine reputation management. The process of monitoring the perceived reputation of a person, brand, company, and so on based on the search engine results that are delivered when a person conducts a search using keywords related to that person, brand, company, and so on.

segment: A smaller subset of a group of consumers who have similar demographic or behavioral traits and are likely to respond similarly to marketing messages.

shareworthy: Content that is useful and meaningful to an audience who is motivated to talk about that content and spread it to their audiences.

short-form content marketing: Any form of content created, published, distributed, and consumed in a very short amount of time for promoting a business or brand.

sidebar: A column on a Web page to the right, left, or flanking the largest, main column.

silo marketing: Silo marketing occurs when a business' varied marketing initiatives are executed independently as stand-alone tactics and without consideration for other tactics.

social bookmarking: A method of saving, storing, and sharing Web pages for future reference. Popular social bookmarking sites include Digg, StumbleUpon, reddit, and Delicious.

social media marketing: Any form of promotion that is executed using the tools of the social Web and is rooted in two-way dialogue and interaction.

social networking: The act of communicating and building relationships with other people online. Popular social networking sites include Facebook and LinkedIn.

social Web: The second generation of the World Wide Web, which focuses on interaction, user-generated content, communities, and building relationships. Also called *Web 2.0.*

spam: Comments submitted on a blog, forum, or Web site for no reason other than to drive traffic to a separate Web site. Spam can also come in e-mail form.

sponsored review: A piece of content written for the purpose of being paid by an advertiser who solicits it. Also called *sponsored post* or *paid post.*

sponsored tweet: A Twitter update published for the purpose of being paid by an advertiser who solicits it.

subscribe: When a person signs up to receive an online content feed in his or her feed reader or via e-mail.

syndication: Online publishers can syndicate their content through licensing agreements or free syndication providers in an effort to get their content in front of wider audiences.

tag: Keywords used to identify and informally categorize content. Tags are also read by blog search engines to provide search results to users.

target audience: The specific segment of a consumer audience that a business markets directly to through specific tactics and strategies. Target audiences typically share demographic or behavioral traits.

tweet: A Twitter update.

Twitter app: A tool developed by a third party to enhance the functionality of Twitter.

unique visitor: When a visitor is counted one time regardless of how many times he or she visits a Web page. See also *visitor.*

URL: The acronym for Uniform Resource Locator. The unique address of a specific page on the Internet consisting of an access protocol (that is, `http://`), a domain name (for example, `www.sitename.com`) and an extension identifying the specific page within a Web site or blog (such as `/specificpage.htm`).

URL shortener: A tool used to shorten lengthy URLs for sharing in short-form or conversational content.

visit: Each time a page on a Web site is accessed, a visit is counted.

visitor: A person who views a page (or multiple pages) on your blog.

vlogging: A fusion of the words *video* and *blog*. The process of publishing episodic videos rather than written blog posts. Also called *video blogging*.

Web 2.0: See *social Web*.

Web analytics: The data used to track the performance of a Web site.

Web log: See *blog*. Also called *Weblog*.

white paper: A research document that is typically based on statistical facts and includes references to source material.

WYSIWYG: The acronym for What You See Is What You Get. The visual editor provided by most blogging applications and forum tools that allows users to type content in a form similar to traditional word processing software where the format seen on screen during the editing process looks similar to how the final, published post will appear.

Index

• M •